History and Theology of Grace
The Catholic Teaching on Divine Grace

History and Theology of Grace

The Catholic Teaching on Divine Grace

John A. Hardon, S.J.

Veritas Press
of Ave Maria College

Ypsilanti, Michigan

Requests for permission to make copies of any part of the work should be directed to:

Veritas Press
of Ave Maria Collge
300 West Forest Avenue
Ypsilanti, Michigan 48197

Imprimatur: † Bishop Raymond L. Burke
Bishop of LaCrosse
September 4, 2001

The *Imprimatur* is an official declaration that a book or pamphlet is free of doctrinal or moral error. No implication is contained therein that those who granted the *Imprimatur* agree with the contents, opinions or statements expressed.

Published by:

Veritas Press
of Ave Maria College

300 West Forest Ave.
Ypsilanti, MI 48197
888-343-8607

Cover Graphic Production: Michael Andaloro

Printed in the United States of America.
Library of Congress Control Number: 2002112825
ISBN 0-9706106-1-0

TABLE OF CONTENTS

INTRODUCTION

We need motivation to learn any subject, whether secular or religious, and some sort of method to make the learning effective. Otherwise interest lags, if it is even aroused in the first place, and what may be useful or important is not taken seriously. Correspondingly, the better defined our motives for entering a field of knowledge, the more profit we derive from the investigation.

The theology of grace is no exception. There is no *prima facie* evidence why a Catholic should know more than his basic obligations and how to remain faithful to the inspirations of God in his soul. On reflection, however, we can see many reasons why a deep understanding is more than useful to the laity, and essential for those who profess what the world around them does not believe. The responsibility this imposes on priests and teachers is obvious, especially with the growing demand among the people for enlightenment and depth in their understanding of the faith, and their unwillingness to be satisfied with a catechism knowledge of fundamentals. Among the mysteries of Catholicism, none is more practically important than the doctrine of grace. It is the very heart of Christianity on its human side, since it describes the panorama of God's dealings with men, and corresponds in theology to the science of psychology, but with implications in every aspect of the Christian religion that have no counterpart in rational philosophy.

All the dogmas of faith take on new meaning for us from the existence of a supernatural order. The Trinity of persons is meaningful because the internal processions within the Deity are the source of external missions outside of God effected by Him in our favor: to become the fountainhead of grace from the Father, through His Son, our Lord, in the Spirit who dwells in the souls of the just.

The Incarnation is the enfleshment of God's Son in order that through Him we might become, by grace, partakers of His divinity as He vouchsafed to be made a sharer of our humanity. In the Eucharist we receive the Author of grace, the same who was born of the Virgin Mary and whose human nature has since become the instrument of our salvation.

By the very fact that we believe, with St. Paul, in things unseen—and hope for the promised rewards of those who love God, we are witnesses to the action of a superhuman power, which is divine grace operating on the mind and will. This grace enables us to see and desire what the natural man cannot perceive.

We say the sacraments are seven signs instituted by Christ to confer the grace they signify.[1] And more broadly we hold that the Catholic Church is the great sacrament of the New Law that Christ founded to be the unique channel of grace to all mankind, with special title to those who are baptized and active members of the Mystical Body of Christ.[2] But no matter how conceived, the sacramental system is so far significant and membership in the Church so much appreciated as we see the great *mysteria Christi* in their true perspective as visible and human agencies for the transmission of invisible divine blessings to the human race.

As we look to the future prospects of a heavenly reward, it is grace again that gives to heaven its only meaning, as a prolongation of the life in God's friendship here on earth. Our faith here becomes vision there, our hope here becomes possession there, and our charity now becomes the measure of our love of God then—in eternity—all aspects of the same mysterious reality that completely distinguishes the Christian religion from every other. We might in justice define Christianity as "the religion of grace." Except for Judaism, from which it arose and above which it stands, Christianity is unique among

---

[1] *Catechism of the Catholic Church (CCC)* 1127.
[2] *CCC* 774–75.

living religions in resting its whole structure on the existence of a supernatural world of which the visible and natural universe is only a feeble analogy.

If the love of God is conditioned on knowledge, the depth of love will be determined by the extent of our knowledge of Him, not only as the Creator of nature but as the Author of grace. And since faith is required to recognize this higher operation of divine goodness, we have in the Catholic doctrine on grace the single most powerful motive for the apostolate.

In sending forth His disciples, Christ directed them before all else to teach, to make disciples and thus to convert the world. It is significant that the Gospel terms, docere (to teach), discipulus (student), magister (teacher), propheta (professional teacher), are all so many aspects of the teaching apostolate. The primary function of the minister of the Gospel is to impart knowledge, specifically knowledge of revelation; from which arises faith and through which the faithful may obtain grace. If the Church's ultimate purpose is to sanctify the souls of men, this purpose would not even be thought of, let alone attained, unless people were first instructed to believe that holiness is necessary and acquirable through the instrumentalities of grace, notably the Mass and the sacraments. This is what God came down upon earth to reveal.

The theology of grace is not simple, as may be seen from the sequence of errors strewn along the path of the Church's history. The complexity of the subject is due as much to its intrinsically mysterious character, since it deals with nothing less than the life of God shared by His creatures, as to our natural proneness to rationalize and explain everything in this-worldly terms. Yet a clear grasp of the basic principles is useful and may at times be indispensable, for directing oneself and others on the road to salvation. It is no coincidence that the great heresies on grace, like Pelagianism and Jansenism, had a profound influence on the morals and spiritual life of those who professed these errors; and that the influence is still exerted centuries after the original aberrations arose. On a smaller scale obscurities or deviations from the authentic teaching can be harmful to individuals who are living otherwise normal Catholic lives; as clarity and certitude can be of immense value for persons who are sincerely trying to serve God and respond generously to His will.

The saints understood the importance and dignity of grace, which they attested is so excellent that neither the gift of prophecy, nor the working of miracles, nor any speculation, however sublime, is of any value without it. For the gifts of nature are common to the good and bad; but grace is the proper gift of the elect. They that are adorned with, influenced by, and sanctified in it are esteemed worthy of eternal life.

No one has spoken more eloquently about grace than the author of the *Imitation* who, through his influence on the Spiritual Exercises of St. Ignatius, has shaped so much of modern spirituality. "Grace," he wrote, "is the mistress of truth, the light of the heart, the comforter of affliction, the banisher of sorrow, the expeller of fears, the matrix of devotion, the producer of tears. What am I without it but a piece of dry wood and an unprofitable stock, fit for nothing but to be cast away." This is not rhetoric but only a faint declaration of the truth, since without grace man is not only left to his own resources and incapable of reaching the Trinitarian destiny to which he was raised but, because of the fall, cannot for long even remain faithful to the laws of his own nature.

1

MEANING OF DIVINE GRACE

Not the least obstacle to the study of grace is the psychological one of meaning. The English word "grace" is simply a transliteration from the Latin *gratia*, first used by the Roman translators of the New Testament for the Greek *charis*, imbedded in the stream of ecclesiastical Latin by Tertullian (A.D. 160–220) and made the center of a whole system of theology by St. Augustine (A.D. 354–430).

In order to get behind the scriptural meaning of grace, therefore; we must examine the import and connotation of the Greek term *charis*, which is, so to speak, our human link with the concept intended by the Holy Spirit in Christian revelation. Hellenist scholars say that the Greek mind has in no word uttered itself and all that lies at its heart more distinctly than in this disyllable, which the authors of the New Testament chose to epitomize God's merciful love for men.

The fundamental notion of *charis* in ancient Greek was the understanding that a person or an object has the power to give joy to the hearer or beholder. And since to a Greek there was nothing so joy-inspiring as grace or beauty, it implied the presence of these. Yet *charis* meant not only their presence as passive qualities, but as gracious or beautiful persons and things in operation, acting outside themselves to communicate to others what they possess within.

One more aspect of the word made it a logical vehicle for the Christian doctrine of divine condescension, locked up in the idea of grace.

1

Charis among the Greek schools of ethics implied a favor freely done, without claim or expectation of return. Thus Aristotle, defining *charis*, laid the whole stress on this very point, that it is conferred freely, with no prospect of reward, and finds its only motive in the bounty and free-heartedness of the giver.[1]

SCRIPTURE AND THEOLOGY

The great expositor of the theology of grace was St. Paul, who speaks of it in all his fourteen epistles, including the short one of Philemon, which he begins and ends with a prayer for the grace "from" and "of our Lord Jesus Christ." In the Pauline letters, supported by the Acts and the letters of St. Peter, the single term *charis* runs the gamut of conceptual meanings which the Christian faith partly borrowed from the Greeks but then sublimated to a level never found anywhere else in classic antiquity.

Underlying these meanings is the basic notion of a benefit freely granted by God to His creatures. The operative word is "freely" or "gratuitously," which is logically opposed to whatever is due or on which a person has a rightful claim. Broadly speaking, of course, the very elements that constitute our nature, our body and soul, are not due to us. They were freely created by the love of God. Yet this kind of gratuity is at best negative, because as contingent beings we had no intrinsic claim on coming into existence. God could have not made us. Once we came into existence, however; a variety of other blessings may be called due to us, such as are needed to make our lives purposeful and enable us to reach the perfection proper to our human nature. Yet even these are not strictly by right, but are divine gifts with the same gratuity as the nature on which they finally depend.

---

[1] *De Rhetorica*, II, 7; *Catechism of the Catholic Church (CCC)*, Second edition (Washington, D.C.: United States Catholic Conference, 1997), 1996, 2027.

Patristic literature often describes these gifts of nature as graces. One of the major heresies in the early Church was built on the theory that human freedom was the only or the highest type of grace we receive; but that is not the understanding of the concept in Catholic theology. When the Scriptures, Fathers or Councils of the Church refer to "grace" properly so-called, they mean that gift which is the fruit of the blood of Christ, by which we become Christians and sons of God, are justified, made holy, and enter into heavenly glory. They often oppose grace to nature, teaching that nature must be repaired, made sound, helped and saved by grace. We are able to do by grace what the lone powers of nature could never do. "By grace, human freedom is not taken away but healed, not destroyed but corrected, not removed but enlightened, not emptied but assisted and preserved."[2] They condemn the Pelagians who equated grace and the gifts of nature by denying that "the grace which the Christian faith professes is not nature but that by which nature is aided and saved."[3]

The appropriateness of the term "grace" for this special benefit of divine love becomes evident once the existence of a higher than natural order is recognized. Certainly if the gifts of nature are gratuitous, those of supernature are given *gratis* to an eminent degree.

Moreover, if we examine the meaning of gratuity, we see that grace, otherwise than gifts of nature, is freely conferred with no positive claim on our part to receive. It is not only that we *had* no claim to whatever we possess naturally—how could we since we did not even exist to press such a claim? But as objects of divine benevolence in the form of grace we *have* no claim to these benefits, although we exist, and enjoy certain rights to the perfection and destiny of our given, existing humanity.

---

[2] St. Fulgentius, *Letter XVII, 20; CCC* 1742.
[3] St. Augustine, "Letter to Innocent I" (177), 7, *Fathers of the Church: Augustine Letters I* (New York: Fathers of the Church, 1955), 99.

This divine benevolence which we call grace may be understood concretely as God, viewed in His own Trinitarian life which He communicated to His natural creatures. All three Persons of the Trinity are concerned: the Father who sent His only-begotten Son to redeem us; the Son who became man and died on the cross to merit the grace of our salvation; and the Holy Spirit, who has been revealed as the term of divine life in our souls through whom the Son, who is generated by the Father, sanctifies those He redeemed.

There are really two gifts involved: one uncreated, which is God communicating Himself to His creatures, and the other created, which is the effect He produces in souls by His new presence to us. Both are graces, and both absolutely undeserved, since their function is to make us capable of living a life that is proper to God alone: of knowing and loving Him as He knows and loves Himself, of possessing Him with the happiness that He enjoys by nature and we are privileged to share by *charis* or the sheer benevolence of grace.

Too often people equate the idea of grace with some special help from God, as though grace was only remedial of human weakness or distress. It is indeed remedial, and to our way of thinking this may seem to be its main function. It is certainly the most frequent object of prayer. However, grace is not primarily a help to human nature but an elevation of it. Grace raises created nature and faculties to an order of being where only the divinity has the right to abide. Its principal function is to make us partakers of the inner life of the Trinity in the beatific vision, where the divine essence is seen intuitively in a face-to-face vision, with no interposition of any creature between the soul and the Triune God.[4]

Accordingly supernatural grace has two elements that characterize it and distinguish it from everything merely natural, its positive and absolute gratuity and its heavenly finality. The first refers to God as

---

[4] *CCC* 1997, 1998, 1999.

efficient cause, who willed to produce a benefit for us beyond the most extravagant conception of a finite mind; the second refers to God as final cause, towards whom we are being directed as our Trinitarian end. Taken together, the two elements give us a definition of grace as a supernatural gift which God confers gratuitously on rational creatures in order to bring them to eternal life.

COMMUNICATION OF DIVINE LOVE

An adequate estimate of grace must see it as a communication of divine love. St. John tells us that "God is love," meaning that in Him reside all the treasures of infinite goodness, perfectly shared among the three Persons, and mercifully communicated to mankind outside the Trinity; first naturally in creation by bringing us out of nothing into existence and endowing us with the divine image of intellect and will; then supernaturally in the Incarnation, which is the source of our life of grace and the meritorious cause of our salvation. While admitting, and almost transmitting, the prior evidence of God's beauty in creating us, St. John says "in this has the love of God been disclosed to us, that God has sent His only-begotten Son into the world that we may live through Him."[5]

Among the species of grace, the primary type is habitual or sanctifying by which we become children of God and heirs of heaven. All other forms are ancillary to this, and take their meaning from the same. At no matter what angle we view habitual grace or, as the Council of Trent calls it, "justification," we see it as a manifestation of God's love in our regard.

The ultimate purpose of this gift from God's part is His glory and that of His divine Son, but from ours everlasting happiness with the Trinity. The agent of this gift is the merciful God, "who freely washes and sanctifies, sealing and anointing us with the Holy Spirit of His

---

[5] 1 John 4:9; *CCC* 458.

promise, who is the pledge of our inheritance." The meritorious source is the "beloved only-begotten Son of God, our Lord Jesus Christ, who, when we were enemies, by reason of His very great love wherewith He has loved us, merited justification for us by His own most holy passion on the wood of the cross, and made satisfaction for us to God the Father." The instrumental means are the sacrament of baptism, in water or at least by desire; and the formality which constitutes the grace of divine friendship in the righteousness, i.e., right orientation to our heavenly destiny. We have this "as a gift from Him and by which we are renewed in the spirit of our mind," since we take on the personality of Christ to become by adoption what He was by nature, sons of God and joint-heirs with Christ of His kingdom.[6]

The value of considering grace as a manifestation of God's love is manifold. We thereby recognize the depth of His charity, which is measured by the freedom and generosity of the benefits conferred which, in grace, are consummately free (with not the semblance of creature-claim) and generous to the limit of God's bounty in receiving us into His own Trinitarian family. We also appreciate what it cost the Son of God to make our supernatural life possible, that we were redeemed "not with perishable things, with silver or gold, but with the precious blood of Christ."[7] We see the selectiveness of God's love in calling us to the true faith and giving us the grace of justification as the pledge of our final glorification. "Those whom He has predestined, them He has also called; and those whom He has called, them He has also justified, and those whom He has justified, them He has also glorified."[8]

---

[6] *Enchiridion Symbolorum: Definitionum et Declarationum de Rebus Fidei et Morum,* ed. Heinrich Denzinger, Adolph Schonmetzer (*DS*), 33rd edition (Barcinone: Herder, 1965), 1529; *CCC* 654, 2009.

[7] I Peter 1:18–19.

[8] Romans 8:30; *CCC* 1821.

Looking upon grace as an expression of divine charity we can rede-fine the providence of God as the constant, solicitous care He has in directing every moment and every detail of our lives to that final goal of union with Himself in beatitude. There is no such thing as chance with God. He plans every creature that crosses the horizon of our experience for a purpose, to have it function as a grace (mediately or immediately) to lead us to our appointed end. Instead of considering grace as a sporadic assistance or even as a static possession, we thus see it as a perpetual outpouring of divine benevolence, channelled through creatures and, for sanctifying grace, as a dynamic power that God intends to have grow and mature under His providential hand.

Above all, if we identify grace with divine love, we place it in the stream of daily life where it really belongs. In the last analysis, grace is an invitation; it is not coercive. Actual graces can be resisted and habitual grace can be lost. They require a loving response on our part to become effective in one case and remain alive in the other.

Cooperation with grace, therefore, is our answer to the prior love of God. This responsiveness becomes more self-sacrificing in proportion as we understand more clearly how generous is the invitation; and how undeserved, because gratuitous, is the gift we possess (in sanctifying grace) or are offered (in actual graces). How ungrateful we are if we resist the advances of infinite mercy or lose the divine life we received.

2

NECESSITY FOR SALVATION

Most Catholics would be surprised if anyone questioned or denied that we need the grace of God to be saved. Built into the Catholic mind is a correlation between grace and heaven so close that the one is unthinkable without the other. The relationship is correct, and the instinct which tells us that we need divine assistance to reach our final destiny is a reflection of the Church's faith over the centuries. Nevertheless, this faith was not preserved without struggle. The calm assurance we now have is the fruit of conflict and of clarification that reach back to the early period of Christianity.

The conflict still continues and is, in fact, the most deep-seated tension in all of human history. There is, on the one hand, the assertion of man's independence in the moral order. On the other hand we have the contrary admission that man is not autonomous, that with all the native powers at his command he is really helpless without special and constant intervention to realize the ultimate purpose of his being.

PELAGIUS TO RATIONALISM

The principal heresy of naturalism was born of Stoic philosophy that infected certain Christian writers from the earliest times. However the full-blown system of Pelagianism into which it developed did not arise until the beginning of the fourth century. A British lay monk, Pelagius, first popularized the theory, together with his disciple Caelestius.

Little is known about the life of Pelagius, except that he was born in England about A.D. 354 and that during a visit to Rome he became alarmed by the low morality of priest and people. He concluded that the only hope of reform lay in placing all the responsibility for sin on the free wills of men, to the point of denying the necessity and thereby the definition of grace.

The premises served as basis for Pelagius's theory. Arguing from the principle that "a person is free if he does what he wills and avoids what he wills to avoid," he said that heaven is attainable by use of our natural faculties alone, since nothing but the free will is needed to practice virtue and keep out of sin. From the axiom that "Adam neither injured nor deprived us of anything," Pelagius decided that men require no special help to repair what Adam is supposed to have lost.

Pelagius and Caelestius went to Africa in A.D. 410, the latter staying to find himself charged with heresy by the Council of Carthage, while Pelagius went on to Palestine and met the same treatment at the hands of St. Jerome. On request of the bishops of North Africa, Innocent I condemned Pelagius, who for a time deceived Pope Zosimus, the next pope, into acquitting him. But the acquittal was promptly changed to papal condemnation in A.D. 418 when the deception was exposed. Though Pelagius leaves the scene at this point, eighteen Italian bishops led by Julian of Eclanum, refuse to submit to the pope and proceed to elaborate Pelagianism into a compact system of doctrine.

Its basic principle is the affirmation of the self-sufficiency of man's free will. We can always will and do good, even when *de facto* we will and do otherwise, depending entirely on our own moral strength.

In the Pelagian scheme there is no room for original sin. What we now call preternatural gifts of bodily immortality and integrity were never really possessed by Adam. He left us only a bad example. The fact that we are prone to sin is not inherited from Adam and Eve, our first parents. We acquire it by our own misdeeds.

Baptism therefore can have no strict remissive function. A person can be saved without it. At most its purpose is to incorporate us into the Church, unite us with Christ, or make us members of a mysterious heavenly kingdom. It can never be understood as being absolutely necessary for salvation.

For the same reason, sanctifying grace is not the necessary basis of supernatural activity, but only a sort of remedy for actual sins or a spiritual adornment of Christians and a sign of their divine adoption. Actual graces are only external, in the form of preaching, miracles, revelation and the example of Jesus Christ. And if, for the sake of argument, real supernatural grace were needed, it would be only as light for the mind but never internal grace in the will. "You destroy the will," Pelagius protested, "if you say it needs any help." The only true "grace" we possess is the faculty of free choice.

Predestination for the Pelagians is a misnomer. It should rather be called foreknowledge. Divine activity does not penetrate into the very heart of human activity, to elevate and transform it. God merely foresees what we are freely going to do; He in no way predestines what our free choices will be. By the same token the Redemption by Christ does not give us a new birth but only lifts us to a higher stage of natural activity; and the influence of Christ's passion and death is not intrinsic but external to our souls.

Semi-Pelagianism

"Half-Pelagianism" or Semi-Pelagianism was historically linked to its predecessor. In this theory grace is admittedly necessary, but not ordinarily for the first steps towards the Christian life, and also not for final perseverance in the grace of God. It came as reaction against certain anti-Pelagian writings of St. Augustine, in which he spoke in extreme terms of the corruption of human nature since the fall, and of the closed number of the elect, apparently preordained from eternity in view of original sin.

Critics of Augustine in his own lifetime took issue with what they considered an error opposite to Pelagius. Augustine defended himself and in turn instructed his critics, notably the African monks of Hadrumetum in a treatise on *Corruption and Grace,* which satisfied the hermits but later gave unwarranted occasion to Calvin and Jansenius for tracing their theories on predestination to St. Augustine.

The reputed founder of Semi-Pelagianism was John Cassian (A.D. 360–435), abbot of the monastery at Marseilles. His sanctity was of a high order but his *Conferences* on the monastic life put so much stress on the power of freedom that, in his opinion, God frequently awaits the good impulses of the natural will before coming to its assistance with supernatural grace. Augustine's disciple, Prosper of Aquitaine (A.D. 390–463), opposed these views of the Massilians. In about A.D. 431 he urged Pope Celestine I to take coercive measures. However the Pope made no definite statement beyond exhorting the bishops of Gaul to protect the memory of Augustine and imposing silence on his traducers.

Prosper carried on a steady polemic with Cassian and Vincent of Lerins (died A.D. 450), whose otherwise excellent *Commonitorium* shows a few strains of Semi-Pelagianism. For centuries the monastery of Lerins was the religious center of Provence and the nursery of a long line of scholars and bishops, including Saints Patrick, Hilary, and Caesarius. Yet during the fifth century its resistance to Augustine made it the stronghold of Semi-Pelagian tendencies. As late as A.D. 470, Bishop Faustus of Riez, formerly of Lerins, wrote a defense of Cassian that is famous for his description of the will as a "small hook" that reaches out and seizes grace. Faustus would also have nothing to do with predestination to heaven and final perseverance as a "special grace."

The decline of Semi-Pelagianism was due mainly to the efforts of a group of Scythian monks and their leader Maxentius, whose campaign against Faustus finally resulted in a proclamation by the Council of Orange (A.D. 529) that Boniface II solemnly ratified in the following year. In twenty-five canons the impotence of nature to super-natural good is vindicated. Also vindicated is the absolute necessity of preceding grace for actions leading to heaven, especially for the beginning of faith, likewise defended is the absolute gratuity of the first grace and of final perseverance. All these were defined as true, while an epilogue on the predestination of the will to evil was branded as heretical.

To avoid misunderstanding, the doctrines of Semi-Pelagianism should be distinguished from the name, which was unknown in Christian history until modern times. Almost certainly the word was coined about 1600 by those who believed they saw a resemblance between the Jesuit Molina's theory of grace and the error of the fifth century Massilian monks. After this confusion was clarified, the term remained in theological circles as a useful name for the ancient heresy.

Luther and Calvin

We hardly think of Reformation principles as questioning the necessity of grace. Did not Luther teach that man is saved "by grace alone," and was not the Reformation motto, "to God alone the glory"?

Yet a series of definitions in Trent emphasize the necessity of grace for salvation and repeat the Church's teaching in Pelagian times. This suggests that, in spite of the verbal insistence on grace in the writings of Luther and Calvin, the objective fact was obscured or explicitly denied.

The current interest in Christian reunion demands clarity about the respective Catholic and Protestant positions. What is the basic truth of man's elevation to the supernatural order, where the original righteousness (comprising sanctifying grace and the perfections of integrity and bodily immortality) are regarded as gifts in our first parents, and not an essential part of their nature? In this context, Luther writes about the Catholic doctrine of the supernatural life:

> The scholastics argue that original righteousness was not a part of man's nature but, like some adornment, was added to man as a gift, as when someone places a wreath on a pretty girl. The wreath is certainly not a part of the virgin's nature; it is something apart from her nature. It came from outside and can be removed again without any injury to her nature. Therefore they maintain about man and about demons that although they have lost their original righteousness, their natural endowments have nevertheless remained pure, just as they were created in the beginning. But this idea must be shunned like poison, for it minimizes original sin.
>
> Let us rather maintain that righteousness was not a gift which came from without, separate from man's nature, but that it was truly part of his nature, so that it was Adam's nature to love God, to believe God, to know God. These things were just as natural for Adam as it is natural for the eyes to receive light.[9]

The logic of this neo-Pelagianism was consistent. Original justice was due to man's nature, by a necessity of essence. Consequently when Adam sinned and lost original justice, his nature was therefore

---

[9] Martin Luther, "Lectures on Genesis" 3:7, *Luther's Work* (St. Louis: Concordia, 1958), 1:164–165; *CCC* 399, 1998.

essentially corrupted and his faculties intrinsically vitiated. As a further result, man is incapable of doing any good, and whatever "virtue" he practices is due to God alone. All man's actions are *per se* sins; only by the mercy of God they are covered over as with a cloak, to hide the shame beneath.

Grace, in Reformation terminology, took on a new meaning. If original justice was not a gift but part of man's nature, any subsequent conferral of "grace" is not really supernatural, albeit gratuitous, but at most a restoration of the native powers that were sinfully lost. The word "grace" may be still used, but it lacks one of the essential qualities of grace in the Catholic sense of the term; it is not intrinsically orientated to a destiny, the beatific vision, which exceeds the capacities of any finite being and belongs by right to God alone.

Under Michael Baius (1513–1579), the Reformation ideas were developed into a compact system, which distinguished three stages in man's relation to God: of innocent nature, of fallen nature, and of restored nature. But the cardinal principle of Luther and Calvin was retained. God made man originally possessed of all the perfections he needed to reach heaven, and these perfections were natural and due to him as man. The theological distinction between natural and supernatural, according to Baianism is invalid and a purely mental construct.

Cornelius Jansen (1585–1638) followed in Baius' footsteps, and carried Luther and Calvin to their logical conclusion. If human nature has been destined to the beatific vision of itself, we cannot say it was raised to the supernatural order, and much less of grace as being physically necessary to reach a hypothetically supernatural end. Too easily we associate Jansenism with moral rigorism, which it also propounded; but this was only a corollary to the fundamental postulate that heaven is not gratuitous.

Rationalism

Though variously defined in different fields, rationalism in theology is that system which declares the absolute rights of natural reason as the only source of religious truth. Common to all rationalists is a dogmatic confidence in the power of human thought, and a conviction that man alone, without revelation, can comprehend whatever he needs to reach his ultimate destination.

As a trend in religious culture, rationalism is as old as Judaeo-Christianity. Among the ancient Jews, the Sadducees denied the resurrection and doubted the existence of angels. The very name "Gnostics" in the first century of the Christian era means "The Knowers" who professed to have a special understanding that was not shared by other believers. Arius insisted on a complete explanation of the hypostatic union. Pelagius settled the problem of grace and freedom by denying the supernatural order. The Jansenists did the same by liquidating free will.

The same attitude, on a more radical scale, was adopted by those who questioned the foundations of the Christian religion in England, France and Germany. Tindal, Collins and Hume, Voltaire and Rousseau, Kant, Hegel and Strauss were all rationalists in the generic meaning of the term. They found Christianity unreasonable by their own standards of rationality.

In modern times rationalism has entered a new phase. We should expect a philosophy that measures truth by empiric knowledge and conviction by human experience to have small respect for the Christian dogmas on the supernatural life, which are revealed mysteries and therefore defy rational comprehension. But we are not prepared for the militant naturalism that will have nothing done of grace and is impatient with any dependence on a higher-than-human agency. "Men have never fully used the powers they possess to advance the good in life, because they have waited upon some power external to themselves and to nature to do the work they are responsible for doing. Dependence upon an external power is the counterpart of surrender of human endeavor.[10]

This impatience with the supernatural has affected not only philosophy but also theology. And the deepest issue in modern religious thought is not between Catholicism and Protestantism, but between those in nominally Christian cultures who admit and those who deny the existence of the supranatural.

Paul Tillich has been called "the theologians' theologian." He calls himself a self-transcending realist. His position is embarrassingly clear.

> Self-transcending realism requires the criticism of all forms of supra-naturalism—supranaturalism in the sense of a theology that imagines a supra-natural world beside or above the natural one, a world in which the unconditional finds a local habitation, thus making God a transcendent object, the creation an act at the beginning of time, the consummation a future state of things. To criticize such a conditioning of the unconditional, even if it leads to atheistic consequences, is more religious, because it is more aware of the unconditional character of the divine, than a theism that bans God into the supra-natural realm. The man of today, who feels separated by a gulf from the theistic believer, often knows more about the "ultimate" than the self-assured Christian who thinks that through his faith he has God in his possession.[11]

What is most disturbing about this attitude is not its assertiveness. Tillich is not saying anything that cannot be found, often more clearly, in Kant, Schelling, and the German idealists. It is the wide

---

[10] John Dewey, *A Common Faith* (New Haven: Yale University Press, 1934), 46.
[11] Paul Tillich, *The Protestant Era* (Chicago: University of Chicago Press, 1948), 82.

acceptance of his premises in ostensibly Christian circles that should cause us concern.

SCRIPTURE AND TRADITION

Before we see the Church's teaching on the necessity of grace, it is imperative to know what kind of grace we are speaking of and what sort of necessity. The grace in question is to be understood strictly, as a purely gratuitous and undeserved gift of God, which He confers internally in the soul (or its faculties) as something physically and intrinsically supernatural. If these qualifications seem oversubtle, they are only reflections of the long history of subtlety created by the hairsplitting refinements of Pelagius, Calvin, Baius, and Jansenius.

This grace, we say, is absolutely necessary, and allows no exceptions. It is simply impossible without grace to perform a salutary action, that is, one which positively leads the person to eternal salvation. Every situation is meant to be covered. A person in God's friendship needs grace to merit heaven. A man estranged from God needs grace either proximately or remotely to become disposed for justification. Grace, therefore, does more than remove obstacles or make it easier to reach heaven. It furnishes the indispensable supernatural energy to take even a single step on the road to heavenly beatitude.

While implicit in the foregoing, we should recognize the need of grace even for the "beginning of faith," in the sense understood by St. Augustine in his controversy with the Semi-Pelagians.[12] They argued that a sinner or unbeliever searching for God can dispose himself for sanctifying grace by his own natural efforts. He is able, they claimed, to become convinced of the necessity of faith (or penance for past

---

[12] *CCC* 153; cf. Vatican Council II. *Dogmatic Constitution on Divine Revelation* [*Dei Verbum*] (1965), 5.

sins), be moved to desire his salvation, and even pray for God's help-all on his own and without the intervention of grace.

Anti-Pelagianism

Aroused by the Pelagian speculations, a series of church councils and papal statements from A.D. 412 to 529 examined the controverted areas and either condemned what were considered aberrations or explained the correct teachings of the Church on the necessity of grace.

About A.D. 435, St. Prosper of Aquitaine gathered together, as he said, "whatever the rulers of the Roman Church had decided" and "certain judgments of the African councils," which the popes had approved. This collection of statements has since become known as the *Indiculus* (small index) and is universally accepted as an epitome of Catholic doctrine, dealing exclusively with grace and its impact on human responsibility.

Running as a theme through the *Indiculus* is the insistence that we need grace not only to help our weakness or dispel ignorance, but absolutely and universally. "God is the author of all good desires and deeds, of all efforts and virtues, with which from the beginning of faith man tends to God. And we do not doubt that His grace anticipates every one of man's merits, and that it is through Him we begin both the will and the performance of any good work."[13]

Under pressure of Semi-Pelagianism, the Catholic position was further clarified. The stress that Cassian and his followers placed on man's effort in the quest of perfection led them to obscure the prior dependence on divine light and strength even to begin to move towards God.

It is remarkable how centuries before Jansenism the Church rightly understood the distinction between the natural and supernatural orders, and rested its case where it really belongs, on the teachings of

---

[13] *DS* 248.

Christ and St. Paul. The Second Council of Orange, north of Avignon in southeastern France, in A.D. 529 condemned the idea that men are able to do anything "pertaining to the salvation of eternal life" by their own strength of nature. Two years later Boniface II (A.D. 450–532) solemnly confirmed the Council's canons against the Semi-Pelagians. The Council declared,

> He is deceived by heretical opinion, who claims it is possible through the power of nature to know or choose anything good, as required, which pertains to the salvation of eternal life; or (who claims it is possible) to accept the salvific, evangelical preaching without enlightenment and inspiration from the Holy Spirit. He fails to understand the word of God who says in the Gospel "Without me you can do nothing," and the statement of the Apostle, "Not that we are sufficient of ourselves to think anything, as from ourselves, but our sufficiency is from God."[14]

The essential elements are specified. If we cannot know or choose anything requisite for salvation by the power of nature (*per naturae vigorem*) alone, we are naturally helpless to attain heaven and therefore need by physical necessity the supernatural energy that only the Holy Spirit can supply. External grace in the form of Gospel preaching is not enough, it is only the sensibly perceptible object to which assent must be given, under the impulse of a special, internal divine action.

Christ's words at the Last Supper quoted by the Council "without me you can do nothing," are the classic source of our doctrine. They must be seen in context to make a full impression.

> I am the true vine, and my Father is the vine-dresser. Every branch in me that bears no fruit He will take away; and every

---

[14] *DS* 378; II Cor. 3:5.

branch that bears fruit He will cleanse, that it may bear more fruit. Abide in me and I in you. As the branch cannot bear fruit of itself unless it remain on the vine, so neither can you unless you abide in me. I am the vine, you are the branches. He who abides in me, and I in him, he bears much fruit; for without me you can do nothing. If anyone does not abide in me, he shall be cast outside as the branch and wither; and they shall gather them up and cast them into the fire, and they shall burn.[15]

The lesson Christ wished to teach through this allegory was that just as a branch cannot bear fruit of itself apart from the vine, so neither can we separated from the influence of Christ. Since His influence is necessarily supernatural, through internal grace, and our fruit of good works are the salutary acts we perform, we conclude that internal grace is required to place any act, no matter how apparently trivial, that directly leads to the heavenly home where Christ said He was going to prepare a place for us.

Throughout the Old Testament the metaphor of the vine and the vineyard signifying the house of Israel is a familiar illustration of complete dependence on Yahweh. It is found in the beautiful canticle of Isaias, "What more should I have done for my vineyard?";[16] in Jeremias' divine pleas against Israel;[17] in a passage of Ezechiel that closely parallels the negative of St. John, "behold it is cast into the fire for fuel";[18] in the Psalms, where the Lord is begged to "look down from heaven, and see, and visit the vineyard, and perfect the same which Your right hand has planted."[19]

---

[15] John 15:1–6; *CCC* 2074.
[16] Isaias 5:1–7.
[17] Jeremias 1–14
[18] Ezeckiel 15:2–8.
[19] Psalm 79.

Six times before, Christ had metaphorically identified Himself: "I am the bread of life, I am the light of the world, I am the door, I am the good shepherd, I am the resurrection and the life, I am the way, the truth and the life." Now He added the seventh and last assertion, "I am the true vine," as the Savior's own image of the need we have of Him to do anything worthy of salvation.

Vital immanence best describes the depth and indispensability of this flow of divine power from Christ to those who would be saved. No figure He might have chosen would more clearly establish our need of Him and, by implication, of His life-giving grace. These six words, "Without me you can do nothing," exclude every sort of Pelagianism. A severed vine-branch is proverbially useless, destined only to be cast out, to dry up and be burned. Nothing could be stronger than St. Augustine's comment, *Aut vitis aut ignis*—either the Vine or hell-fire.

Beginning of Faith

Perhaps the expression "beginning of faith" (*initium fidei*) is not the happiest to cover all that the Semi-Pelagians meant by saying that God "awaits man" to give him the grace for which he has predisposed himself. A better rendition would be "beginning of salvation" (*initium salutis*), although even this is inadequate.

The Semi-Pelagians admitted original sin and the need for internal grace for meriting heaven. Their problem was to make theological sense of St. Augustine's wholesale rejection of Pelagianism. In the process he seemed to make so much of grace that free will was practically denied. If, as Augustine appeared to say, grace is necessary for the whole stream of salvific acts, beginning with faith and ending with perseverance, and all this was absolutely gratuitous from God; if man himself cannot merit grace or even positively dispose himself to receive it—what is left of free will?

Cassian and others felt that Augustine had gone too far in making man's salvation depend entirely on divine grace and leaving no room for human activity. They believed there is some beginning of salvation, a kind of natural prelude, of which men are capable by their native powers. Grace is not required for this *initium salutis*. What is more, God waits for the natural effort on our part. If we offer Him the initial preparation, He gives us the grace we need for salutary acts, and, indeed, because of our previous disposition. But if we fail to present this preliminary mite, we get no grace and have only ourselves to blame for the deprivation.

This human predisposition was variously identified with our good resolutions, pious aspirations, or at least the indication of good will; which the Semi-Pelagians held can be produced by the soul alone, aided by its natural forces, and prior to the influx of grace. The Second Council of Orange, in France, where these theories were dominant, answered them in the most sweeping manner possible. Every angle was explored and every loophole closed to the notion that we, and not God, make the first move in the path of salvation.

First on the question of prayer, we cannot say that "the grace of God can be obtained by human (natural) prayer, and that it is not grace itself which causes us to invoke God" profitably for heaven, at the risk of contradicting St. Paul who quotes Isaias quoting the Lord, saying, "I was found by those who were not looking for me; I was clearly shown to those who never asked about me."[20] God must inspire our prayer before we can pray efficaciously for His grace.

Of great importance for dealing with non-Catholics and those separated from God is the fact that "increase in faith, as well as the beginning of faith, and the very impulse by which we are led to believe in Him who justifies the sinner" is not our own achievement

---

[20] *DS* 373; Isaias 65:1; Romans 10:20; *CCC* 2567.

"by nature," but comes to us "as a gift of grace, that is to say, through the inspiration of the Holy Spirit."[21] Faith is a free benefit from God, which He is not constrained to confer but gives, as He wills, and to which He leads the souls of the elect by His own prevenient light and strength.

Finally, we are forbidden to say that "without the grace of God, the divine mercy is accorded to our faith and wills, our desires and efforts, our labors and prayers, our watching and studies, our begging, searching and knocking for entrance." Rather we must see that "our ability to believe, to will, and so all these other things, as necessary (for salvation), are due to the infusion and inspiration of the Holy Spirit in us." We may not, in fine, "subordinate the aid of grace to human (natural) humility or obedience," but admit that our salutary "humility and obedience are the very gift of grace." Otherwise we should contradict the express teaching of St. Paul who asked, "What have you that you have not received," and confessed that, "By the grace of God, I am what I am."[22]

Reformation to Jansenism

The sixteenth century Reformers began with the settled conviction that Adam's original justice was not a superadded gift but a possession of his nature; and that his sin therefore not only deprived us of graces or preternatural blessing but depraved our very being.

In a later section we shall examine the consequences of the Protestant doctrine on its human side: the denial of freedom and the predestination to which it necessarily leads. Now we emphasize that the Council of Trent was not merely "painting the background" for its decrees on justification when it seemed to go back to Pelagian times to

---

[21] *DS* 375.
[22] *DS* 179; 1 Cor. 4:7, 15:10.

redefine the necessity of grace at every stage in the economy of salvation. For although few words occurred more frequently in the writing of Luther or of Calvin than grace, the meaning was changed from what Augustine defended or the Council of Orange had defined. It was at best a remedy for perverse human nature, and not, as Christian tradition always believed, first an exaltation of man to the family of God.

However, a new tone entered the scene. Where previous statements of the *magisterium* treated of grace more abstractly and referred to the person of Christ mostly to support the argument, the Council of Trent placed the subject into a Christological setting, no doubt because the Reformers charged the Church with usurping the honor and authority of the Savior.

And there is another difference in Trent. Since the papacy and scholastic theology were accused of canonizing good works to the exclusion of grace, before man's cooperation could be safely explained the absolute and prior need of God's action had to be clarified.

Accordingly, in the case of adults, "without divine grace through Jesus Christ (no one) can be justified before God by his own works, whether they were done by his natural powers or by the light of the teaching of the (Mosaic) Law." We receive grace through the Redeemer not merely to assist us to live justly and merit everlasting life, as if we could accomplish either, by our own free will without grace, even if we stipulate it would be difficult. It is simply unthinkable that, "without the Holy Spirit's preceding inspiration and without His help man can believe, hope and love or be repentant, as is required, if the grace of justification is to be given to him."[23]

These declarations are clear enough. But the precise point on the supernaturality of grace was rather implied than explicitly declared. Then Michael de Bay (Baius) denied the supernatural order and said it

---

[23] *DS* 1551–53; *CCC* 1813, 1989.

was gratuitous only because sinners are unworthy of divine mercy, thus echoing the Reformation theory about man's original state before the fall. De Bay was condemned by St. Pius V (1567) to give us the first formal statements by the Church on the intrinsic supernaturalness of divine grace.

Among the seventy-nine censured propositions of Baius, two are especially pertinent. Positively, he asserted that "the exalting of human nature to a participation of the divine nature was due to the integrity of man in his first state, and for that reason should be called natural, not supernatural." And negatively, "It is absurd to say, as some do, that man was elevated from the beginning, by means of some supernatural and gratuitous gift, above the condition of his nature, in order to worship God supernaturally by faith, hope and charity."[24] Much the same sentiments were expressed on the preternatural gifts, notably freedom from concupiscence, that Jansenius was later to develop into a new theological system.

A graphic commentary on the devious ways of heresy was the famous *comma Pianum,* missing in the original draft of Pius' condemnation of Baius, and supplied by the latter's followers to suit their own fancy. The Pope had said, at the end of the catalogue of false propositions that, "although some of them might be defensible under a certain aspect, in the strict and proper sense of the words intended by those who profess them We condemn (these statements) as heretical, erroneous, suspect, temerarious, scandalous and offensive to piety." Baius and his friends inserted a comma after "who profess them," to make the Pope say that some of the prepositions are tenable in the sense understood by their defendants.

Jansenius was condemned almost a century later, (1635) in a synthesis of five opinions that have made theological history. Only

---

[24] *DS* 1921–23.

one, the fourth, has relevance here. According to the Bishop of Ypres, "the Semi-Pelagians admitted the necessity of internal, preparatory grace for individual acts, even for the beginning of faith; they were heretics for this reason that they wished this grace to be such that the human will could resist it or obey it."[25]

Both statements are untenable, the one as a matter of history and the other on dogmatic grounds. It is not true that the Semi-Pelagians admitted the necessity of internal grace for the "beginning of faith"; they were condemned for denying it. But by implication the Jansenists condemned themselves for calling it heretical to say the human will can resist or obey the internal inspirations of God. Liberty is just a name unless it has the option of accepting or rejecting grace.

Characteristically the Jansenists tried to evade Innocent X's censure of their founder. They piously agreed with the Pope that the five propositions he termed heretical were erroneous indeed, but, as it happened, they were never taught by Jansenius. Their real author was Antoine Arnauld (1612–1694), who aroused the enmity of the Jesuits for criticizing their educational experiments. The Jesuits avenged themselves by saddling the errors on the late Bishop of Ypres and getting Rome to pass sentence.

As a result Jansenism continued to propagate as though Rome had never spoken. This went on for three years, until the next pontiff, Alexander VII, published his Constitution *Ad Sacram Beati Petri Sedem* (October 16, 1656) that is rightly considered the highpoint of papal authority prior to the First Vatican Council. The Constitution was the first explicit case in papal history where a solemn definition, binding irrevocably, dealt uniquely with an object connected only extrinsically with the deposit of faith, namely, did Jansenius teach what the Pope condemned. Alexander, therefore, published, "We

---

[25] *DS* 2004.

declare and define that the five propositions were taken from the book of the aforementioned Cornelius Jansenius, Bishop of Ypres, whose title is *Augustinus*, and that they were condemned in the sense intended by the same Cornelius."[26]

Still the evasion continued, until nine years later when Alexander composed a formula of submission to his own and predecessor's Constitutions, to be taken under oath and "*sincero animo*," as a condition for ordination to the priesthood and consecration to the episcopate. Among those who refused to take the oath were the organizers of the Old Catholic Churches, who are affiliated by "intercommunion" with the Anglicans and Episcopalians.

Modern Times

By the time of the First Vatican Council Western religious culture had radically altered. Influenced by Kantianism, authors were no longer discussing the relative importance of faith and goodworks, or arguing, as did the Jansenists, whether divine inspiration overcomes free will. They called into question the very existence of revelation, without which grace and the supernatural are fabulous myths. Kantian rationalism furnished the framework for much of the Vatican teaching on the necessity of grace for divine faith, "which is the beginning of human salvation."

Immanuel Kant (1724–1804) is often called the greatest of modern philosophers. He was certainly the most influential. His notion of religion was consistent with his general theory of knowledge and reality. He believed that man should recognize no authority superior to his own conscience, and therefore everyone should make his own judgment in religion and morality.

---

[26] *DS* 2012.

Historical events and personages may yield man an occasional clue; certain institutions may afford him a modicum of social support; and even revelation, were its authority beyond cavil, might hasten his discovery of the eternal verities. Yet all these aids are no more than adventitious, and the strong man will avoid undue reliance upon them trusting, so far as possible, in himself alone. For, irrespective of racial heritage, social environment or personal traits, the inner voice of reason is always his surest guide; and the fact that his own conscience commands him to be perfect bespeaks a corresponding ability to obey its behest through his own efforts.[27]

Consequently, just as Kantian ethics are independent of any other postulate than the mind, so religion is a creature of pure reason and moral strength has no need of help from the outside.

The Vatican I dogmas on faith and the Church were specially concerned with this modern anthropolatry, as the *Acta* of the Council clearly indicate. They went over the ground covered before in conflict with Pelagianism and during the Reformation, and carried the Christian teaching still more deeply on the necessity of divine grace for salvation—on three levels: as external grace in the form of revelation, internal grace to accept revealed truth in humility of faith, and social grace in the supernatural society founded by Jesus Christ.

On the level of the external grace of revelation, the Council outlined the two kinds of necessity under which we labor and because of which God must come to our aid. One is the moral necessity of enlightenment on the truths of natural religion, God's existence and the rest; the other is a physical necessity that arises from our elevation to a higher than natural end. On both counts we need divine grace, in the form of

---

[27] Immanuel Kant, *Religion Within the Limits of Reason Alone* (Chicago: The Open Court, 1934), 74–75.

external communication to the mind, supernaturally transmitted by God, and inviting our acceptance on the word of an all-wise and truthful Revealer.

Thus, "it is owing to this divine revelation that, even in the present condition of the human race, those religious truths which are by their nature accessible to human reason, can easily be known by all men with solid certitude and with no trace of error."[28] Mankind, in other words, needs the gift of revelation to know the truths of the natural law with ease, objective certainty and subjective conviction.

The reasons for such help are not hard to find. For the truths that have to do with God and our relations to Him transcend the sensible order; and where they call for practical application and realization, demand self-surrender and self-abnegation. In acquiring these truths our intellect is hampered not only by the impulses of sense and imagination, but also by evil passions stemming from original sin. As a result, men readily persuade themselves in religious matters that what they do not wish to be true is false or at least doubtful.

But this is minor compared with the greater need of the external grace of revelation, which is "absolutely necessary only because God, out of His infinite goodness, destined man to a supernatural end, that is, to a participation in the good things of God, which altogether exceed the human mental grasp; for 'eye has not seen, nor ear heard, nor has it entered into the heart of man, what things God has prepared for those who love Him.' "[29]

To still speak of the inner voice of pure reason as man's surest religious guide is to deify, as Kant did, the autonomous human intellect; and to open the way, as his followers did, for that apostasy from God which the Vatican Council foresaw in 1870 and which twentieth-century secularism and Communism completely verified.

---

[28] *DS* 3005; *CCC* 38.
[29] *DS* 3005; 1 Cor. 2:9.

However, the fact of revelation is not enough to believe and profit from the benefits of faith, whether of naturally-knowable truths or of strict mysteries. Internal and strictly supernatural grace is also required to make faith itself possible. Again the First Vatican Council harked back to Pelagian times, but the urgency then was nothing compared to the crisis now. It underlined those elements which modern man has most need to recall: that he is a weak, finite being completely subordinate to God; that he needs faith to be saved and grace to believe; that humility of soul is required to accept the mysteries which reason cannot by itself perceive; and that the reward of faith is a firm hope on earth of an eternal reward after death.

> Because man depends entirely on God as his Creator and Lord, and because created reason is wholly subordinate to uncreated Truth, we are obliged to render by faith a full submission of intellect and will to God when He makes a revelation.
>
> This faith, however, which is the beginning of human salvation, the Catholic Church asserts to be a supernatural virtue. With the inspiration and assistance of God's grace, by that faith we believe the things He has revealed are true—not because their intrinsic truth is seen with the natural light of reason—but because of the authority of God who reveals them, of God who can neither deceive nor be deceived. For, on the word of the Apostle, "Faith is the substance of things to be hoped for, the evidence of things that are not seen."[30]

Certain semi-Rationalists in the Catholic camp said we may need grace to believe, but only for the faith which includes all the theological virtues. We can believe quite on our own if only faith, minus sanctifying grace, is involved. This was a new angle suggested by

---

[30] *DS* 3008; *CCC* 156.

Georg Hermes (1775–1831), professor of theology at Munster, in an effort to adjust Catholic principles to the supposed requirements of Kant's philosophy.

Hermes distinguished two kinds of faith: a faith of knowledge, or intellectual adherence to religious truths on the basis of reasoned arguments; and faith of the heart, or a habitual state of will completely submissive to God and conforming one's whole life to what is believed. Only the latter, living faith, was truly free and needed supernatural grace from God.

The Council condemned Hermesianism by reasserting the indispensability of grace for divine faith, which is not an irrational instinct (as some Rationalists claimed) nor a purely natural act of the mind (as Hermes had taught), but a free response to God's inspiration that can be rejected if we choose. So that, "even though the assent of faith is by no means a blind impulse, still, no one can assent to the gospel preaching as he must in order to be saved without the enlightenment and inspiration of the Holy Spirit, who gives all men their joy in assenting to and believing the truth. Hence, faith itself is essentially a gift of God and the act of faith is a work that pertains to salvation. By this act man offers to God Himself a free obedience since he concurs and cooperates with God's grace, when he could resist it."[31]

There is another aspect of grace, the social, on whose necessity the First Vatican Council passed judgment. The Catholic Church is at once a cosmic external grace and the source of internal, supernatural helps that men need to find and remain in the faith "without which it is impossible to please God."

Granting we must believe "to enter into the company of God's sons, no one has ever obtained justification without faith, and no one will reach eternal life unless he has persevered in the faith to the end." In

---

[31] *DS* 3010; *CCC* 153, 143–44.

His mercy God did not leave the acquisition of this important commodity to our own initiative or trust that we should keep it if left alone. "In order to enable us to fulfill our obligation of embracing the true faith and steadfastly persevering in it, God established the Church through His only-begotten Son, and endowed it with unmistakable marks of its foundation, so it could be recognized by all as the guardian and teacher of the revealed word."[32]

Accordingly the Catholic Church was established primarily as a grace to mankind, to teach men the truths they need to be saved and protect them from error that might endanger their salvation.

The implications of this doctrine are profound. Fifteen centuries after Pelagius and Cassian, the Church is still defending the need of grace for salutary acts, but now the type and range of necessity have changed, and the shift is most significant. Formerly the question arose as something speculative, among people who otherwise professed the Christian faith; it was mainly a moral and volitional problem and concerned more with individuals than with huge segments of society. Now the issue does not merely verge on the practical, as any theory allowed to ferment long enough in men's minds is bound to; it is a crucial situation that faces a large part of Western civilization, whose supernatural moorings are being swept away by generations of uninhibited naturalism.

Formerly the almost academic question was whether a person could rightly use his will without grace and reach a heaven in which the Christian people of the time still believed; now the very existence of a supernatural destiny beyond the grave is ignored, and the power of human reason so extolled that any help from outside of man is simply denied. Modern Pelagianism is the heresy of intellectual self-sufficiency.

Conscious of this state of affairs, the Church has added a new dimension to her teaching on the necessity of grace, the pragmatic one

---

[32] *DS* 3012; *CCC* 846, 851, 2104.

of how to bring a whole culture back on the road "that leads to life" from which it had strayed. Hence the stress on proclaiming the Church's mission in the world, "like a standard lifted up for the nations," as a visible grace inviting those who see her to accept the faith she proposes and through it enter the pathway to heavenly glory.

SPIRITUAL IMPLICATIONS

The simple fact that we need grace to perform actions conducive to salvation has corollaries that touch on every phase of the spiritual life and the apostolate. Many of these implications are bound up with special aspects of the subject, to be treated later in detail. But even at this point certain consequences should be brought into the open, to strengthen appreciation of this "kindness and generosity of God our Savior," and extend the horizons of our zeal.

Universal Need

The more common teaching of theologians is that sanctifying grace alone is not enough to act supernaturally; that in addition God must furnish us with actual graces every time we place a salutary act. Of course unbelievers cannot begin to approach Him "heaven-wise" without these transient infusions in the mind and will; nor can people in sin return to God without His prevenient help; and even those who enjoy the divine friendship need special, supernatural assistance in a multitude of ways, from overcoming severe temptations to remaining in God's love until death.

All this is assured, and will be seen in context as the questions arise. But we are saying that the state of grace must be supplemented constantly by the providential activity of God. The general divine concurrence would not suffice, even though we possess the infused virtues and our faculties are elevated by divine love. In the words of

Trent, "Christ Jesus Himself is constantly pouring strength (*iugiter virtutam influat*) into the justified, even as the head gives strength to the members, and the vine to the branches. This strength always precedes, accompanies and follows (*semper antecedit et comitatur et subsequitur*) the good works of the justified and without it the good works cannot be at all pleasing to God or meritorious."[33]

St. Thomas puts this need for constant infusion of actual grace to the character of the virtues of faith, hope, and charity we possess. "Man is not so perfectly directed by them to his final end that he does not besides always have to be moved by a kind of higher instinct of the Holy Spirit."[34] It is comparable to the action of the faculties on the natural level, which must receive motion from God, the first cause, concurrent with their native powers. Raised to a higher order of being, they need another elevated impulse to go into action on this more sublime plane.

Humility and Prayer

Why this incessant, supernatural dependence upon God? The saints saw it as a mark of divine bounty. "If anyone marvel that God made all His creatures such that they should always need aid of His grace, let him know that God did it out of His double goodness. First to keep them from pride by causing them to perceive their feebleness, and to call upon Him; and secondly, to do His creatures honor and comfort."[35]

One of the surest remedies for pride, and safeguard against its rise is the self-consciousness of necessity. A man is proud in the degree to which he considers himself independent, and the acme of pride is the belief in perfect self-sufficiency. In the natural, physical order our

---

[33] *DS* 1546; *CCC* 2000, 2024.
[34] St. Thomas Aquinas, *Summa Theologiae*, I–II, q. 68, a. 2.
[35] St. Thomas More, *Treatise on the Passion* (New Haven: Yale University Press, 1976).

dependence on others is realized by us from the dawn of reason, and by reflection back to the first moment of existence. "What have you that you have not received?" is a description of man's life from conception to the last act of charity we receive before we die.

It is less obvious that behind all we receive from others is the perennial goodness of God, the real fountainhead of altruism and the source, not only of human charity but of every blessing that enters our lives. Yet we must pause to reflect on God's part to appreciate His generosity.

The same with grace. Here not reason or memory but faith must tell us we are beneficiaries of a continuous, supranatural inflow of which God is the author more immediately and directly than ever happens in nature, where secondary agents are more than mere instruments of the First Cause. More than ever, we have cause to say in humility, "I am what I am because of the mercy of God."

This consciousness of perpetual reliance on the Author of grace should inspire unceasing prayer. It is not coincidental that all the terms Christ used to designate prayer have to do with begging for favors from God. Since we are constantly in need of divine help, and God as constantly must furnish it, once we realize both realities, we are inspired constantly to pray. Indeed the spontaneity with which we turn to God in prayer is an index of our spiritual life. To be religious is to have the habit of prayer, or to pray always. "As our bodily life discovers itself by its activity, so is the presence of the Holy Spirit in us discovered by a spiritual activity, and this activity is the spirit of continual prayer. Prayer is to the spiritual life what the beating of the pulse and drawing of the breath are to the life of the body."[36]

The constant need we have of grace is not only calculated to keep us humble, or move us to pray. Its function is also to show us what those who lack faith cannot conceive: that God cares for His creatures

---

[36] John Henry Newman, *Parochial and Plain Sermons* (London: Longmans, Green, 1908), 7:209; *CCC* 2569–660, 2742–45.

with a minute constancy that scandalizes the natural man. What does it mean for us to depend so completely on God, except that He providentially makes Himself our perpetual support?

If the norm of charity is solicitude for another's needs, the depth of divine love for man must be extreme, since the interest that God has in our welfare extends to the least salutary action we perform. This, in turn, is another motive for prayer, not only of petition for help but of gratitude for favors received.

From Christ the Head to His Body

The remarkable feature about our need of grace is that it simply means our need of Christ, and the proof in revelation for this necessity is the declaration of the Savior that, "with out me you can do nothing."

If we study the concept more closely, and especially see its expansion in St. Paul, we find that the source of this gracious indispensability is not merely Christ in His physical person as the God-man but Christ in the wholeness of the mystical personality He entered by incorporating us into His Church. When He said, "I am the true vine, you are the branches," He gave us His own image of the Mystical Body, which is the extension of Himself, the total Christ, the Catholic Church of Pauline and Christian theology.

It is as Head of the Mystical Body, therefore, that Christ communicates to us the graces we need to be saved and sanctified. Holiness, whether substantial in the possession of sanctifying grace or superior in striving after perfection, begins from Christ and Christ is always its cause. No action of our leading to glory can be placed unless it comes from Him as its supernatural source.

If we grieve and do penance for our sins; if we turn to God with filial fear and hope of reward, it is because Christ is leading us. Grace flows from Him, our Head, as from an inexhaustible fullness.

Our Savior is continually pouring out His gifts of counsel, fortitude, fear and piety, especially on the leading members of His Body, so that the whole Body may grow ever more and more in holiness and in integrity of life. When the sacraments of the Church are administered by external rite, it is He who produces their effect in souls. He nourishes the redeemed with His own flesh and blood, and thus calms the turbulent passions of the soul; He gives increase of grace and prepares future glory for souls and bodies.

All these treasures of His divine goodness He is said to bestow on the members of His Mystical Body, not merely because He, as the Eucharistic Victim on earth and the glorified Victim in heaven, through His wounds and prayers places our cause before the Eternal Father. He also selects, He determines, He distributes every single grace to every single person, "according to the measure of the giving of Christ."[37]

In order to have a clearer picture of this important relationship of Christ with the Church, it will help to examine briefly the different kinds of grace that are found in Him and which of these precisely flows into His Body. Following St. Thomas, theologians commonly distinguish three types of benefit conferred *gratis* on the human nature of Christ. "The first is the grace of union, whereby the human nature, with no merits preceding, received the gift of being united in person to the Son of God. The second is the singular grace whereby the soul of Christ was filled with grace and truth beyond all other souls. The third is the grace of being Head, in virtue of which grace flows from Him to others."[38] We find the three forms described in sequence by St. John the Evangelist. Regarding the grace of union, he

---

[37] Pius XII, *On the Mystical Body of Christ* [*Mystici Corporis*] (1943), 51; *CCC* 957.
[38] St. Thomas Aquinas, *Compendium Theologiae*, cap. 214.

says, "The Word was made flesh"; of His singular grace of sanctity, he adds, "We saw his glory, glory as of the only-begotten of the Father, full of grace and truth;" and of the grace of headship, "of his fulness we have all received."[39]

All three types are, in their way, infinite. The grace of union is evidently more than finite because in His human nature Christ received the gift of becoming the Son of God not by participation but by nature. And since natural divinity is infinite, also the union by which the divinity was received is infinite by its very essence.

We might suspect that sanctifying grace with its concomitants is not infinite in Christ, "Since such grace is a created gift, we have to acknowledge that it has a finite essence."[40] Yet it may be considered infinite because the whole of Christ's human nature was filled to ultimate capacity, because He received all that pertains to the nature of grace and, especially, because by the hypostatic union His soul was united to the divinity, which is perfectly inexhaustible. As a corollary, therefore, the grace of headship in the Mystical Body is likewise infinite. What Christ possesses He communicates. "And since He has received the gifts of the Spirit without measure, He has the power of pouring forth without measure all that belongs to the grace of the Head. Consequently His grace is sufficient for the salvation not only of some men but of the whole world, as expressed by St. John that "He is the propitiation for our sins; and not for ours only, but also for those of the whole world; and we may add, of many worlds, if such existed."[41]

Now arises the subtle question: in what sense do we receive from the fulness of grace that is in Christ? It would not be accurate to say that the created gifts in Christ are so abundant that they "flow over" from Head to members in such a way that our portion is numerically

---

[39] John 1:14, 16.
[40] St. Thomas Aquinas, *op. cit.*, cap. 215.
[41] Ibid.

the same as His. Also not a few graces that we possess, like faith and sorrow for sin, are not formally present in Christ. Theologians for these reasons prefer to speak of the grace of headship in its relation to the whole organism of the Mystical Body as the uncreated gift of the Holy Spirit, who dwells in Christ to an infinite degree. And it is this numerically identical gift that flows into the Body and its members with finite limitations according to the measure of Christ's donation and suited to the dispositions or office that each one in the Body occupies. Thus "although the habitual gifts are not the same in the soul of Christ and in ourselves, yet the same Holy Spirit who abides in Him is the one that fills those who are to be sanctified."[42]

Grace to Mankind

There is no difficulty accepting on faith the mystery of sanctification, wherein the members of the Mystical Body are animated by the Spirit of Christ and from Him receive all the blessing of the supernatural life. But can we extend the principle to include also those who are not actually in the Body of Christ? Do they also depend on the invisible Head of the Church for all the graces they receive? They must, since there are not two Christs, one who is Head of the Mystical Body and another who is not.

We go a step further. Is there a legitimate sense in which non-Catholics derive supernatural grace not only from Christ who is Head of the Church but from Christ precisely as Head of the Mystical Body? While the answer is affirmative, it needs to be carefully distinguished. When we speak of Christ as Head of the Church we mean the Savior in His capacity of governing the society of human beings of which His own divine Spirit is the animating principle. He governs this society in two ways: the first by imparting sanctity to individual persons and the

---

[42] St. Thomas Aquinas, *In Joannem*, cap. 1, lectio 10.

second by uniting these individuals into a living organism that is destined to last for all eternity.

The two are quite distinct. A person can be in the Mystical Body and not be in sanctifying grace, as he can be in the state of grace without being an actual member of the Church. But in the latter case, he obtains justification only because he is somehow in conjunction with the Church. For an infant this means baptism by water. For an adult it means that degree of response to the divine will which God will recognize as implying the desire to be incorporated into His Body. It matters little that *psychologically* a non-Catholic is not aware of the full implications of his generosity; *ontologically* God sees the implications and credits the soul accordingly.[43]

Equally important and more subtle is the second way that Christ operates as Head of the Mystical Body. We are liable to forget that personal sanctification is not the only purpose of the redemption. In the plan of God, we are not only to be personally sanctified but also united with Christ and each other in union whose intimacy is incomprehensible to the natural man. If a person is in the state of grace but not actually in the Church, Christ's function will be to draw him into ever closer approximation to actual membership, until (at least after death) he is fully incorporated into the Body of Christ.[44]

Consequently the teaching of the Vatican I Fathers stands firm: "there is no communication of the Spirit except in the Church," i.e., in relation to her by some kind of volitional response to her teaching, either actual profession or such generosity as objectively (though unwittingly) includes the desire to become a Catholic. Also "there is not communication of the Spirit except through the Church," i.e., through her invisible Head, who sanctifies individuals wherever He finds the necessary

---

[43] *CCC* 846–48; cf. Vatican Council II, *Dogmatic Constitution on the Church* [*Lumen Gentium*] (1964), 14–16.
[44] *CCC* 1045.

good will, and incorporates them into Himself. The very analogy with a human organism permits us to see how the Body of Christ can be active beyond its own physical self, by radiating power that affects others besides its own members and by assimilating elements from the outside for its growth and amplification.

However, we are not to suppose that Christ acts independently of the Church in His action of sanctifying and incorporating non-Catholics to Himself. He uses the Church on every level of her ministration, especially the Sacrifice of the Mass and the prayers and sacrifices of the faithful.

The most important medium in the Church for the salvation of the non-Catholic world is the Sacrifice of the Mass. On the altar is renewed the oblation of Calvary because it is the same Priest and Victim who offered Himself on the Cross. Moreover, the appointed ends are the same, notably the expiation of sin and impetration of grace from Almighty God.

To be emphasized is the universality of the fruits of the Mass. "No one was better fitted," wrote Pius XII, "to make satisfaction for all the sins of mankind than Christ. Therefore He desired to be immolated upon the Cross as a propitiation for our sins, and not for ours only but also for *those of the whole world*. In like manner, He daily offers Himself upon our altars for our redemption."[45] These are the sentiments of the Church in her liturgy, where at every Offertory of the Mass she prays that "the chalice of salvation may ascend for our salvation and *that of the whole world*." Thus anticipating before the consecration the words of Christ Himself at the Last Supper: "This is the chalice of My blood, of the new and eternal covenant, which shall be shed for you and for many, unto the remission of sins." The expression "for many" has always been understood to mean "for all mankind."

---

[45] Pius XII, *On the Sacred Liturgy* [*Mediator Dei*] (1947), 73.

As far back as we go in the Church's tradition, she has always recognized the Mass as a universal instrument for the salvation of the gentiles who were still outside the City of God. One of the most eloquent comes to us from the fifth century under the authority of the then-reigning pontiff, St. Celestine. When priests "fulfill the sacerdotal office entrusted to them, they are *pleading the cause of the human race* before the divine clemency, and while the whole Church mingles its sighs with theirs, they beg and pray that faith may be given to the infidels, that idolaters may be freed from the errors of their impiety, that the light of truth may appear to the Jews, that heretics may return to wisdom with the true comprehension of the Catholic faith, that schismatics may receive the spirit of charity once more revived in them and that those who are lapsed may be given the remedy of repentance."[46] This doctrine, says the pope, "was handed down from the Apostles," and therefore represents the mind of Christ, whose prayer for unity at the Last Supper is perpetuated in every Sacrifice of the Mass.

Correlative with the Mass are the prayers and sacrifices of the faithful, impetrating from Christ the graces which He dispenses outside the Mystical Body. As with the Mass, the tradition goes back to the early Church and is based on the dogmatic principle that the fruits of the Redemption are applicable to all the members of the human family. Following the example of his Master, Stephen prayed for his persecutors and Paul for the recalcitrant Jews, even to becoming anathema if this were necessary to win their salvation.

However, besides the salvific will of God another principle is also operative in this tradition of apostolic prayer and sacrifice in favor of the non-Catholic world. While believing that conversion to Catholicism and especially final perseverance is a gift of divine liberality, we recognize

---

[46] St. Celestine, "Epistola ad Episcopos Galliarum," *Patrologia Latina (MPL)*, ed. J.P. Migne, 50:535.

the corresponding need of human activity antecedent to the reception of grace, notably the necessity of prayer. It may be the prayer that a person says for himself, asking for divine guidance and strength to follow the will of God; it may also be the prayer that others say in addition to his own or in his stead. For Catholics as well as non-Catholics the latter altruistic prayer is indispensable. We need the prayers of the living members of the Mystical Body of Christ to reach our heavenly destiny.

In a famous letter that St. Augustine wrote against the Pelagians we have all the essentials of this doctrine with reference to those who are eventually converted to God. Augustine pleads with his correspondent to recognize the Church's duty of praying for those outside of her fold. "Surely you will not forbid the Church to pray for unbelievers that they may be believers, for those who refuse to believe that they may be willing to believe, for those who are at variance with God's law and doctrine, that God may give them what He promised by the prophet, 'A heart for understanding Him and ears for hearing.'" He argues from the practice of St. Paul in favor of the unbelieving Jews, saying that "my prayer to God is for them unto salvation."[47]

As a general principle, therefore, "these and other divine testimonies prove that God by His grace takes away the stony heart from unbelievers and forestalls merit in men of good will. . . . This is shown both by thanksgiving and by prayer: prayer for unbelievers; thanksgiving for believers. Prayer is to be made to Him that He might do what we ask; thanksgiving is to be offered when He has done it."[48] Both would be useless and "a mockery," unless the prayers of the Church effected the sanctification of those estranged from God and thanksgiving were demanded in gratitude for the Church's prayers having been answered.

---

[47] St. Augustine, "Epistola ad Vitalem," *MPL* 33:900.
[48] Ibid.

Pope Pius XII gave voice to the same tradition when, in his capacity as Vicar of Christ, he declared that "We have committed to the protection and guidance of heaven those who do not belong to the visible Body of the Catholic Church," and united with "the prayers of the whole Church, We desire nothing more ardently than that they may have life and have it more abundantly."[49]

If we couple the individual prayers of the faithful with the public worship of the Church, and add to these the sacrifices and sanctity of the whole Mystical Body of Christ, we have in cosmic outline the ultimate basis for the Church's necessity for the salvation of all mankind. By divine ordinance she is the great sacrament through whom graces are dispensed to the entire human race. Within her Body, members receive these gifts as by a special privilege to which, by God's mercy, they have a supernatural title. But even outside her Body, whoever is eventually saved, must credit his salvation to the instrumentality of the Catholic Church, whose invisible Head is the fountain of all life and holiness and of whose fulness anyone who is sanctified must have received.[50]

---

49 *Mystici Corporis* 103.
50 *CCC* 846; cf. *Lumen Gentium* 14.

3

POWERS AND LIMITATIONS OF FALLEN NATURE

Man is a bundle of contradictions. Newman called him the strange composite of heaven and earth, cloaking corruption yet weakness mastering power. "What sort of freak then is man," wrote Pascal, "How novel, how monstrous, how chaotic, how paradoxical, how prodigious! Judge of all things, feeble earthworm, repository of truth, sink of doubt and error, glory and refuse of the universe!"[51]

Over the centuries poets and philosophers have written at length on the paradox of human nature, at once glorious and hideous, capable of mystic union with God or of eating with swine in the parable. Depending on the mood or theme, we get representations of human idealism as in Virgil's *Aeneid* or of human depravity as in Schopenhauer. Both aspects have their element of truth, and common experience shows that men are more complex than the simple definition "rational animal" would lead us to suspect.

This complexity is more than might be expected of joining spirit and matter in one being. It arises from two other sources, both above the grasp of mere reason: that man has been elevated not only above brute creation but raised to a destiny with God by grace, and that man is not now what he once was or that God originally intended him to be. He has been sublimated to a supernatural order by divine love, and debased himself by his own sin.

[51] Blaise Pascal, *Pensees,* 131, trans. A. J. Krailsheimer (London: Penguin, 1995), 34.

Faced with this mass of contradictions, Catholic theology has steered a middle course between so exalting humanity that, without grace, we could aspire to heavenly beatitude, and so depressing our nature that nothing is left but sin. To maintain this balance, the Church has had to defend the true mean against extremists on either side, beginning with the Pelagians for whom free will is the only grace a man needs, and ending, or rather continuing with those who despair of man's ability of himself to know any truth or do any moral good.

AUTONOMY AND IMPOTENCE

The adversaries' position on the necessity of grace may be viewed from the standpoints of either ultimate destiny or the obstacles that stand in the way. On the first level, the stream of theories from Pelagius to Luther and Calvin has been remarkably constant. Man's destiny as originally intended by God is not a gratuitous elevation to the supernatural order but a function of his nature, to which humanity had a legitimate claim.

But there the parallel ends. Pelagianism and classical Protestantism equally recognized the fact of original sin. Their estimate of the fall, however, and of the consequences it had on man's efforts to reach heaven was radically different. Pelagius and his followers were theological optimists, who saw no serious results of Adam's sin infecting the human family; the Reformers were dogmatic pessimists for whom the fall of the first man meant the collapse of human nature and the loss of every intrinsic good. Between them historically, and beyond them to the present day, is a variety of theories on the powers and limitations of the mind, soul, and will. All these theories can easily bewilder us unless we see them in their proper setting.

Pelagian Optimism

In the extant writing of St. Augustine we have a detailed exposition of the doctrine of Pelagius, Caelestius, and their disciples. He often quotes them verbatim and always clarifies their meaning in spite of the deliberate ambiguity of these classic exponents of moral naturalism.

The Pelagians at first made no mention of grace but only stressed man's native ability to keep all the commandments, to practice all the virtues, and to attain eternal life. "They are such enemies of the grace of God as to claim that a person can keep all the divine mandates without it, which, if true, makes useless the Lord's words to us, 'without me you can do nothing.' "[52]

Under pressure from Augustine and others, the critics of grace shifted ground, at least verbally. To avoid condemnation they pretended to admit the necessity of grace, which for them was nature itself and its endowment of free will. "I am not denying God's grace," Pelagius protested, "since I defend human liberty." On which Augustine commented, "How clever, but transparent."[53]

At this point they developed the famous set of distinctions between *possibility, will,* and *action.* Realizing they had to make some compromise on grace, they held that the possibility of willing and doing good comes from God alone, since He gave us our nature and the faculties of choice and action. But the choice and action themselves are only from man, with no help from God. They proceed solely from our own free will and are of our own making.

Further pressed by the opposition to recognize grace as something distinct from the free will, the Pelagians began to speak of grace according to the Scriptures, as a composite of such gifts as the Law

---

[52] St. Augustine, "De Haeresibus," 88, *MPL* 42:47.
[53] St. Augustine, "Sermo 26," 7, *MPL* 38:174.

and sacred doctrine by which God assists human weakness to help us
know what to do and what to avoid. They added the "grace" of the
forgiveness of sin. Still later, the benefits of the virtues were noted and
Jesus Christ was proposed as a model for us to imitate.

These admissible graces, however, were all external. A distinction
was made between *possibility* and *assistance* to possibility. By possibility they understood nature itself, by assistance they meant the Law,
doctrine, revelation, example of Christ, miracles, and the like, to help
us acquire and persevere in the justice of God. They were eloquent in
extolling graces of this type, but equally clear that there was no question of absolute indispensability. "Their function is only to enable men
more easily to accomplish through grace what they are commanded to
do by their own free will."[54]

Meanwhile, the controversy reached a critical stage. What finally
led to the exposure of Pelagianism and its condemnation, after previous acquittal by Pope Zosimus, (A.D. 418), was the question of baptism. Under Roman inquiry, Celestius published a book in which he
declared that infants should be baptized "according to the rule of the
Church, and according to the meaning of the Gospel. For the Lord has
determined that the kingdom of heaven (the Church) should only be
conferred on baptized person." But when he came to explain what this
means he denied that infant baptism removes original sin.

> We did not admit, however, that infants must be baptized
> for remission of sins, as though to affirm there is sin by trans-
> mission. This is very alien from the Catholic meaning,
> because sin is not born with a man; it is subsequently com-
> mitted by man. For it is shown to be a fault, not of nature, but
> of the will. It is fitting, therefore, to confess this, lest we seem

---

[54] St. Augustine, "De Gratia Christi et de Peccato Originali", I, 29, *MPL* 44:375.

to make different kinds of baptism. Moreover it is necessary to lay down this preliminary safeguard, lest, by the occasion of its mystery, evil should be said to be conveyed to man by nature, before it had been committed by man—to the disparagement of the Creator.[55]

At first Pelagius was either afraid or ashamed to make the same blunt admission. Augustine compares the two men by saying the one, Celestius, was more open; the other more reserved: Or, at any rate, that one was more candid and the other more astute. But eventually Pelagius supported his "more pertinacious" disciple and declared openly that "Everything good, and everything evil, on account of which we are either laudable or blameworthy, is not born with us but done by us. For we are born not fully developed, with a certain capacity for either conduct. We are procreated as without virtue, so also without vice. Previous to the action of our own proper will, that alone is in man which God has formed."[56]

In these words the dogmas of both men were contained. Infants are born without the contagion of sin from Adam. He fell, no doubt, but "Adam's sin was injurious to himself alone, and not to the human race."[57] At worst he set a bad example which the opposite good example of Christ may be said to counteract.

A final nuance to the Pelagian theme, after Zosimus' censure, was to admit the possibility of some kind of special illumination of the mind, without letting go of the major premise. That is the notion that we have, antecedent to grace, the natural capacity to do good, avoid sin, and even reach Christian perfection.

---

[55] St. Augustine, "De Gratia Christi et de Peccato Originali", II, 5–6; *CCC* 403.
[56] St. Augustine, "De Gratia Christi et de Peccato Originali", 14; *CCC* 404.
[57] St. Augustine, "De Gratia Christi et de Peccato Originali"; *CCC* 405.

Cassian's Compromise

The Semi-Pelagian theory arose from an uncritical attitude towards St. Augustine, whose critique of Pelagianism seemed to have left no room for free will.

Basically the difficulty was rooted in a certain confusion of the natural and supernatural by the ascetic Cassian, who was no theologian and whose interests were wholly practical. He did not see why man cannot achieve at least something by his own power in the supernatural order. He never claimed, as did Pelagius, that man was healthy in the order of grace; but neither would he go along with Augustine to say he was absolutely dead. He preferred to speak of man as being sick.

Cassian was right to affirm the integrity of the human will; he was mistaken to conclude from this that man of himself (*a semetipso*) could achieve anything towards the Beatific Vision.[58] In a later context we shall examine more closely Cassian's idea of what we can do naturally to dispose ourselves for sanctifying grace; here we wish to see mainly his basic principles and their relevance to man's power of persevering in grace and dying in the same.

There was never any doubt for Cassian that grace is supernatural, interior, and penetrates to the very soul. In this he differed completely from Pelagius. But grace in the Cassian system not so much intended to *cause an act of the will*, as to cause a *perfect act of the will*. In other words, the last word in the economy of salvation should be given not to grace but to man's free will.

On the subject of predestination, Cassian insisted on God's will to save all men; but he paid no attention to another sobering aspect of divine volition—God's consequent will. The same Lord who sincerely wants all mankind to be saved does not in fact save all mankind. Augustine faced this issue squarely, in order, as he said, to

---

[58] St. Cassian, "Collationes," XIII, 12, *MPL* 49:925.

abase human pride and defend the teachings of faith on the eternity of hell. Cassian, therefore, was led by his own premises to deny God's special regard for the elect and reduce predestination to a mere prevision of merits.

In the Semi-Pelagian theory, just as an unbeliever can by his powers merit supernatural grace to start on the pathway to heaven, so by his natural effort he can merit and obtain those helps of grace needed to persevere and grow in divine friendship. By the same token, it was held that perseverance is doubly dependent on man's freedom. He can merit grace remaining in the state of justification, and "no one receives such perseverance as he is not permitted to resist, but such as anyone may voluntarily weaken or nullify."[59]

The fixed prejudice in Semi-Pelagianism was the inability to see that God by His efficacious will grants to some and not to others the gift of final perseverance. From God's viewpoint, He equally wills the salvation of all men, which depends, in the last analysis, on them alone. To be consistent, it was even proposed that the grace of baptism is given to some and denied to other infants through a divine prevision of the futurible merits or demerits. From beginning to end, from the *initium salutis* to *finalis perseverantia,* the will takes the initiative; grace does no more than cooperate—which is an inversion of man's relation to God.

Medieval Perfectionism

A strange form of Pelagianism arose in the late Middle Ages and has since been associated with two groups of semireligious groups, the Beghards and Beguines. The Beguines were members of certain sisterhoods, founded in the Netherlands in the twelfth century. They lived a quasi-monastic life of considerable austerity, but were allowed to hold

---

[59] St. Hilary, "Letter to St. Augustine," *MPL* 33:1009.

private property and to leave the community and marry. Their male equivalents were the Beghards, who were usually weavers, dyers, or fullers. They had a common purse and no private property.

It is believed these communities derived their names from Lambert le Begue (the stammerer), a revivalist preacher who died in 1177 at Liege. They soon spread to France, Germany, and elsewhere. Their main purpose was to engage in the corporal works of mercy, along with specified times of contemplation and prayer; yet they had no common rule, mother-house, or superior.

Pious, devoted to works of mercy, and highly influential in promoting medieval devotion to Christ's humanity and passion, these lay religious at one time, in some localities were characterized by erroneous ideas on grace and free will. Finally, in 1215, the Lateran Council took steps to curtail their spread by decreeing that henceforth no religious order might be founded except in conformity with those already existing. A century later they were condemned by the Council of Vienne (1311–1312) for holding that "a man is able to acquire in this life so much and such a degree of perfection that he becomes impeccable and incapable of growing any more in grace."[60] The argument adduced was that otherwise a person could become holier than Christ if he kept growing in sanctity. Behind this strange notion was the belief that grace is a kind of *ad hoc* assistance we occasionally receive from God, instead of a perennial inflow that we need to remain in God's love, let alone to grow in holiness and avoid even venial sins.

Protestant Origins

The "black judgment" of the Reformers on human nature is common knowledge. It is impossible to read a page of Luther's *Commentary on Genesis* or of Calvin's *Institutes* without feeling we have entered a

---

[60] *DS* 891.

different atmosphere of religious thought. What is less obvious is the consistency of the Reformers' position, in which the necessity of grace became an absolute at the expense of man's volition; and yet fundamentally the need was based on a revival of the Pelagian thesis that Adam's original possessions were part of his essential nature.

Basic to the Reformed theology of grace was the principle that original justice was due to human nature by a strict right of essence. "Original righteousness," wrote Luther, "was part of man's nature (*originalem justitiam esse de natura hominis*)."[61] This cardinal principle is never lost sight of, and forms the keystone to other, better known, features of classic Protestantism.

As a logical consequence, when Adam fell and lost the righteousness he had possessed, his nature became essentially corrupt and his faculties were intrinsically vitiated. Nothing in Reformation literature is more emphatically asserted against the "scholastic innovators" who misinterpreted revelation and the Fathers.

"See what follows," urges Luther, "if you maintain that original righteousness was not a part of nature but a sort of superfluous or superadded gift. When you declare that righteousness was not a part of the essence of man, does it not also follow that sin, which took its place, is not part of the essence of man either?" If this were so, then "there was no purpose in sending Christ the Redeemer," and what can be said that is more unworthy of a theologian?[62]

He was impatient with those "who speak of our depraved nature in the manner of the philosophers, as if it were not depraved." As theologians, "let us maintain that the reason in men is most hostile to God." Instead of making light of the depravity we acquired, "let us emphasize it. Then we shall both regret deeply this state of ours and have a

---

[61] Luther, *Commentary on Genesis*, 3:7, 167.
[62] Ibid., 166.

profound longing for Christ, our Physician, who was sent by the Father to heal those evils which Satan brought upon us through sin."[63]

John Calvin was equally explicit. His concern was less about exhorting people to absolute trust in God than showing men how helpless they are before the divine majesty. While the *Institutes* dwell on the same theme, the classic treatment is in Calvin's commentary on Romans, where the apostle graphically portrays the condition of fallen man.

> Let us, then, be agreed: that men are as they are here described not merely by the defect of the depraved custom, but also by depravity of nature. The reasoning of the apostle cannot otherwise stand.
>
> First of all he strips man of all righteousness, that is, integrity and purity; then of understanding. Indeed, apostasy from God proves lack of understanding, for to seek Him is the first degree of wisdom. This lack, therefore, is necessarily found in all who have forsaken God. He adds that all have fallen away or become corrupt so that there is no one who does good.
>
> Then he adds the shameful acts with which—once they have been let loose in wickedness—defile their very members. Finally he declares them devoid of the fear of God, to whose rule our steps ought to have been directed. If these are the hereditary endowments of the human race, it is futile to seek anything good in our nature.[64]

All a man's actions are consequently sins. Melancthon, friend of Luther and principal author of the Augsburg Confession, left no doubt of the fact. "Granted there was a kind of constancy in Socrates, chastity in Xenocrates, and temperance in Zeno, they are not to be

---

[63] Ibid., 3:1, 143–44.

[64] John Calvin, *Institutes of the Christian Religion* (Philadelphia: Presbyterian Board of Christian Education, 1936), II, 3, 2.

considered true virtues but vices. Yet Pelagians (that is Catholics) deny that the force of original sin was so grave that all the works of mankind, and every effort of man, are sins."[65]

Given the postulate that man's nature is totally estranged from God, the human will is necessarily held in bondage. Except for divine grace, everything it does is a sin. The Reformers did not question that we have volitional power, but they denied its freedom to choose anything but evil. "Because of the bondage of sin by which the will is held bound, it cannot move toward good, much less apply itself thereto." Nevertheless, "the will remains, with the most eager inclination disposed and hastening to sin." If we do any good, the whole reason is God and no credit to us. "Therefore simply to will is of man; to will ill, of corrupt nature; to will well, of grace."

Lest there be any doubt on this crucial point, Calvin, following Luther and followed by all the Reformed school, compares the necessity of man's sinning with the necessity of God's goodness or the devil's malice.

> Now, when I say that the will bereft of freedom is of neces-sity either drawn or led into evil, it is a wonder if this seems a hard saying to anyone since it has nothing incongruous or alien to the usage of holy men. But it offends those who know not how to distinguish between necessity and compulsion. Suppose someone asks them: Is not God of necessity good? Is not the devil of necessity evil?
>
> Therefore, if the fact that He must be good does not hinder God's free will in doing good; if the devil, who can do only evil, yet sins with his will—who shall say that man therefore sins less willingly because he is subject to the necessity of sinning?[66]

---

[65] Philipp Melanchthon, *Loci Communes* (Erlangen: A. Deichert, 1890), 22.
[66] Calvin, *Institutes,* II, 3, 5.

This estimate of human nature was not changed when the Reformers allowed that, although a man sins in all that he does, yet in those
who are justified, their sins are not imputed because they are covered
by faith. Sins are verily imputed to the unjustified, so that all their
actions are not only sinful, *ex hypothesi,* but deserve everlasting
punishment of and by themselves because they are the fruits of a
fallen will.

Baianist Prelude

There is a direct link between the Reformation and Jansenism, in
the person of Michael de Bay, who identified the original status of
Adam with the natural order. The Flemish theologian saw Protestantism at first hand; he represented the University of Louvain at the
Council of Trent, convened to meet the Reformation crisis; and he was
perturbed over the complacent intransigence of other Catholics on the
crucial subject of grace and fallen nature.

Shortly after his appointment to Louvain, he announced his twofold
aim. First, he would free dogma from all the foreign elements that the
Scholasticism of the Middle Ages had introduced into it and that
constituted the sole obstacle to the conversion of Protestants. Second,
he would study the Catholic doctrine on grace in its true sources, not
the anathemas against Pelagius, but in the Sacred Scriptures and the
writing of the early Fathers.

According to de Bay, when man came from the hand of God he
possessed perfect righteousness, which theology has called sanctifying grace, but which ought rather be called natural because it was
Adam's by right of nature. In fact, man is truly man only when he
accomplishes works meritorious of heaven. So far Baius was teaching
straight Protestantism. But then he added a clarification and a corollary. Our will has been ruined by concupiscence, and is capable of

nothing but evil in the spiritual order. "All the works of infidels are (therefore) sins, all the virtues of the philosophers are vices."[67]

Baius, like Luther and Calvin before him, went to St. Augustine to discover his doctrine. And like them he drew the same conclusions. It is true there are patristic texts, especially in Augustine's strong anti-Pelagian writings, in which it is forcibly asserted that from the beginning man was called to eternal life and to a special order of morality which alone is proportioned to that sublime end. But Baius, like the Reformers, saw in these polemic statements a destiny not only of fact but of right. Hence his persistent refusal to admit the supernatural character of those primitive gifts to Adam and Eve: his Pelagian optimism on the psychology of fallen mankind.

Baianism was a prelude to Jansenism. It began with the principle that original justice was due to man by an exigency (demand) of his nature. When Adam fell he lost his pristine state and with it his free will. We no longer have freedom from necessity (internal liberty of indifference) but only from external coercion.

Then comes the important Baianist contribution. In place of the free will, there is a twofold love necessarily attracting the will—a vicious love or the love of perfect charity; so that as long as charity does not rule, malicious cupidity takes over. In sinners, of course, charity does not rule and therefore all the words, thoughts, and actions of sinners are sins of and by themselves. To make sure he was not misunderstood, he said, "Whatever a sinner, or slave of sin does, is a sin," and "negative unbelief," that is, nonacceptance of the Gospel, "among those to whom Christ has not been preached is a sin."[68]

Bringing infidels into the picture was not a sophism. Its purpose was to emphasize the essentially sinful condition of man's will in and

---

[67] *DS* 1925.
[68] *DS* 1935, 1968.

by itself, as exemplified in persons who have not been touched by the saving grace of Christ.

After Baius' condemnation, he submitted formally to the Holy See, although his subsequent writings show that he never actually gave up his opinions. He died nine years later in the peace of the Church. His influence might have ended there, except for Jacques Janson, Baius' successor at Louvain, who discovered and encouraged one of his young students, Cornelius Jansen, to carry on the work of the former university chancellor.

Conquering Delight

How thoroughly devoted Jansenius was to the memory of Baius may be seen from the original name of his magnum opus, on which rests his sole title to fame. He was going to call it *Baii Apologia,* but later changed his mind to call it *Augustine, seu Doctrina Sancti Augustini de Humana Naturae Sanitate, Aegritudine, Medicina Adversus Pelagianos et Massilienses.* Every word is significant. The avowed function of the book was to defend the orthodoxy of Baius, and to reform Catholic theology on the subject of grace in the light of St. Augustine's doctrine against the Pelagians and French (Marseilles) Semi-Pelagians. Since Jansenius shared the former chancellor's dim view of human nature, the terms *aegritudo* and *medicina* are misleading, except in the sense that grace can supply what man had lost without restoring him to a supernatural goal to which he was never destined.

Jansenius' treatise was not published until 1640, after his death as Bishop of Ypres, a commune in northwest Belgium. It was the fruit of a lifetime of cold research, mostly of St. Augustine whom Jansenius said he had read ten times. His biographer declares that he saw an old armchair with one arm turned into a writing table. It was in this chair that Jansenius studied and almost lived, for he rarely went to bed.[69]

The logic of the *Augustinus* is perfect, beginning with its threefold status of human nature—innocent, fallen, and repaired—each so technical that the whole structure of Jansenism depends on every detail. A theme running through the book is a preoccupation with the human will in its different stages of relationship to God.

In the state of original innocence, according to Jansenius, Adam had real liberty of active indifference regarding good and evil, to enable him freely to chose to sin or serve God. Along with this liberty he received divine assistance, a *sine qua non* help to which his nature had a right and of which it had need for a composite of body and soul. However, Adam could receive or reject this assistance, which was subject to his will. In addition he possessed other gifts and the prospect of eternal life.

Once the first man fell, the whole of human nature was changed through concupiscence to become diffused in Adam's posterity. All that we have left is liberty from external constraint, unless on some rare occasion we are physically coerced to do another's bidding. Yet merit and demerit remain, since they do not require internal freedom but only liberty from compulsion. Parallel with this theory of freedom, Jansenius followed Baius in claiming that whatever is not heavenly charity is vicious cupidity, and charity cannot be had without the grace of Christ. Unless a man has this grace he sins in everything he does.

Finally and most subtly, in the state of restored nature, Christ did not restore to us the pristine liberty enjoyed by Adam. He gives grace instead, which consists in the delectability of heavenly charity which the Holy Spirit infuses in the heart, in opposition to the pleasurableness of cupidity. In other words, because of the fall the moral will is a

---

[69] Claude Lancelot, *Memoires* (Geneva: Slatkine Reprints, 1968), I 103, II 308.

passive faculty which always leans on the side where the weight of attraction is stronger. Thus we can be influenced by two contrary delights: an evil one that proceeds from concupiscence (whether sensual or spiritual), such as the longing for honors, riches, worldly enjoyments, or simply egoism; or a good delight that emanates from God as our first principle and last end. This latter is beyond the capacity of nature alone, i.e. to elevate itself to such a motive of action and to be influenced by it. Hence only grace can effect our being, thus moved by God, to have God as our source and final destiny.

Such is our lot as fallen men. If grace is given to the will, we act irresistibly; if grace is not given, concupiscence will fatally conquer.[70] Nor is this all. Jansenius also described a balance or kind of tension between the two delights (of grace or concupiscence) that constantly operate on the will. The heart of Jansenist theology is the concept of *delectatio victrix* (conquering delight). According to him, "we necessarily act according to that which more delights us."[71] Consequently, if the attraction of grace is greater than the proposed enjoyment of cupidity, it infallibly prevails and draws the will to what is good. Then we receive what Jansen called *magna gratia,* which means a *delectatio victrix* or conquering delight. But if this attractiveness of grace is less *parva gratia* then it produces only sterile action and no fruit of moral good.

As a logical corollary, Christ must not have died for all men but leaves a large number as a *massa damnationis.* To others He gives small graces, *gratiae parvae* which lead them to faith. On still others He confers the great graces that lead to justification. No one, however, receives sufficient grace to avoid all sins. Some divine precepts are simply impossible and no grace is given to render them possible.

On the same grounds, Jansenius called it Semi-Pelagianism to say that man can resist grace. Either he receives grace in the form of a

---

[70] *CCC* 1732, 1742, 2515.
[71] Jansenius, *De Gratia Christi,* VIII, 6.

conquering delight, or he does not receive it, except, perhaps, in that futile guise of a *parva gratia*. If the grace comes, he inevitably consents; if it fails to come, he sins with equal inevitability. Those for whom Christ died receive grace and they will be saved; the others do not receive grace, (which is always efficacious) and are consequently lost.

Reflexions Morales

Where Jansenius was heavy and speculative, two of his disciples, Arnauld and Quesnel, had a consummate mastery of their native tongue and were eminently practical. Except for them Jansenism would very likely have remained an academic theory with small impact on the lives of people, or at least it would never have become so widespread or devastatingly popular. We shall see Antoine (the Great) Arnauld in a later context. Our present interest is with Pasquier Quesnel (1634–1713), the ex-Oratorian, whose writings precipitated a theological revolution.

Quesnel was educated by the Jesuits and at the Sorbonne. At twenty-three he entered Berulle's Oratory where he was given charge of the junior members of the congregation. In 1672 he published *Abrege de la Morale de L'Evangile,* with a laudatory preface by the Bishop of Chalons-Sur-Marne. Its later editions, expanded and revised, became famous under the title *Le Nouveau Testament en Français, Avec des Reflexions Sur Chaque Verset,* usually abbreviated to *Reflexions Morales.* As against the formalized methods of spirituality in the manuals, the work emphasized the close study of the Scriptures in order to grow in perfection.

Three years later he published a scholarly edition of the works of St. Leo the Great which, however, was placed on the Index owing to the Gallican theories developed in the footnotes. All the while Quesnel also favored Jansenism, though in company with his colleagues in religion he had signed the formula of Alexander VII three or four times. Because of his Jansenism he left the Oratory in 1685, though he continued to describe himself as "Priest of the Oratory." In 1703 he was imprisoned by the Archbishop of Malines on orders from Philip V, but escaped to Holland. His subsequent life was spent defending himself and the *Reflexions* which, commended by the Archbishop of Paris, Cardinal Noailles, went through many editions, though it was condemned by Clement XI in 1708, and again five years later by the same pontiff in the dogmatic Constitution, *Unigenitus*.

Quesnel never accepted the condemnation, and though he asked for and received the last sacraments, he appealed (against a papal prohibition) to a future general council for his vindication.

The *Reflexions* are saturated with the ideas of Jansenius, though the author avoids identifying himself with them too openly. Jansenius' five propositions are hardly ever found in unequivocal form, but in the shape of brief comments, short prayers, and reflections he links with the text of the New Testament maxims for the spiritual life derived from the thought of his master. St. Augustine is frequently quoted and so woven into the format that the characteristic edges and corners of Jansenism are well disguised.

Thus from Jansenius' assertion on the irresistibility of grace there follows that sinners and pagans who have not been truly converted are wholly forsaken by grace and antecedently predestined for damnation. Quesnel offers this in such a way that most people would miss its appalling harshness. Again he casually mentions that faith is the "first grace," or that forgiveness of sins is the "first grace" bestowed by God on the sinner, so that logically the unconverted sinner or pagan has never received grace of any kind, otherwise true faith and conversion would no longer be the first grace.

Constantly throughout the *Reflexions,* Quesnel proclaims that without grace, meaning efficacious grace as understood by Jansenius, man is utterly helpless to do any good. But his thesis is shrouded behind seemingly harmless and edifying expressions. Basing himself on St. Augustine, he prays, "In vain you command, O Lord, unless you give us to do what you command." Or "assuredly, O Lord, all things are possible for him for whom you make them possible by Yourself working them in him." He describes grace as "an effect of the all-Powerful hand of God, which nothing can hinder or restrict."

Consistent with his master's teaching, Quesnel upholds the claim that God's salvific will extends effectively only to the elect; but here, too, he avoids crude expressions. In a note on Luke 5:13, for example, he says, "When God is willing to save a soul and touches it interiorly with the hand of His grace, no human will resists Him."

Individual statements, out of context, often had an orthodox sound to them. But when the *Reflexions* repeated the same idea in varied terms, the average reader would certainly be affected by this unqualified Jansenism. What complicated the issue and did much to foster Quesnel's ideas among the faithful was the Gallican policies of the French king and parliament. Their compromising attitude on papal authority favored the spread of a theory on man's impotency that would otherwise have remained where it originated, in the churches of the Reformation.

The general impression of Quesnel is that he did not advance the Jansenist theses beyond Jansenius, but only slightly modified them and reduced their application to the realm of morals and spirituality. Actually Quesnel went beyond his preceptor by advocating a new concept of the Church, outside of which he said no grace is received. The Church in his vocabulary was not the visible, hierarchical society subject to the Holy See.

The characteristic mark of the Christian Church is that it be Catholic, comprehending all the angels of heaven, and all the elect and just of the earth and of all ages.

What is the Church except the assembly of the children of God abiding in His bosom, the adoptive ones of Christ, subsisting in His person, those redeemed by His blood, living with His spirit, acting by His grace, and awaiting the gift of the future life.

The Church, or the whole Christ, has the Word Incarnate as Head and all the saints as members.

Nothing is more extensive than the Church of God; because all the elect and all the just of all ages compose it.[72]

Accordingly, since only the elect or predestined are members of the Church, "No grace is given outside the Church." If it were, grace would not be infallibly efficacious; it could be resisted by a free will that was still fundamentally sound. Quesnel's dilemma, therefore, was either to admit that not only the predestined belong to the Church, but also persons who received the gift of faith but willfully failed to cooperate with divine grace—which undermines a cardinal principle of Jansenism, or to restrict the Church to the elect and equate its members with those who receive grace—while excluding simultaneously the nonpredestined from church membership and God's efficacious grace from those who are not predestined.

Synod of Pistoia

In spite of repeated condemnations, Jansenism not only continued in existence but spread to other countries outside of Holland, Belgium and France. Under pressure from Louis XIV, Jansenius' great apostle,

---

[72] *DS* 2472–75; *CCC* 830–31, 834, 836–38.

Antoine Arnauld, took refuge in Holland, where his followers were supported by the sympathetic Calvinist government. They elected one of their number, Cornelius Steenhoven, to the episcopate, and had him receive consecration from a Catholic bishop who was at the time under suspension. The schismatical sect established a diocese in Haarlem in 1742, and their organization, known as the Old Roman Catholic Church (De Oud-Roomsch-Katolieki Kerk), has survived to the present day.

Another, more significant, group of Jansenists was established in Italy. Here the movement followed aristocratic rather than popular lines, as in France. Consequently its impact on the masses was less effective. Clerics in the highest ranks of society in Italy either openly or sympathetically espoused the principles of Jansenius and Arnauld. Among these, the most famous was Scipione de Ricci, nephew of the last Jesuit General before the suppression of the Society, and subsequently Bishop of Pistoia.

Born in Florence in 1741, he died in the same city in 1809, having ruled the diocese of Pistoia from 1780 until his forced resignation in 1791. Although related to the Jesuit General, Ricci conceived a hearty dislike for the Society already in his student days in Rome, when he came under the influence of Jansenist sympathizers. Returning to his native city, he wrote and spoke openly in favor of the Jansenists in France and Holland, and within a year of his ordination was publicly expounding Jansenius' doctrine on grace. Not long after his elevation to the See of Pistoia, he joined the Grand Duke of Tuscany in an overt attempt to Jansenize the dioceses under his jurisdiction, if need be at the cost of severance from Rome.

Ricci's extant sermons breathe the unmistakable spirit of Jansenius. It is a principle of faith, he held, that very few adults will be saved. Priests must ever keep this fact before the minds of the people, in order to draw them away from evil and move them to salutary repentance.

Consequently, it is contrary to this established truth to give absolution freely or admit to Holy Communion the majority of penitents.

The climax in Ricci's effort to reform his diocese was reached at the Synod which opened at Pistoia on September 18, 1786, in the Church of St. Leopold, under the presidency of the bishop. There were 234 participants, including 171 parish priests and thirteen religious. The theologian Tamburini, known for his Jansenism, was appointed "promoter" of the Synod. As Ricci remarked in his memoirs, Tamburini was to be "the leading spirit in this movement against 'the old machine of papal monarchy.' "[73] After ten days of session, the Synod published its decrees which, together with the Acts of the Council, fill two volumes in the modern edition.

In his correspondence with the Jansenist Church in Holland, Ricci expressed the hope of a similar establishment in Italy. Fortunately for the Catholic future of that country, this full flowering of Italian Jansenism was not supported by Ricci's fellow bishops in Tuscany; only two of sixteen are known to have been in sympathy with his ideas. He was also opposed, with violence, by the Tuscan laity. With his innovations, Ricci had outraged the most sacred sentiments of the people. They gave full vent to their fury, which did not subside until Ricci had taken flight. When the cathedral chapter joined the popular demonstration, the bishop had no choice but to resign, which he did on June 3, 1791.

Efforts were made to forestall a formal condemnation of the Synod of Pistoia, but Pius VI, "to fulfill his apostolic and pastoral duty," caused eighty-five tenets to be cited from the records and decrees, each one to be censured separately to avoid any possible misunderstanding. On August 28, 1794, the Pope issued the Constitution, *Auctorem fidei,* incorporating the cited passages and corresponding censures.

---

[73] *Memoria de Scipione de'Ricci,* (Firenze: F. Le Monnier, 1865), I 490.

Among the synodical declarations of Pistoia was a series taken almost bodily from the *Augustinus* and the *Reflexions*. One especially stressed the familiar distinction between the two kinds of grace, the small and the large, with a new touch that was absent in the older Jansenists.

> The light of grace, when alone, only serves to make us aware of our unhappy state and of the gravity of our sin. In such cases grace produces the same effect which the Law (of the Old Testament) produced. God must, therefore, create a holy love in our heart and inspire a holy delight contrary to the love that is dominant in me. This sacred love and delight is, properly speaking, the grace of Jesus Christ and the inspiration of charity, by whose light we act with a holy love. This is the root from which good works are germinated. This is the grace of the New Testament that liberates us from the slavery of sin and constitutes us sons of God.[74]

The involved diction and preoccupation with a divine love that displaces self are typically Jansenist. Only one form of God's action on the soul was a grace, they held: that which makes us do good (*facit ut faciamus*). It is not really a grace if the Holy Spirit merely touches the heart of man by His illumination and inspiration, leaving us the option of resisting His touch if we will.

Traditionalism

Not long after Pistoia, another form of doctrinal depreciation of man's nature arose in France and Belgium. Commonly known as Traditionalism, its main tenet was the assertion that all spiritual, moral and religious knowledge is based on a primitive revelation of God to man handed down in an unbroken tradition. Its origins were

---

[74] *DS* 2621.

theologically based on the Reformation, since human reason was denied the power of attaining by itself to any truths, especially those of natural theology: it made divine faith in a revealed tradition the source of all religious knowledge. Historically it was a reaction against eighteenth-century Rationalism in the direction of the other extreme. Where the Rationalists claimed that reason was alone capable of all truth, the Traditionalists pointed to the debacle in religion and philosophy which this arrogance produced; they said the opposite—reason of itself is incapable of any truth.

Among its chief advocates were L. G. A. de Bonald (1754–1840) and F. R. de Lammenais (1782–1854), whose four volumes *Essai sur l'indifference en matiere de Religion* was most influential. In order to restore belief to the modern world the traditionalists aimed at removing it from discussion by individual reason and at imposing it by the authority of the common consent (*sens commun*) of mankind. Lammenais invested this common agreement with infallibility. He made submission to authority, proximately to human institutions but ultimately to God the revealer, the fountainhead of man's knowledge.

Without authority there is no existence, no truth, and no order. Principle and rule of our thoughts, affections and duties, authority reigns supreme over the soul which, in turn, lives only by faith, and which dies the moment it ceases to obey. Not to listen to the voice of authority is to know nothing, to understand nothing. Man's intellect has no other foundation, no other source of certitude, no other basis than the great testimony which originally came from God Himself, the infinite, unchangeable, and all-pervading wisdom.[75]

The tragic irony of de Lammenais' exaltation of authority over reason was that he ended his life by repudiating the Church's authority and

---

[75] Felicite' de Lammenais, *Essai sur l'indifference en Matière de Religion* (Paris: Tournachon-Molin & H. Seguin, 1820), 197–98; *CCC* 35, 36.

denying such basic Christian mysteries as the divinity of Christ, eternal punishment, and the supernatural order. He carried to their conclusion the premises which underlie Traditionalism: a despair of man's nature that postulates a denial of his elevation by grace and a concept of grace that means only an extrinsic remedy for human depravity.

Not all Traditionalists were so extreme. Modified forms of the doctrine were held by L. E. M. Bautain (1796–1867), A. Bonnetty (1798–1879), and G. C. Ubaghs (1800–1875). Gerhard Ubaghs was the chief representative of the Traditionalist Ontologism of Louvain. Professor of philosophy and later editor of the *Revue Catholique,* Ubaghs expounded a mitigated Traditionalism according to which the knowledge of metaphysical and moral truths is based on a primitive divine revelation handed on by oral tradition. This teaching he combined with the Ontologist doctrine of the direct contemplation of God by the intellect in the "objective ideas," not unlike Calvin's notion of the indwelling Spirit who teaches us now as He once taught the prophets of the Old Law.

Ubaghs and the Louvain school departed from Fideism (rigid Traditionalism) in not requiring divine revelation as the unique cause of our knowledge of all suprasensible realities. For them it was only a necessary condition. But they were at one with the Fideists in denying to the mind, without supernatural illumination, the power to know the truths of natural religion. Reading Ubaghs, one gets the impression of a religious mind that seeks to exalt God at the price of depressing man.

> We cannot attain to the knowledge of any external metaphysical truth, such, namely, as pertains to anything which does not come under our senses, without first having received instruction from someone else, and, in the last analysis, without divine revelation.

External metaphysical truths cannot be demonstrated in the strict sense of the word.

The existence of God can never be demonstrated. We deny that the existence of God can be demonstrated.

Proofs for the existence of God are in the final analysis a kind of faith, or are founded on faith, by which we believe rather than understand. In other words, we are naturally persuaded that this idea is to be believed, although we cannot conclude it from mere intrinsic evidence.[76]

Traditionalism was condemned in several documents: de Lammenais in two Encyclicals, *Mirari Vos Arbitramur* (1832) and *Singulari Nos Affecerunt Gaudio* (1834). Ubaghs was censured by the Congregation of the Index in 1843; he submitted and soon after resigned his post at Louvain.

Centrality of Sin

It is well to know that the Reformation estimate of human nature as a *Massa damnata* is not a historical relic. The notion that by the fall man did worse than injure his faculties because he lost the gift of integrity, that he debased his very nature, is more prevalent in modern thought than appears to the casual observer. A sign of its prevalence is the stature and acceptance of Reinhold Niebuhr, widely acclaimed to have been America's greatest theologian of the twentieth century.

Until his retirement in 1960, Niebuhr was for more than thirty years professor of Christian Ethics, then dean and finally vice-president of Union Theological Seminary. A shelf of sixteen books, including the monumental *Nature and Destiny of Man*, suggests his influence in

---

[76] G.C. Ubaghs, *Theodiceae Elementa* (Louvain: Vanlinthout et Vandenzande, 1843), 73, 220.

shaping what critics have called a system of theological pragmatism, but which others insist is a blessed amalgam of religious ultimacy and vigor in dealing with social problems.

More than one commentator believes that the central overwhelming idea of Reinhold Niebuhr is sin. Perhaps the general impression was best stated by a friendly critic who said that in spite of Niebuhr's "profound sense of comprehensiveness of Christianity," he has been guilty of overemphasizing sin in his reaction to modern sentimental versions of the Christian faith. Concerned over the neglect of man's fallen nature, he is so busy rehabilitating this fact that other and equally important aspects of Christianity suffer from underemphasis.

In existential terms he defines sin as the unwarranted human claim to finality. "Man is mortal. That is his fate. Man pretends to be not mortal. That is his sin." The variety of forms which this pretense assumes is myriad. Will to power and lust of the flesh are only generic names for a malady that infects even the noblest of man's actions.

Pride, he explains, may be individual or collective. On the individual level it may be a thirst for domination exhibited in those who already enjoy social security and those who wish they did. When social forms persuade men they are secure, an incredible blindness to their finite nature overcomes them. Tyrants and dictators fondly imagine they are exempt from the common laws of suffering and death. Those who are socially insecure show their lust for power under the guise of a laudable search for security. It is the sin of those who, knowing themselves to be insecure, seek sufficient power to guarantee their security, inevitably at the expense of other life.

Less obvious but equally sinful is pride of intellect, found in those who pretend they are in possession of the final insight into truth. "Intellectual pride is thus the pride of reason which forgets that it is involved in a temporal process and imagines itself in complete transcendence over history."[77] The mind begins innocently enough, in the pursuit of knowledge. But soon it goes beyond this modest aim and ends by saying that a final system of truth has been reached.

Moral pride is the pretension of finite man that his highly conditioned and imperfect virtue is the final righteousness, and that his very relative moral standards are absolute. The conflict which Jesus had with the Scribes and Pharisees is a classic example. They refused to submit to the test of divine law, preferring to set their own moral security independently. Being most subtle, the pride of morality is also the most vicious. Self-criticism and tolerance are unknown. "The whole history of racial, national, religious and other social struggles is a commentary on the objective wickedness and social miseries which result from self-righteousness."[78]

At the acme of wickedness stands spiritual pride, which not only claims to possess final truth and virtue, but identifies these possessions with the will of God. Other prides are only means which lead to this quintessential form, when the individual leaps out of himself and brazenly claims self-deification. The zenith is reached when "our partial standards and relative attainments are explicitly related to the unconditioned good, and claim divine sanction."[79]

Since the social unit is formed of many individuals, the nature of collective pride remains the same. The group is more arrogant, hypocritical, self-centered, and ruthless in the pursuit of its ends than the individual. For one thing, the collectivity can more easily mask individual pretensions; it also tends to favor the outlook of the most aggressive and dominant members of society who, by definition, are the most proud.

---

[77] Reinhold Niebuhr, *The Nature and Destiny of Man* (London: Nisbet & Co. Ltd., 1945), 208.

[78] Ibid., 213.

[79] Ibid.

Niebuhr singles out for special mention the Catholic idea of natural law. The purpose of the natural law, as he sees it, is to define for the free individual the proper performance of his functions, the normal harmony of his impulses, and the normal social relation between himself and his fellows within the limits of the natural order. Yet there is no easy way to decide what, if anything, should be included in natural law. There are too many possibilities of man's involvement in a limitless number of circumstances. Niebuhr makes no effort to catalogue what the law of nature prescribes, or even to state its basic elements.[80]

Instead he castigates all forms of finality on the content of the moral law, with stress on the Catholic pretension to fix the limits of man's duties to God. The roots of this fixation, he says, reach back into the medieval theory of the Fall and its tenuous distinction between pure nature and the additional gifts of grace. "The primary mistake of Catholic theory is precisely the sharp and absolute distinction which it makes between the two. It speaks of an original righteousness which was lost in the Fall and a natural justice which remains essentially uncorrupted by the Fall."[81]

His distrust of reason makes him impatient with any system of ethics which pretends to be fundamentally rational.

> The sin of man perennially insinuates contingent and relative elements into the supposedly absolute standards of human reason. Undue confidence in human reason, as the seat and source of natural law, makes this very concept of law into a vehicle of human sin. It gives to the peculiar conditions and unique circumstances in which reason operates in a particular historical moment the sanctity of universality. The confidence

---

[80] *CCC* 1954–60; cf. Vatican Council II, *Dogmatic Constitution on the Church in the Modern World* [*Lumen Gentium*] (1965), 10.
[81] Niebuhr, op. cit., 297.

of medieval Catholicism in the ability of an unspoiled reason to arrive at definitive standards of natural justice thus became the very vehicle of the sinful pretensions of the age. The social ethics of Thomas Aquinas embody the peculiarities and the contingent factors of a feudal-agrarian economy into a system of fixed socio-ethical principles.[82]

Niebuhr believes that all so-called natural or rational standards of morality are involved in sin. "There is no uncorrupted natural law," and the only effect of claiming the contrary is to raise "ideology" to a higher degree of unreality, while it illustrates the force of sin in the pretense of sinlessness.

CATHOLIC MIDDLE GROUND

Since the dawn of Pelagianism to the present day, the Church has consistently veered a middle course between the two shoals of despairing of man's native powers because of the fall, or ignoring original sin and so exalting human nature that nothing is supposed to be impossible to man.

There is no set pattern to the rise of these contrary tendencies. They are always in evidence. Broadly speaking, however, they seem to follow a dialectic form where one emphasis, in theory or practice, evokes another of the opposite kind.

Thus Pelagianism in the early Church revolted against the complacency of those who so relied on grace as to ignore the correlated demands of the will. Semi-Pelagianism reacted against the polemic rhetoric of St. Augustine, which the zealous monks of Marseilles mistook for a threat to man's liberty. In the early Renaissance the growing disregard for sound morals among the clergy and civil author-

---

[82] Ibid., 297–98.

ities provoked criticism of the Church among the Waldenses, Lollards, and Hussites that exploded in the Reformation and placed all the emphasis on grace to the obscuration and denial of man's freedom.

Since the Reformation, every major adversative position on grace in Christian thought has been deeply influenced by the classic Protestant thesis of man's total depravity. Still extant in dominant areas and propounded by such leaders as Karl Barth, it directly occasioned Kantianism, which was nominally rationalistic, but actually despaired of man's intellect to understand the *noumena* of things; it indirectly provoked the Enlightenment that went to the other extreme of extolling the mind and making reason, without grace and even without God, the measure of all truth; it helped to shape Jansenism and Traditionalism; the one postulating grace as a substitute for freedom in mastering concupiscence, the other making revelation replace reason in acquiring any knowledge.

At the present time, both extremes are still prevalent, of absolute self-sufficiency in modern secularism, and of near despair in the existentialism of Camus and Sartre—with satellite positions on either side that affect every aspect of human thought and behavior.

Few aspects in the Catholic doctrine on grace are more relevant to contemporary life and problems than the Church's teaching on the powers and limitations of the mind to know truth and the will to do good. If divine guidance is needed in any field of knowledge, it is imperative in these fundamentals, because the whole structure of Christian faith and morality and, in fact, human society ultimately rests on them.

It seems best to dispense here with the strictly historical sequence of ecclesiastical documents and rather follow a more logical order: examining first the positive capacities of human nature, what can be done without grace or revelation, and then the negative limit of these powers, where the fallen state of man requires divine assistance.

Substantial Integrity of Mind

Experience and authority suggest that man's intellect has been terribly if not completely darkened by some primordial fall. Pascal's graphic description is a fair picture of what the natural man is often tempted to paint. "I know not who put me into the world, nor what the world is, nor what I myself am, I am in terrible ignorance of everything. I know not what my body is, nor my senses, nor my soul, not even that part of me which thinks what I say, which reflects on all and on itself, and knows itself no more than the rest."[83]

The early Reformers were not always consistent in denying man's ability to know religious truth. In one place Calvin wrote "there is within the human mind, and indeed by natural instinct, an awareness of divinity."[84] Elsewhere in the same *Institutes* he was more logical. "We are drunk with the false opinion of our own insight and are thus extremely reluctant to admit that it is utterly blind and stupid in divine matters." This means that "flesh is not capable to know God and what is God's, unless it be illumined by the Spirit of God."[85]

Yet the Council of Trent did not explicitly go into the question, perhaps because in Reformation times the great need was to defend freedom of the will in its encounter with God's grace, and because the Reformers sometimes rose above their own principles; they preached total depravity but when it suited their needs were willing to compromise on the extent of its effects.

Not until the rise of Rationalism and its reactionary Traditionalism do we have a series of intense Church documentation on the subject. The problem raised by Traditionalists was the delicate one of the relation of faith to reason. If, as they claimed, man's mind is naturally so darkened it cannot of itself know any religious truth but depends for

---

[83] Blaise Pascal, *Pensees,* 194.
[84] Calvin, *Institutes,* I, 3, 1.
[85] Ibid., II, 2, 19.

everything on a primitive revelation, what if someone should challenge our Christian faith and demand evidence that Christianity is true? Are there no rational grounds for accepting the Christian revelation in preference over the Hindu or Mohammedan? If there are not, then one religion is as good as another, or at least we have no way of knowing which supposedly revealed religion, if any, is true.

This explains the Church's preoccupation with establishing the mind's competence to know what are called the preambles of faith, namely, those verities on which the credibility of the Christian revelation depends.

In 1840 Louis Bautain was required to subscribe to the thesis that: "Even though reason was rendered weak and clouded by original sin, it still has a sufficiently clear power of perception to lead us with certitude to the knowledge of the existence of God and to the revelation given to the Jews through Moses, and to the Christians through our adorable God-man."[86]

Six years later, Pius IX came back to the same issue, stressing in his Encyclical *Qui Pluribus* the endowment of mind left intact by the Creator to allow us sufficient grounds for making a rational acceptance of faith. In fact, the obligation to inquire into Christian revelation when presented rests on this prior sufficiency of intellect, which can also recognize the dignity of submitting itself in faith to the infinite mind of God.[87]

Shortly after, Augustine Bonnetty's writings were censured and he was ordered to accept several propositions similar to Bautain's, except more detailed. "The reasoning process," it was declared, "can prove with certitude the existence of God, the spirituality of the soul, and the freedom of man. Faith is subsequent to revelation and, one cannot validly appeal to it against atheism to prove the existence of God nor

---

[86] *DS* 2756.
[87] *DS* 2778; *CCC* 156, 274, 1706.

against a disciple of naturalism and fatalism to prove the spirituality and freedom of the rational soul."[88] By implication, the unbeliever has sufficient intelligence to have these truths proved to him rationally. So that for all men, "the use of reason precedes and with the help of revelation and grace leads man to the same."[89]

On the eve of the First Vatican Council and incorporated into its official *Acta* was a decree of the Council of Cologne (1860) that spelled out in detail all the essential elements in the Catholic teaching on the mind's innate capacity for truth.

> We declare that just as the will is able to perform certain good works, so also the intellect of fallen man can understand, with certitude and of its own resources, certain truths which pertain to natural religion, notably the existence of God. For the Apostle teaches regarding the gentiles that God, surely the true God as distinct from the world, can be known and was known from the natural manifestations through created things, and that the gentiles were to have given Him thanks. There was no question of a doubtful or uncertain knowledge; since what is manifested and what the intellect perceives is obviously most certain. Hence St. Augustine with other holy Fathers clearly teaches that some knowledge of God, commonly called natural religion, is produced by nature.[90]

The First Vatican Council canonized this doctrine by comparing the two modes of knowledge open to us by the author of Creation, the one natural and the other supernatural. After declaring that God created heaven and earth and governs all things by His providence the Coun-

---

[88] *DS* 2812.

[89] *DS* 2813; *CCC* 35–6.

[90] *Collectio Lacensis*, ed. G. Schneemann (Friburgi Brisgoviae: Herder, 1890), 4:17, 299.

cil affirmed: "The same holy Mother Church holds and teaches that God, the origin and end of all things, can be known with certainty by the natural light of human reason from the things He created; for since the creation of the world His invisible attributes are clearly seen, being understood through the things that are made!"[91] Then follows an anathema against those who should hold the contrary.[92]

In 1910, during the heyday of Modernism, St. Pius X drafted an oath which was recited annually in all Catholic seminaries, attesting that God's existence is knowable by the natural light of reason (*naturali rationis lumine*) from the visible effects in creation. The knowledge is certain and even demonstrative on scientific grounds.[93]

Theologians further refine the nature of this knowledge and the character of man's power to acquire it. They say it comprehends certain natural truths, including those that have to do with God and the moral law, though necessarily the scope and depth of understanding differ with different persons. "Some truths to some extent" is a simple, if not very precise, formula commonly used. We cannot, of course, make this comprehension too accurate or its possession too certainly convincing, otherwise there is risk of obscuring the moral necessity of revelation, also defined by the Vatican. Yet the function of revelation regarding natural truths must never be absolute. Its purpose is not to supply what could otherwise not be secured, but to expand in amount and clarity of knowledge, intensify in subjective certitude, correct in objective truth, and facilitate in acquisition.

By saying the mind can come to this minimal understanding, theology explains that both the external grace of revelation and the internal graces of the Holy Spirit are dispensable, without denying they may be present. The point is this. Our minds are not so debilitated by hereditary

---

[91] *DS* 3004, *CCC* 32.
[92] *DS* 3026.
[93] *DS* 3537–42.

sin that they cannot know anything in the suprasensible order without remedial grace from God. On our part the capacity is not only physical, because we still have a mind, but also moral, in that the obstacles to such elementary knowledge are not so great that scarcely anyone overcomes them.

Native Capacity of Will

If man's nature were totally corrupt, his incapacity in things spiritual would span both faculties of mind and will. Historically the will was first impugned and the whole atmosphere of the Counter-Reformation was colored by this concern, to vindicate man's ability, minus grace, to accomplish some spiritual good.

Several items complicate the issue. Catholic tradition has never questioned the weakening effects of original sin on the human will. In fact, St. Thomas believed these effects were more grave than on the mind. "Human nature," he said, "has been more infected by sin in its appetite for good than as regards its knowledge of truth."[94]

Moreover, as normally found in the manualists, it seems a purely academic question whether infidels and sinners can perform any naturally good acts. The manuals simply follow the declarations of the Church. These in turn were conditioned by the theories of the Reformers, de Bay, and the Jansenists. Though put speculatively in the documents, the issue behind the censured theories was anything but speculative. It centered uniquely on the highly practical question of whether man's freedom remains intact after the fall. By supposition, infidels and sinners were assumed to be without habitual grace, the first with none and the second without infused charity.

Can such people do anything morally good, or is every act they perform sinful? If not all of their actions are sinful, their wills are not

---

[94] St. Thomas Aquinas, *Summa Theologica*, I–II, 109, 2, 3.

wholly vitiated; if all they do is a sin, their nature must be essentially estranged from God.

The Reformers had a very dim view of man's condition after the fall. What is less familiar is their thematic insistence that all the deeds of sinners are themselves additional sins. This had special reference to the acts of faith, hope, and sorrow that the Catholic religion had always taught were necessary predispositions for the reception of sanctifying grace. Since in the Reformation system justification of a sinner is entirely God's work, and man's contribution is nil, whatever he does before being justified is sinful, even though ostensibly he performs acts of virtue or piety.

It is instructive to know that John Huss (1371–1415), the Czech Reformer, anticipated Luther and Calvin by over a century. His grievance was not unlike theirs: prelates and civil rulers who were not leading edifying lives. To deprive them of authority he hit on the idea of identifying their right to govern with the possession of grace. A sinful bishop or king, therefore, need not be obeyed. The Council of Constance condemned Huss and later had him burned at the stake. Among the censured opinions was one on the perfect disjunction between two kinds of acts.

> The proximate division of human actions is as follows: they are either virtuous or vicious, because if a man is bad, then whatever he does is vicious; but if he is good, then whatever he does is virtuous. For just as vice, which is called a crime or mortal sin, universally infects the actions of a bad man, so virtue animates all the acts of a man who is virtuous.[95]

The canons of the Council of Trent are crisp in their clarity on the exact point at issue raised by the Reformers. They outlawed every

---

[95] *DS* 1216.

theory which calls into question the power of the will to prepare itself for God's sanctifying grace, claiming that "all works performed," for example through faith or with actual grace, nevertheless "are truly sins or merit God's hatred; or that the more zealously a person strives to dispose himself for grace, the more grievously he sins."[96] Similar anathemas were leveled at anyone who calls it sinful to fear hellfire or make an act of imperfect contrition as motives for humble repentance.[97]

Jansenism, whether in its prelude under Baius or development through Quesnel, also held to the same theory, although somewhat refined. Unless a man has the Christian faith and operates under the influence of charity, whatever he does is sinful. A statement censured by Rome as late as 1690 indicates that Jansenism was in the full stream of the Reformed tradition on the status of sinners before God.[98]

However, the main interest of the Jansenists was more sophisticated. In the state of repaired nature, they held, Christ did not restore to man his former liberty of will, but gives him grace instead. This efficacious drawing to the good (conquering delight) is not given to unbelievers, in whom concupiscence dominates. That is why whatever they do is automatically sinful.

We have already seen Baius' proposition, censured in 1567: "that all the works of infidels are sins."[99] A like statement occurs in the catalogue of Jansenist opinions proscribed under Alexander VIII, that "an unbeliever necessarily sins in every action he performs."[100] But the most detailed exposition of Jansenism in its attitude towards those who lack the faith occurs in the dogmatic Constitution of Clement IX

---

[96] *DS* 1552.
[97] *DS* 1558, 1677–78; *CCC* 1451–53.
[98] *DS* 2311.
[99] *DS* 1925.
[100] *DS* 2308.

in 1713, which was a hundred and fifty years after Baius first came into conflict with St. Pius V.

A remarkable feature about the whole controversy was the Church's position on St. Augustine, to whom Reformers and Jansenists appealed for all their arguments. Augustine was never censured. He was, in fact, quoted by ecclesiastical authorities in support of Catholic doctrine. To understand this paradox it is necessary to see the patristic tradition before and after Augustine, and between East and West.

Before Augustine's time, the Greek and Latin Fathers spontaneously recognized that pagans were quite capable of placing morally good actions, though without too clearly distinguishing whether these were done by natural powers alone or also with actual grace. The Greek tradition was so strong it may sound (without being) almost Semi-Pelagian. "We must first select the good," wrote St. John Chrysostom, "and then God adds what pertains to His office. He does not act antecedently to our will, so as not to destroy our liberty."[101] Unlike the West, the Eastern Fathers did not have to deal with Pelagianism. Their polemics were directed against an oriental fatalist *gnosis*. They recognized antecedent grace, as did Chrysostom when he said: "Although you cite faith, you owe it nevertheless to call," and had no trouble admitting, as Nazianzen did, that unbelievers could "have good works precede true faith." But without the contest against Pelagianism, they were never pressed to so emphasize grace that future generations could later quote them on the side of man's total depravity or of unbelievers always committing sin.

Augustine could be thus quoted and had to defend himself against the charge laid by his own contemporaries. It is no coincidence that in Calvin's *Institutes,* Augustine is directly cited more than eight hundred times, as often as all other ancient authorities (about fifty) put together.

---

[101] St. John Chrysostom, *Homilia XII in Hebraeos.*

Yet time and again he "corrects" Augustine, pointing out that he misunderstood a passage in Scripture or otherwise went beyond the evidence. The truth is that St. Augustine certainly admitted that not all the works of sinners or unbelievers are sinful, since he recognized that they, too, have free wills.

Writing to his friend Simplicianus, he said "He does not sin in every act who has not yet been reborn nor has charity diffused in his heart."[102] Or again, "There is a charity that is divine, and another human; and the human may be licit or it may be illicit. It is licit human charity by which a wife is loved. But see that this kind of charity is possible also among sinners, namely, among pagans, the Jews and heretics."[103]

It must be granted, however, that Augustine more than once appears to say that all the actions of unbelievers are sinful. What did he mean? It seems he meant that the state of original sin extends to whatever a person does, depriving all his actions of true ordination to a supernatural end. Analogously, therefore, we can say they are, in a sense, suffused by the stain or original guilt. But their sinfulness is really no more or less than that of the original sin itself. Consequently these "sins" do not constitute a new guilt deserving of new punishment, as Baius and the Jansenists had taught. Without defending Augustine's terminology, we can at least spare his reputation for orthodoxy, although he was the principal authority used by John Calvin and the subject of Jansenius' classic book.

Augustine's name is connected with a theory that arose among Catholics in the heat of the Jansenist controversy, which said that without the grace of at least imperfect charity an unbeliever sins, if not mortally, then venially. Since God never gives such grace to people who do not know Him, they sin venially in all their actions.

---

[102] St. Augustine, *Ad Simplicium*, 1, 2.
[103] St. Augustine, *Sermo* 349, 1.

Three men are associated with the theory—H. Noris, F. Belleli, and J. L. Berti—who belonged to the so-called Augustinian school in the eighteenth century.

Henri Noris (1631–1704) was the outstanding representative among the Augustinians. His most important work was *Historia Pelagiana et Dessertatio* on the Pelagian heresy, followed by a defense of the Augustinian doctrine of grace against that held by Luis de Molina. Approved by Rome, the book stirred a great deal of opposition and the author was denounced to the Holy Office for renewing Jansenism. Noris was acquitted of heresy, but forty years later *Historia* was placed in the *Index*. In 1748 Benedict XIV ordered Noris' writings removed from the *Index*, but his theories, shared by Belleli and Berti, are now abandoned by theologians.

However, the principles behind these speculations are not obsolete. According to the Augustinians, every good act requires the motive of supernatural charity, and an explicit intention of pleasing God as one's final end—neither of which can be had without grace. It is hard to see how these conditions differ, in practice, from the demands made by Quesnel. If nothing else, they would confuse the faithful who rightly believe that an action is good provided it conforms to conscience and the natural law, and that an explicit intention to please God is nowhere required in the Church's teaching as a necessary condition for placing every single act of virtue.

Observance of the Natural Law

While the Church has resolutely defended human nature as intrinsically sound in spite of the fall, it fully recognizes that not all is well with man since Adam lost original justice and we have inherited his guilt.

Catholic theology agrees that because of original sin, the human race lost sanctifying grace, bodily immortality, integrity, and the state of happiness enjoyed by our first parents. In patristic language, man was *spoliatus in gratuitis*. Although we are still capable of knowing God by the light of pure reason, and our free will has not been completely destroyed, we have become, in the words of Trent, "worse in body and soul."[104]

St. Thomas distinguished four injuries that were inflicted on human nature through the fall of Adam: the wound of ignorance, in as much as reason has lost its facility for the knowledge of truth, especially in the religious and moral order; the wound of malice, through which the will is deprived of its ready inclination to good; the wound of weakness, which makes us weak in overcoming the trials incident to the practice of virtue, resulting in a deficit of the constancy and effectiveness demanded by the moral law; and the wound of concupiscence, or loss of integrity in the control of the appetitive faculties, so that pleasant things are spontaneously desired and tend to attract, antecedent to the dictate of reason and even in spite of it, while the unpleasant are instinctively shunned.

The first consequence of this condition is our need of grace to keep intact the moral law for any length of time. To isolate the essential elements involved, theologians use the hypothetical case of an unbeliever in original sin, destitute of all grace, whether habitual or actual, and ask if such a person could observe the natural moral law for some time, say for a few years or under grave temptations for several months. They answer negatively and derive their conclusion with dogmatic certainty from defined doctrines of the Church.

It may be well to anticipate the objection that this is purely academic, since God does not leave such a person for long without some help of grace. True, but in showing his need of grace we come to recognize with precision the limitations of our nature on its voli-

---

[104] *CCC* 37, 399, 400, 1008.

tional side, similar to its debility intellectually in needing revelation for an adequate knowledge of natural religion. In both cases, the physical capacity is there but also there is the moral necessity for help from the outside because of the obstacles involved.

Pelagians would naturally claim that we have both the physical and moral competence to keep the whole law, on their basic assumption that original sin did not directly affect anyone but Adam. Indeed on their principles, we could avoid all sin, even the slightest, for a lifetime, if only we put our wills to it; since the principal source of our weakness in moral matters is the ravages of inherited sin, which the Pelagians simply denied.

At the other end of the scale, classic Protestantism and Jansenism emphatically agree that without grace there is no observance of the natural law. But the need, they say, is more than relative (moral necessity) due to weakness. It is absolute and physical because all the progeny of Adam have had their freedom so thoroughly destroyed that only God's intervention can supply what was lost.

Not to see the thoroughness of Reformed doctrine here is to miss the Church's concern to safeguard man's ability, of himself, to keep the divine commands, at the risk of denuding human nature of its most precious natural possession. Luther was lucidly clear. "Free will," he repeated, "is purely passive in every one of its acts (*in omni suo actu*) which can come under the term will. A good act comes wholly and entirely (*totus et totaliter*) from God, because the whole activity of the will consists in the divine action which extends to the members and powers of both body and soul, no other activity existing."[105]

Among the most comprehensive statements on the need of grace to observe the moral law occurs in the *Indiculus* against the Pelagians. "No one," it declares, "not even he who has been renewed by the grace

---

[105] Luther, *Werke* (Weimar: H. Böhlau, 1884), 2:421.

of baptism, has sufficient strength to overcome the snares of the devil, and to vanquish the concupiscence of the flesh, unless he obtains help from God each day to persevere in a good life."[106]

The conclusion is that if even those baptized and in sanctifying grace need supernatural help, *a fortiori* the infidel in sin; and if such need is required each day (*quotidianum adjutorium*), certainly without it the law could not be observed for any length of time.

All that we read in the Scriptures confirms this sober judgment. St. Peter exhorts us to be ever watchful because the devil, like a roaring lion, goes about seeking whom he may devour.[107] St. Paul bids us put on the armor of God, to be able to withstand the snares of the devil, by every prayer and supplication, praying all the time.[108] Christ Himself instructed us to pray, "lead us not into temptation," and to watch and pray lest we enter into temptation.[109]

All this insistence on the necessity for constant prayer would be meaningless if the graces it seeks to obtain were not needed just as constantly to keep out of sin. This includes explicitly those in the divine friendship, and also by implication, those in original or personal sin.

Perseverance in Grace

A new problem occurs as we approach the limitations of a person already in the state of grace. Can he persevere in God's love without additional actual graces? If he can, for how long? And if he needs supernatural assistance to retain the infused virtue of charity, is something more required to die in the state of sanctifying grace?

The answer to these questions is a humbling admission of our complete dependence upon God. For though we are justified, we cannot

---

[106] *DS* 241.
[107] 1 Peter 5:8.
[108] Ephesians 6:11.
[109] Matthew 6:13, 26, 41.

long persevere in this possession without God's special ongoing help which, we must add, He never denies. Moreover actual, final perseverance is another great gift we can infallibly obtain through prayer.

Theologians fairly agree on certain qualities of this special help to persevere for any time in supernatural charity. It is to be distinguished from such habitual graces as the theological virtues, gifts, or fruits of the Holy Spirit; and also from the general divine concursus in the natural order. It is not a permanent habit nor a special privilege but an assistance in the form of actual grace.

There is less agreement on the exact nature of this assistance. A minority see it only as the gift of final perseverance by anticipation, which seems hardly satisfactory since not everyone who is now in the state of grace will necessarily die in that condition. Something extra appears necessary. Others prefer to call it the sum of all the actual graces a man receives through life or, best of all, an altogether distinct benefit over and above the stream of actual graces. As a common denominator, it consists in that special sequence of actual graces which gives the justified man or woman the energy needed to persevere in the state of grace for a long time, in spite of any array of temptations to commit sin.

In Pelagian times, the Church emphasized the necessity of prayer against those who would have dispensed with this duty on the grounds of having all the strength in nature to meet any moral crisis. "Those reborn and healed (by baptism) must always beg for the help of God so they might persevere in good works and attain to a good end."[110]

The Council of Trent returned to the same theme on the absolute necessity of prayer in order to keep the divine precepts. "No one should say it is impossible for the just man to keep the commandments of God, for that is a rash statement censured with anathema by the

---

[110] *DS* 380; *CCC* 2744.

Fathers," notably St. Augustine in his treatise on *Nature and Grace*.[111] "For God does not command the impossible; but when he commands, He warns you to do what you can, and to pray for what you cannot do, and He helps you so that you can do it."[112] Then to clinch the doctrine, those are censured who would say the contrary.[113] The need of assistance is specified against anyone who claims that "without God's special help it is possible for a justified man to persevere in the justice he has received, or says that with God's special help it is impossible."[114]

Behind the conciliar teaching stands the whole background of Scripture, with its frank statements about the dangerous struggle which the just man must undergo on the road to heaven. The correlative duty is therefore constantly to pray for help, without which the uneven contest between man and forces of evil cannot be won. Christ explicitly taught us only one prayer, which is a composite of seven petitions and in which are imbedded the terms "this day" and "daily" to show the constant call we should make on the divine mercy. We need God's help to remain faithful to Him.

For our consolation, we know that the help we need will not be denied to us. The first proposition of Jansenius condemned by Innocent X read, "There are some of God's commandments that just men cannot observe with the powers they have in their present state, even if they wish and strive to observe them; nor do men have the grace which would make their observance possible."[115]

The whole tenor of revelation runs counter to such blasphemy, by telling us of God's readiness to help in our necessities. The Psalms are a mosaic of divine assurance and of motives for perfect trust.

---

[111] St. Augustine, "De Natura et Gratia," 43, *MPL* 44:271.
[112] *DS* 1536.
[113] *DS* 1568.
[114] *DS* 1572.
[115] *DS* 2001.

The Lord turns His eyes to the just and His ears to their appeal. They call and the Lord hears and rescues them in all their distress. The Lord is close to the broken-hearted, those whose spirit is crushed He will save. Many are the trials of the just man, but from them all the Lord will rescue Him.[116]

As a father has compassion on his sons, the Lord has pity on those who fear Him. For He remembers of what we are made, He remembers that we are dust. The love of the Lord is ever-lasting upon those who hold Him in fear. His justice reaches out to children's children, when they keep His covenant in truth, when they keep His will in the mind.[117]

Christ emphasized that His yoke is sweet and His burden light. "This is the love of God," St. John wrote, "that we keep His commandments; and His commandments are not burdensome."[118]

However, retaining sanctifying grace for any length of time is one thing, and dying in the state of grace is something else. No doubt God's help is not wanting to enable us to remain in His love until death, yet we know that some people do not persevere. Possible perseverance does not necessarily mean actual perseverance, for which another and greater gift is required. If required, how can we acquire it?

There should be no cavil about calling the grace of final perseverance a gift, but its specialized character needs explanation. It is special because it is distinct from the power of perseverance and distinct also from all other gifts of God. It is given only to the predestined, and those who receive it attain to eternal life. It is absolutely gratuitous on God's part, since we cannot merit this gift in strict justice nor may anyone claim it merely because he is just. We might describe it as a

---

[116] Psalm 33:8–10.
[117] Psalm 102:6, 8.
[118] 1 John 5:3.

complex of God's special providence and protection, by which He arranges that the elect should conquer sin, practice virtue, and be taken away by death at the time when they are in the state of grace.[119]

This paramount benefit can be assured by humble and confident prayer, with an infallibility founded not in formal justice but in the generous promise of God. The prayer must be persevering—not once and again, but daily—and as often as conditions allow, especially when temptations arise or circumstances remind us of our dependence on God. Hence the value of certain formularies like the Lord's Prayer, with its plea to be delivered from the evil of eternal damnation, and the Hail Mary which ends with the invocation, "now and at the hour of our death."

It is not surprising that the earliest declarations of the Church on the gratuity of final perseverance were made in Pelagian times, when the supernatural order was reduced to human activity. There could be no question that it is a special gift to die in the state of a grace whose very existence was denied. Yet the most explicit teaching occurs in the Council of Trent, which calls for some apologia.

Superficially we think of the Reformers as the last ones to call into question the gift of final perseverance. Their entire theology was bound up with grace and even protested against its compromise by Catholics, who also required good works. But faced with the stark implications of their theory, they reconstructed tradition by shifting the emphasis from faith as an act of knowledge to faith as an operation of the will. The bedrock of the Christian edifice, therefore, became absolute confidence in God's mercy, trusting uncompromisingly in His goodness and in the imputed merits of His Son.[120]

Accordingly, where Catholicism had always defined faith as primarily an intellectual assent to God's revealed truth, the Reformers saw

---

[119] *CCC* 2016.
[120] *CCC* 154–55.

it as mainly a volitional reliance on the divine liberality. A man trusts implicitly that he is one of the predestined and this confidence makes him a believer.

> He alone is truly a believer who, convinced by a firm conviction that God is a kindly and well-disposed Father toward him, promises himself all things on the basis of His generosity; who, relying on the promises of divine benevolence toward him, lays hold on an undoubted expectation of salvation. No man is a believer, I say, except he that, leaning upon the assurance of his salvation, confidently triumphs over the devil and death.[121]

Luther was more dramatically clear. "Every Christian must beware of ever doubting as to whether his works are pleasing to God. The just man lives by faith (confidence). Whoever has this shall not be damned, even though he commit sin."[122]

In the light of these positions, it is less surprising that so much of Trent's decree on justification should deal with the humble trust in God's mercy while forbearing to presume that we are absolutely predestined for heaven. Both Trent and the Reformers might speak of perseverance as a gift, but the Catholic notion was poles apart from the other. In one case, the gift was independent of our merits and consequently not real perseverance at all. In the other it depended not only on God's predestinating will but also on our full cooperation with His grace, which could be resisted (and for which we might be called to give an account of our stewardship) when actually estranged from God.

"This gift," the Council declared, "can be had only from Him who has the power to determine that he who does stand shall stand with perseverance, and who can lift up him who falls. Let no one feel

---

[121] Calvin, *Institutes*, III, 2, 16.
[122] Luther, *Werke*, 2:44 ff.

assured of this gift with absolute certitude, though all should have a most secure hope in the help of God."[123] In the same way, "No one, so long as he lives in this mortal life, should be so presumptuous about the deep mystery of predestination as to decide with certainty that he is definitely among the number of the predestined, as though it were true that, because he is justified, either he cannot sin again, or, if he does sin again, he should promise himself certain repentance. For it is impossible, without a special revelation, to know whom God has chosen as His own."[124] There was no provision in Reformation thought for lapsing from the divine friendship or, at least, from not being reinstated after a fall.

While not defined by the Church, it is common teaching in the schools that the grace of a happy death can be infallibly impetrated from the Divine bounty. The term "impetration" is technical and means an efficacious petition of a favor. Here it means a supplication which so moves God that He grants the petitioners actual persever- ance. St. Thomas explains that "by prayer we impetrate even those things which we do not merit," as when "a man by asking impetrates of God the gift of perseverance, either for himself or for others, although it does not belong to merit."[125]

In practice, the Church has imbedded pleas for perseverance into the Mass and liturgy, into countless prayer formulas, in the whole spirit of the faith, and even in certain approved private revelations which express the authentic Catholic mind: that God will call His faithful out of life when they are properly disposed, provided they fulfill the condition of earnestly asking Him for this gift. Yet no absolute certitude is possible, short of a personal divine communica- tion to remind us that "we cannot command our final perseverance,

---

[123] *DS* 1541; *CCC* 1817.
[124] *DS* 1540.
[125] St. Thomas Aquinas, *Summa* I–II, 14, 9.

but must ask for it from God,"[126] or, with St. Francis de Sales, that "though perseverance . . . does not come from our power, yet it comes within our power" through explicit or implicit prayer.[127]

Avoidance of Venial Sin

A final question has still to be answered. Granting that a person in sanctifying grace needs further actual graces to avoid mortal sin, and to receive the great gift of perseverance to enter eternity while justified, does he also need special graces to avoid venial sins for any length of time? He does, and by that necessity hangs the final thread of our constant dependence on God.

It is remarkable how this aspect of the need for grace already figured in the ancient controversies. But then we remember that the whole issue was first raised by monks, for example, Pelagius and Cassian, whose main concern was precisely with the relation of grace to free will in the pursuit of perfection, which, by definition, presumes the avoidance not only of grave but also of venial sins.

Pelagius and Celestius began preaching their doctrine in North Africa in A.D. 410. Within eight years, Pope Zosimus anathematized their doctrine in a catalogue of censures that became the foundation of our theology of grace.

The stress is on man's continued lapse into sin, and the practical impossibility without special divine assistance to avoid all failing in the service of God. Pelagian perfectionists had reinterpreted St. John's statement that "If we say we have no sin, we deceive ourselves" to mean a pious exaggeration, spoken in humility.[128] But they were wrong, "for the apostle could have said, 'If we say we have no sin we

---

[126] St. Thomas Aquinas, *De Veritate*, XXIV, 14.
[127] St. Francis de Sales, *Treatise on the Love of God*, trans. Rev. Henry Benedict Mackey, O.S.B. (Westminster, MD: Newman Book Shop, 1942), III, 4:140.
[128] 1 John 1:8.

exalt ourselves, and humility is not in us.' However, since he says, 'We deceive ourselves, and truth is not in us,' he clearly shows that the person who says he has no sin is not speaking the truth.'"[129]

Another Pelagian proof text was the petition of the Lord's Prayer, "forgive us our debts," which they claimed was not spoken by holy persons (*sancti*) for themselves but for others, "because such a request is not necessary for them." The theory is untenable since we read everywhere in Scripture of saintly men who included themselves in the humble acknowledgment of sins. "The apostle James," for example, "was a holy and just man when he said, 'In many things we all offend,' why was the word *all* added? Was it not to express the same idea as we find in the Psalm, 'Enter not into judgment with Your servant, for in Your sight no man living shall be justified.'"[130]

In Reformation thought no distinction was made between venial and mortal sins: Where grace operates, they said, it is always effective and no sin results, but where it is absent the whole weight of a man's evil nature stands behind the fault. The Council of Trent took issue with this hard doctrine and gave it scriptural perspective.

> Those who are sons of God love Christ; and those who love Him (as He Himself testifies) keep His words, which they certainly do with God's help.
>
> For granted that in this mortal life, however just and holy men are, they sometimes commit at least slight daily sins, which are also called venial. Still they do not on that account cease to be just. For the just say truthfully and humbly, "Forgive us our debts."[131]

---

[129] *DS* 228.
[130] *DS* 229; James 3:2; Psalm 142:2; *CCC* 827.
[131] *DS* 1536–37.

Otherwise good people should feel a special obligation to walk in the way of justice, since they already possess substantial holiness, and "advance through Jesus Christ, through whom they have had access to grace" in the first place.[132] Positively, therefore, the gift of sanctifying grace imposes the obligation of progress in virtue. It does not mean that "a man once justified cannot sin again and cannot lose grace, and that consequently the man who falls and sins was never truly justified." Nor can it mean that a man once justified can avoid all sins, even venial sins, throughout his entire life without a special privilege of God (*ex speciali Dei privilegio*), as the Church holds in regard to the Blessed Virgin."[133] Our dependence upon supernatural support is not constant, but coterminous with life and coextensive with the whole spectrum of moral conduct, down to shadows of venial sin.

Where does this inability to avoid all venial sin come from? Its root cause is concupiscence, the disorderly appetites of will and flesh that seek their objects independently of reason and the teachings of faith. Contributing factors are dullness of mind to recognize moral evil the moment it appears, and vacillation of freedom caught between choosing what pleases and what displeases God. Evil habits of long standing also exert their pressure as unexpected temptations from the outside may catch us offguard. The devil's malice is always scheming to exploit our tendencies and break down our reserve.

We must distinguish, however, between semideliberate lapses and sins that are fully deliberate. Open-eyed wilfulness is one thing, but when a person does something wrong though conscious it is sinful. Another matter are those surprise attacks that catch us unawares, in which neither full attention nor complete consent are present, although the matter is venially wrong.

---

[132] *DS* 1537.
[133] *DS* 1573; *CCC* 411, 493; cf. *Lumen Gentium* 56.

Even canonized saints committed venial faults of surprise when they were momentarily betrayed into some thoughtless remark, imprudent action, rash judgment, word against charity, or act of deceit to cover up a fault. Newman's famous observation stands: "The Catholic Church holds it better for the sun and moon to drop from heaven, for the earth to fail, and for all the many millions in it to die of starvation in extremest agony, as far as temporal affliction goes, than that one soul, I will not say, should be lost, but should commit one single venial sin, should tell one wilful untruth, or should steal one poor farthing without excuse."[134] And the conduct of the saints in deploring their least failings confirms this judgment. But the Church also understands the cast of our nature and the liability to sin because of the fall. While holding firmly to the objective malice of sin, it recognizes the subjective weakness of man.

Semideliberate failings, therefore, are not eradicable without God's exceptional privilege, such as we may certainly affirm only of the Blessed Virgin. It is a privilege in the same category as the Immaculate Conception. We do not mean that God established, as it were, an "iron law of sin"; but that there is a general law by which He permits venial sins. He does not, in the present dispensation, wish to give persons in His friendship (not even the saints) such extraordinary graces that they always avoid all venial sins, including those of surprise or semideliberation.

Yet with prayer, sacrifice, and the sacraments, even semideliberate faults can be decreased and finally overcome. Benedict XII in his definitive Constitution on the beatific vision speaks of the "apostles, martyrs, confessors, virgins and others of the faithful" who may have "no need of purification at the time of their death," thus clearly indi-

---

[134] John Henry Newman, *Apologia Pro Vita Sua,* (London: Longmans, Green, 1906) 5; *CCC* 311.

cating that complete purity of soul is possible at least towards the end of one's life.[135] In the same sense we can say that certain outstanding saints and mystics, described by St. John of the Cross, may become freed from all venial sins after extreme purification by God and with the help of His special assistance—which is still not the lifetime or long years' deliverance that requires an extraordinary privilege, in the technical sense of a *privata lex* or "private law" that relates to one person only and that runs counter to the general, in this case divine permissive, law of God.

In order to clarify what may otherwise be misunderstood, the situation herein described is not hypothetical. Actually and really, God does not give this privilege except rarely, to a few or only one—to Mary. Whereas when we spoke of an unbeliever needing grace, and the justified needing special help to avoid mortal sins for a long time and to die in sanctifying grace, the cases were purely fictional, albeit useful to point up the doctrine, since God will not deny the grace and special help according to His merciful providence.

THE PERFECT PRAYER

Catholic doctrine on the necessity of grace for salvation and the limitations of fallen human nature is epitomized in the Lord's Prayer. According to St. Augustine, "Whatever else we say when we pray, if we pray as we should, we are only saying what is already contained in the Lord's Prayer," which he also called "the hallmark of predestination."[136]

The recitation of the *Pater Noster* has been woven into the fabric of Catholic piety since the days of the catacombs. It forms an integral part of the Mass and Canonical Hours, having Christ Himself as

---

[135] *DS* 1000–1001.
[136] St. Augustine, Letter 121, 12, *MPL* 33, 466; *CCC* 2762.

the author. "The same Lord who made us also taught us how to pray, that our petitions may be more easily heard when we speak in the words offered to us by His Son."[137] In the early Church, the faithful were required to recite the Our Father at least three times a day. "He who made us to live, taught us also to pray, with that same benignity, to wit, wherewith He has condescended to give and confer all things else; in order that while we speak to the Father in that prayer and supplication which the Son has taught us, we may be the more easily heard."

Significance in the Theology of Grace

A thematic implication that pervades all the teaching of the Church on the necessity of grace is the corresponding need of prayer as the normal channel for obtaining, retaining, or growing in that gift without which no one can reach God. In view of this correlation it is more than passibly important to know that we have in the *Pater Noster* a compendium of all the lessons that Christians should learn about prayer: How we should pray, what priority of values to observe, what objects to request, and how to state our petitions.

Moreover within the petitions themselves is enclosed the whole of the Christian religion in miniature. Christ has given us a composite of faith and supplication that has an efficacy, compared in patristic writings, with one of the sacraments. It is the one prayer most often recommended to obtain the gift of final perseverance. St. Augustine, and after him the Council of Trent, singled out the *Oratio Dominica* (Lord's Prayer) as a quasisacramental means of obtaining remission for daily venial sins. "Since we live in the midst of the world, where

---

[137] *St. Cyprian,* "The Lord's Prayer," *The Treatises of Cyprian,* trans. Rev. Ernest Wallis, Ph.D., *The Writings of the Fathers Down to A.D. 325: Ante-Nicene Fathers* (Peabody, MA: Hendrickson Publications, 1995), 2, 448; *CCC* 2607, 2610, 2614.

no one can live without sin, the forgiveness of our faults is found not only in the sacred waters of baptism, but also in the daily repetition of the Lord's Prayer. It is like our daily baptism."[138]

St. Thomas's analysis of the structure of the *Pater Noster* leans heavily on Augustine and emphasizes theological intimations that might otherwise be overlooked. Since prayer is an interpretation of our desires, he says, we should pray for those things which are proper for us to desire. In the Lord's Prayer, we are asking of God everything that may lawfully be ambitioned. It is therefore not only a catalogue of petitions but also a corrective for the affections.

Thus the first object of our desires is our last end. The second is the means to arrive at that end. But our destiny is God, to whom our affections incline in two ways: by desiring His glory and wishing to enjoy a share in His glorification. The first belongs to the charity by which we love God in Himself, the second to the charity by which we love ourselves in God. So the first petition asks that God's name be hallowed, that He may be glorified, and the second that we may come to the enjoyment of this glory.

Furthermore we are directed to the end of our existence either by something essential or something accidental to salvation. A thing can be essential either directly, according to the merit by which we deserve beatitude because we are obedient to God (and in this sense we ask that God's will be done on earth as it is in heaven), or it may be only instrumental, although essential, because it helps us merit heaven (and in this sense we say, "Give us this day our daily bread," whether we understand this of the Eucharist or of the bread of the body, which is symbolic for a sufficiency of food).

We are also directed to heaven accidentally, by the removal of obstacles that stand in the way. There are three possible barriers to the

---

[138] St. Augustine, *Enchiridion* 81, *MPL* 40, 270.

beatific vision: sin, temptation, and evils, from whatever source they arise: hence the last three petitions for remission, protection, and deliverance from everything that may hinder our journey to God.

The structure of the Lord's Prayer, according to St. Thomas, can be schematized in a way that shows each petition as a successive step in the logical process just described. Our destiny may be considered either (1) objectively, as the glory of God, or (2) subjectively, as man's beatitude in heaven, which is attained positively, and (3) directly, by doing the will of God, or (4) instrumentally through the bread of the Eucharist and our bodily sustenance, and negatively, by removing the obstacles, which are (5) sin and its prelude, which is (6) temptation, and its just retribution, which is (7) the evil of God's punishment for sin.

Doctrinal and Moral Interpretation

No other formula of prayer in the Church has been more widely commented upon. Practically all the Fathers of the East and West have written either full-length treatises or extensive studies in their homilies on the Gospels according to Matthew and Luke. They considered it, with Tertullian, a summary of the whole Gospel (*breviarum totius evangelii*)[139] and therefore worthy of repeated exploration. Among theologians the outstanding commentary is that by Thomas Aquinas; among mystics it is the spiritual classic of St. Teresa of Avila.

For our purpose we shall follow the lead of St. Robert Bellarmine (1542–1621), whose opusculum *Expositio Orationis Dominicae* has a rare combination of features that specially commend it in a study of divine grace. Bellarmine based his analysis on the earlier and more elaborate treatment by St. Augustine, the great expositor of grace in

---

[139] *CCC* 2761.

Catholic Christianity; he was the prime mover in facing the challenge of Baianism, recognizing its insidious character and paving the way for the later conflict with Jansenism, which was nothing but Baianism reborn. Living in the maelstrom of the Reformation, Bellarmine's basic positions on grace and free will did more than any of his contemporaries to clarify and critically compare the teachings of the Reformers with the teachings of traditional Catholicism.

However, the commentary which follows is not a bare translation of Bellarmine. Using him as a basis, it draws upon other writers, notably Augustine, Peter Canisius, and modern ecclesiastical authorities among the Roman pontiffs. The ensemble is intended to give a deeper insight into the most efficacious prayer for grace known to the Christian faith. Bellarmine recalls that "if, as Christ Himself says, whatsoever we shall ask the Father in His name He will grant us, what should be our assurance of being heard if we pray to God not only in the name of Christ but in the very words that passed His sacred lips?" We might add, in the very words He taught us to pray for that supernatural influx without which no one can see God.

"Our" in the Lord's Prayer is an eloquent reminder to the rich and prosperous not to pride themselves on their possessions of mind or body or despise others as less honorable. In the term "Our" they confess all Christians to be their brethren under God. All the faithful are reminded of the peace and unity that should exist among them if they expect God to answer their prayers. If we are all children of one Father, there should be among us only one heart and soul, symbolized in the unity of the one expression, "Our Father."

Judging by the comments of men like Cyprian, Ambrose, and Chrysostom, one lesson Christ wished to teach by having the *Pater Noster* begin with the first person plural was that a generic form of prayer is preferable to the more specific. Not that specific petitions should not be made, but, other things being equal, joining my prayers with those of others carries a unique motive power with God. It gives voice to the spirit of charity on that most personal level of our dealings with the invisible world. And even looked at "selfishly," the general form is more beneficial to the one praying. While each person is praying for everyone else, all are praying for one another. If I said only, "My Father," no one would be praying for me except I myself; whereas in the form prescribed by Christ all Christians the world over are praying for me. This is spiritual utility raised to its highest degree.

To whom is the Lord's Prayer addressed? To all three persons of the Trinity, although nominally we seem to be speaking only to God the Father. Whatever God does outside of Himself, here being invoked in our favor, is done by the whole Trinity, since among the persons there is only one will, one power, one nature and one divinity.

Although addressed to the triune God, the Lord's Prayer is specially directed to God as our Father, not only or immediately as our Creator but as the Father who adopted us into His own divine household in the supernatural life. The *Pater Noster* is, in effect, the characteristic prayer of the New Testament. As the Jews on Mount Sinai were impressed with their position as the *servants* of Yahweh we are now not servants but *sons* of God, and so are bidden to pray, "Our Father, who art in heaven."

Two interpretations are given of what is meant by "heaven." One is that heaven refers to the minds and hearts of the faithful in whom the Lord dwells by grace as in His tabernacle. More literally we should understand the physical heavens above, which are symbolic of the abode where God dwells. He is still everywhere but there the glory of His presence is most fully manifest to the angels and saints who behold Him face to face. Since heaven is our real home, we are urged to turn our hearts away from earthly things as much as possible and fix them on that eternal country where a loving Father waits to hear our prayers and grant us what we wish.

"Hallowed be Thy name" does not imply that the name of God is not holy. God is infinitely perfect so that nothing can be added to His perfection or taken away from it. Yet the Lord can be sanctified and His name hallowed by men. We therefore ask that the name of God may be better known and more honored among His creatures. It is the expression of an ideal towards which to strive, and that the world more closely reaches with every unbeliever who finds the true faith, every sinner who gives up his sin, and every person who grows in reverence and submission to the name of God.

The second petition follows logically from the first, since we are to seek our own beatitude only subordinately to the glory of God. But what Kingdom are we asking to come when we pray *adveniat regnum tuum,* because the Scriptures speak of kingdom in various senses, from the kingdom of nature to that of heavenly glory?

There can be no question of a natural kingdom as an object of prayer, since God already rules over all created things. This kind of kingdom has existed in the past and will continue into eternity, no matter how the wicked try to subvert the order of God's providence. In this sense Mordechai spoke to Yahweh, "O Lord, almighty king, all things are in Your power and there is none that can resist Your will."[140]

The kingdom of grace extends to all the faithful in the Church of God, where the Lord rules over His elect by dwelling in their hearts. It was of this kingdom that Christ prophesied that "the Son of Man will send forth His angels, and they will gather out of His kingdom all scandals."[141] Accordingly when we pray for the advent of God's

---

[140] Esther 13:9.
[141] Matthew 13:41.

kingdom we ask for the speedy coming of the kingdom of faith in which the things of God and not the creations of man will hold first place. We ask for the subversion of the kingdom of ignorance and error, of that kingdom in which sinners cast themselves into everlasting fire. We pray for the coming of the kingdom of divine grace, that it may reign in us by the indwelling Spirit, and that the kingdom of malice may be destroyed. For the Lord reigns in the hearts of the just as the devil rules in the souls of the wicked. Sinners prefer slavery to Satan over the freedom which comes from obedience of sons to God their Father.

When we pray, "Thy kingdom come," we ask for the establishment of the Catholic Church throughout the world, that it may grow and advance not only in numbers but in holiness of life. We ask that soon there may be but one flock and one shepherd, that the enemies of peace and unity may be humbled, that the Church may be guided by leaders and priests who are outstanding in virtue and remarkable for the depth of their faith.

But the kingdom of God in the truest sense is the kingdom of glory, already begun in the souls of the blessed and destined to reach perfection on the last day.[142] From that time on, all the power of demons and wicked men over the souls of the just will cease. Only God and His adopted sons will reign. Therefore we ask that this kingdom which was promised may certainly come to us. We ask that what we have hoped for may not have been sought in vain. We ask that our desire of becoming heirs of God and coheirs with Christ may be fulfilled according to His words, "Fear not, little flock, for it has pleased your Father to give you a kingdom."[143]

Theologians commonly distinguish two kinds of will in God—the divine signified will and His will of good pleasure. The former includes

---

[142] *CCC* 2816, 2821.
[143] Luke 12:32.

all the commands and prohibitions which He imposes on rational creatures, and by which He indicates what He wants done or avoided. His
will of good pleasure, however, is absolute, is always fulfilled and no
creature can impede it. Illustrative of the first type are the words of
Christ, "Whosoever does the will of my Father, who is in heaven, he is
my brother, and my sister and my mother."[144] The Old Testament
abounds in examples of the second type. "All things, whatsoever He
will, the Lord has done in heaven and on earth."[145] Consequently the
principal object of the third petition is not the absolute but the signified
divine will, since we are asking that God may give us the grace necessary to not only obey His commands, but to go beyond the simple
obedience to precepts and to live also according to His counsels.[146]

Remarkably the petition does not say, "Do Thou perform Thy will in
us," nor even, "May we do Thy will," but simply, "Thy will be done."
This is to make us understand that obedience to the law of God,
expected of us with the help of His grace, is not exclusively the work of
God, or entirely the fruit of our will. It is the result of a combined action
between God and ourselves.

However, while we pray especially for the strength to fulfill the
signified will of God, we do not exclude the other. Quite as necessary
as obedience to the divine law is the patience we need to accept the
will of God's good pleasure without murmuring or complaint, no
matter how painfully His hand may rest on us. It was this will that
Christ asked might be fulfilled when He prayed in His agony, "Not my
will but Thine be done."[147]

The phase "on earth as it is in heaven" has been variously understood.
By heaven we may understand the spirit, and by earth the flesh, as

---

[144] Matthew 12:50.
[145] Psalm 113:3.
[146] *CCC* 2822, 2823, 2826, 2827.
[147] Luke 22:42.

suggested by St. Paul, that "the flesh lusts against the spirit, and the spirit against the flesh."[148] We ask, then, for a perfect harmony between flesh and spirit, so that just as the spirit is conformed to the law of God, the flesh may be subject to the spirit, and thereby also conformed to the divine law.

The most common explanation is the literal one, where heaven is generic for the Church Triumphant in glory and the earth means the Church militant in its present exile. We plead that by God's grace we may obey Him with something of the obedience of the angels and saints in heaven, who serve the Lord with joy and exultation, with alacrity and no constraint. They are so inflamed with the love of God that nothing gives them greater pleasure than the ready fulfillment of all His commands.[149]

A correlative interpretation is that just as the heavenly bodies—the sun, moon, and stars—perfectly obey the will of God and follow the course He laid out for them, so we may act in the moral conduct of our lives.

The supplication "Give us this day our daily bread" is one of the most critical passages in the Gospels. Everything depends on what we mean by "daily bread." This in turn depends on two basic dogmas of faith: the Real Presence and the prevenient grace that invites cooperation but may be resisted by the free will.

There is no problem seeing in the bread requested all the material sustenance that we need. From the moment we enter the world, we need food, drink, clothing, sleep, health, and a home to live in—all of which are implicitly contained in the one word "bread." But the fourth petition only begins there. It would be incredible that the Lord would have us beg for bodily food and ignore the spiritual nutriment of the soul, especially since He cautioned in the same sermon, "Do not be

---

[148] Galatians 5:17.
[149] *CCC* 2823.

anxious, saying, 'What shall we eat,' or 'What shall we drink,' or 'What are we to put on?' For your Father knows that you need all these things. But seek first the kingdom of God and His justice, and all these things shall be given you besides."[150]

It is not surprising that the Reformers, like Calvin and Melancthon, would have nothing but material food understood by the "bread" of the Lord's Prayer, excluding spiritual sustenance which patristic tradition has always included. They denied the bodily presence of Christ in the Eucharist and did not recognize grace as a gift which could be accepted or rejected, implied in the notion that bread offered could be either taken or refused.

Among the spiritual nutrients of the soul, none is more necessary than the Holy Eucharist, which the ancient Fathers and the councils of the Church saw expressed in the bread for which Christ told us daily to pray. "I am the living bread that came down from heaven," Christ described Himself when making the promise of the Eucharist. Unless we eat this Bread, there can be no strength, no consolation, no growth in the spiritual life. Without this Bread, on the words of Christ, we shall die.[151]

St. Augustine was so sure of the Eucharist as the primary sustenance intended by the Lord's Prayer that he went to great lengths to excuse the contrary custom of not receiving Holy Communion daily, which by then had crept into the Eastern Churches. "Although this bread is called a daily bread," he said, "in the Eastern countries there are very many who do not partake of the Lord's Supper every day; nevertheless they occasion no scandal by not partaking. They are not condemned as disobedient, because their ecclesiastical superiors do not command them to partake."[152] He might have added, however, that the bishops in the East

---

[150] Luke 12:22, 31; *CCC* 2830.
[151] *CCC* 2837.
[152] St. Augustine, *Sermon on the Mount,* II, 7, 26; *CCC* 1389.

were by no means pleased that the immemorial custom of receiving Communion daily had fallen into disuse. Speaking a few years after Augustine, St. John Chrysostom gave a series of homilies at Antioch, in which he deplored the infrequency with which many approached the Holy Table, and he urged the daily reception of the Sacrament.

When St. Pius X restored the traditional practice in modern times, he explained in the prologue of his decree on Frequent Communion that in reception of the Blessed Sacrament "frequent" means daily. Arguing from the analogy of food used by Christ, and the "all but unanimous interpretation of the Fathers" that daily bread in the Lord's Prayer means daily Communion, he concluded that "the Eucharist Bread should be our daily food."[153]

The petition "forgive us our trespasses as we forgive those who trespass against us" refers to our sins and the offenses of others. This is clear from the parallel passage in St. Luke, "forgive us our sins, for we also forgive everyone who is indebted to us," and from the explicit statement of Christ which follows on the Lord's Prayer, that "if you forgive men their offenses, your heavenly Father will also forgive you your offenses. But if you will not forgive men, neither will your Father forgive you your offenses."[154]

Sins are called trespasses or debts because whoever sins does injury to God, thus becoming indebted to Him and owing satisfaction. When a man sins he disturbs the objective order, which carries with it the sanction of reparation. Atonement or restitution is owed by the one who violated the law. God has also entrusted to each one a soul that He expects to be cultivated and tilled like the vineyard of the Scriptures. He looks for this vineyard to bear fruit in its time. To this end He has given us talents of nature and grace to assist our labors until He

---

[153] Pius X, *On Frequent and Daily Reception of Holy Communion* [*Sacra Tridentina*] (1905), paragraph 2.
[154] Luke 11:4, Matthew 6:14–15.

comes. We owe to God—even if we have failed Him, and don't have it—the profit He expected.

Since we are all bidden to pray "forgive us our trespasses," it must mean that we are all sinners. With the certain exception of the Blessed Virgin, all men are at some time infected with the stain of sin. This is why even the saints could rightly ask for pardon, not just from humility, but because they had really sinned.

The context of the petition shows that not all sins are mortal, but some are only venial or, as the Council of Trent calls them, "light and daily sins." A person does not cease to love God if he commits them, although they are offensive to His majesty and demand sorrow and expiation. The implication is that after baptism we still have a chance for repentance, and that the Lord's Prayer has remissive power not only for venial faults but is also useful to move the divine mercy after grave sins are committed.

We do not add the words "as we forgive those who trespass against us" with the idea that God would imitate us and learn to have mercy after our example. But we bear witness to ourselves that mercy is pleasing to Him and the forgiveness of injuries an infallible means of obtaining pardon for our sins. Christ will be satisfied with nothing less if we hope to obtain His mercy. "Forgive, and it shall be forgiven unto you." According to St. Augustine, no matter how earnestly a man prays or how sorry he may be for his sins, unless he is also ready to forgive his neighbor, God will not pardon him. "Would he make out infinite Truth to be a liar, when Christ said, 'If you will not forgive men, neither will your Father forgive you'?"[155]

Two requests are implied in the petition "lead us not into temptation." We pray to be delivered, as far as possible, from temptations that God would otherwise permit to assail us, and to be protected from falling under those temptations which He actually allows.

---

[155] *CCC* 2842–45.

The most important thing about temptations is that we cannot escape them in this life, which is one unremitting temptation, "for the flesh lusts against the spirit."[156] No matter where we turn, temptations are there to meet us: we are tempted in food and drink, in hunger and sobriety, in riches and poverty. But if temptations are inevitable, are they useful? Yes, and even necessary. Through temptation we become familiar with our weakness, and so enabled to fulfill the maxim *Cognosce te ipsom.* Through temptation we are saved from the demon of self-exaltation, our souls are cleansed and enlightened, and we are effectively moved to come to the assistance of others because our sympathy for them has been aroused by the knowledge of ourselves.

Take away temptation and what happens to patience, fortitude, and constancy? Without trial how can these and other virtues not only exist but also be preserved and made to grow? "All that will live godly in Christ Jesus," says the Apostle, "shall suffer persecution," which is synonymous with temptation. The more holy were God's saints, the more severely He tried them in the crucible of temptation.

While temptations are useful, they are still dangerous. Struggle with them is an uncertain issue. It would be presumption to ask for them. It is a mark of humility to decline them and ask God not to lead us into them, if that be His will.[157]

But how to reconcile this with the statement of St. James, "My brethren, count it all joy when you shall fall into divers temptations"?[158] The reason is that although temptation is not to be asked for, in the sense of relished and desired, once it has come upon us, we should bear it not only bravely but even gladly. We also know that what is tolerated is not necessarily loved. Speaking of temptations, St. Augustine observed that Christ bade us to bear them, not love them,

---

[156] Galatians 5:17.
[157] *CCC* 2847.
[158] James 1:2.

for no one loves what he bears, even when he loves to bear it. And though he rejoices to bear what he suffers, still he would rather be spared what he has to bear. Sometimes we read in the lives of the saints that after a revelation about their eventual victory over temptations they asked for more trials, exposed themselves to more dangers, or went out in search of more persecutors. These may be examples we can rightly admire but not imitate.

Those who are seriously striving to please God must be specially on their guard against temptations that might be called native to them: discouragement and pusillanimity, as though they were abandoned by grace; instability in their state of life; a lack of esteem for the guidance of authority, particularly in what concerns the worship and service of God; aspiring to heights which exceed their capacities by adopting uncalled-for practices of zeal and devotion; failing to weigh and examine daily their defects and remorses of conscience; taking half-hearted measures to conquer natural inclinations and bodily emotions; not consulting God before entering on a duty or when faced with a decision; lacking in that prayerful spirit which befits a soul that is walking in the presence of her Lord; and looking at the example of those who are tepid and weak instead of those who are fervent and strong.

No matter what view we take of this petition of the *Pater Noster*, the object of prayer is to avoid sin in the future. In one sense the stress is on the intention of the one praying, in the other on the words of his prayer. For we are asking for two things: to be strong in resisting temptation, and to be spared the temptations themselves. In either case we appeal to God's mercy for help, knowing our own weakness and the power of evil in the world, the flesh and the devil. One aspect that might be overlooked is the function of enlightening grace in forestalling and conquering temptations. The divine light we receive enables us to avoid needless exposure to heavy trials that God foresees would be too much for us; it also tells us what means to use in overcoming present temptations, which call not only for volitional strength of resistance but also mental alertness to outwit the evil spirit and conquer unruly passions by strategy.

Nowhere does the spirituality of the East and West appear more different than in the explanation of the last petition "deliver us from evil." The Greek Fathers without exceptions say the evil from which we beg to be delivered is the evil spirit. They are partly led to this interpretation by the Greek version which reads "from the evil one." But more cogently their preoccupation with the devil in the contest of man's salvation is very distinctive, more so than in the West. The Latin Fathers, like Ambrose, may include the devil as partial object of this petition but they prefer to say we are asking for deliverance from all the evils that afflict us in consequence of Adam's sin or that may befall us after death.[159]

The Church's authority stands behind this broader object, since the Canon of the Mass adds the following prayer immediately after the *Pater Noster* as a form of corollary: "We beseech You, O Lord, to deliver us from all evils, past, present and to come, so that, strengthened by the aid of Your mercy, we may ever be free from sin and secure from all disturbance."[160]

We may look upon the last petition as an extension of the preceding one. It is as though we said, "We pray to be spared not only from temptations that would lead us into sin but, as far as expedient for our salvation, from every kind of evil."

Thus we pray that the penalties we have to suffer may be truly medicinal and corrective, and may not rather weaken our defense against the avowed enemies of the soul. We pray to be delivered even in this life from those dreadful punishments that God's anger is justified in sending for our own and others' sins. We recall how the human

---

[159] *CCC* 2850–53.
[160] *CCC* 2854.

race has been made to suffer because of Adam's fall, and how David's own fault of pride brought vengeance on all his people.

We pray not to be broken or depressed under the weight of adversity, and not to become impatient lest the evil we suffer make us worse instead of better. We pray to be delivered from the fires of purgatory, deserved for our many sins. It will be no comfort that purgation after death is not eternal; it is more grievous than any sufferings we shall ever experience on earth, and should be considered God's retribution for those who had sinned and failed to expiate the penalty by salutary penance and prayer. When God punishes a man in this life, or moves him by grace to punish himself, He means to spare him in the life to come. No one is ever punished twice for the same crime.

Finally we ask to be delivered from the everlasting pains of hell, possible only through the remission of sin. Conscious of our misery and unworthiness to be forgiven, we implore the divine mercy and trust in God's goodness that He will not demand in the end what our rebellion against Him had justly deserved.

A number of Greek and Syriac manuscripts, mostly of a later date, have a doxology after the seventh petition, "For Thine is the kingdom, and power, and glory forever. Amen." Several Greek Fathers, notably Chrysostom, also comment on these words in their explanation of the Lord's Prayer. However, it is certain that the addition was not part of the original Gospel text but introduced by way of the Eucharistic liturgy. It occurs in the *Didache* (from the first century) and, in a longer form, in the Byzantine rites of Sts. Basil, James, Mark, and John Chrysostom. Thus it corresponds to our formula, "We beseech You, O Lord, to deliver us," in the canon of the Mass according to the Latin rite.[161]

---

[161] *CCC* 2855.

4

SANCTIFYING GRACE

The nature of grace cuts so deeply into the Christian religion that a proper understanding of what revelation means by this gift of divine love practically identifies the Catholic faith as distinct from all other forms of Christianity, whether as historical phenomena or still existing church institutions.

Since the order of grace is analogous to that of nature, we should expect that just as naturally God exercises His goodness towards us in two different ways. He gives us the nature we have as human beings and by concurring with that nature through His sovereign providence, He acts supernaturally in similar fashion. By giving us a supernature which places us into the divine family where we are enabled to offer our minds and wills toward acquisition of, retention of, and growth in the supernatural order to which we have been raised.

The first species of grace was implied in the statement of St. Athanasius, that "God has not only made us out of nothing; but He gave us freely, by the grace of the Word, a life in correspondence with God". The second was described by St. Ambrose that "every holy thought is the gift of God, the inspiration of God, the grace of God."[162] In technical terms, the first is called sanctifying grace, the second actual grace, although the terminology is fluid and a variety of synonyms is used for both concepts. Our concern here is with the habitual, supernatural state of soul, as distinct from the transitory

---

[162] St. Athanasius, *De Incarnatione Dei Verbi,* 5; St. Ambrose, *De Cain et Abel,* I, 45.

assistance received from God, comparable to the principle of rational life which makes us men as distinguished from the passing divine influence that concurs with our every action.

EXTRINSIC IMPUTATION

Catholic teaching on sanctifying grace reaches back to patristic times when the early Fathers commented on the numerous passages in the New Testament which speak of a grafting into Christ, a renewal of life through incorporation onto the Vine or, in the words of St. John, parturition of those who are born not of blood nor of the will of flesh nor of the will of man, but of God.

But the first detailed examination of what this doctrine implies was occasioned by the Reformation, when Luther, Calvin, and the early Reformers reinterpreted the teaching of St. Paul in a way consistent with their prepossessions on the nature of fallen man. Since they regarded man himself as thoroughly corrupted by the sin of Adam, so that all his actions were intrinsically vitiated and sinful, they logically conceived of man's restoration as a purely extrinsic operation on the part of God. In the exercise of his will, man has no real power of free choice. Whatever good he does is attributable solely to God. Thus the whole process of justification is entirely God's with no vital contribution on man's side to change his status from the essential sinfulness to which original sin had reduced him.

Once a Christian is righteous by faith, Luther taught, he should not console himself that he is no longer a sinner. "He is righteous and holy by an alien or foreign holiness," which means "he is mercy and righteous by the mercy and grace of God." But lest he be misunderstood, he added, "this mercy and grace is not something human (intrinsic to man); it is not some sort of disposition or quality of heart." Indeed, "it consists completely in the indulgence of another and is a pure gift of God, who shows mercy and favor for Christ's sake."

The Christian is not formally righteous (*formaliter justus*), he is not righteous according to substance or quality—I use these words for instruction's sake. He is righteous according to his relation to something; namely, only in respect to divine grace and the free forgiveness of sins, which comes to those who acknowledge their sin and believe that God is gracious and forgiving for Christ's sake, who was delivered for our sins and is believed in by us.[163]

This theory is contraposed to the Catholic notion of a formal righteousness, whereby a man is not only considered but actually is right with God.

Throughout his writings, but especially in the commentary on the Psalm *Miserere,* Luther insists on the paradox that a man is *simul justus et peccator,* at once righteous and sinful: righteous by reason of the imputed merits of Christ and a sinner because his inherited guilt remains. He admitted the function of the word of God and baptism in purifying the soul, yet the cleanness is not within. According to this purity, "the Christian is rightly said to be purer than snow, purer than the sun and stars, even though the defilements of spirit and flesh cling to him. These are concealed and covered by the cleanness and purity of Christ, which we obtain by hearing the Word and by faith." However, "we should note diligently that this purity is an alien purity, for Christ adorns and clothes us with His righteousness. So if you look at a Christian without the righteousness and purity of Christ, as he is in himself, even though he be most holy (*sanctissimus*), you will find not only no cleanness, but what I might call diabolical blackness."[164]

John Calvin professed the same theory, but developed and amplified it in more theological language. A man is justified, he said, who

---

[163] Luther, *Enarratio in Psalmum* 51, 2.
[164] Ibid., 7; *CCC* 2023.

although a sinner, "is reckoned in the condition not of a sinner, but of a righteous man." Accordingly, "we explain justification simply as the acceptance with which God receives us into His favor as righteous men. And we say that it consists in the remission of sins and the imputation of Christ's righteousness."[165] The expression "remission of sins" should not mislead. Calvin meant to combine the two ideas— remission and imputation, i.e., an imputed remission which left the sinner internally unchanged.

> We are justified before God solely by the intercession of Christ's righteousness. This is equivalent to saying that man is not righteous in himself (*hominem non in se ipso justum esse*), but because the righteousness of Christ is communicated to him by imputation (*quia Christi justitia imputatione cum illo communicatur*),—something worth carefully noting.
>
> You see that our righteousness is not in us but in Christ, that we possess it only because we are partakers in Christ; indeed with Him we possess all riches.
>
> To declare that by Him alone we are accounted righteous, what else is this but to lodge our righteousness in Christ's obedience, because the obedience of Christ is reckoned as though it were our own.[166]

All the Protestant churches followed the same tradition and profess it in their modern creeds. The eleventh of the Thirty-nine Articles of the English (and Episcopalian) Church reads that, "We are accounted (*reputamur*) righteous before God, only for the merit of our Lord and Saviour Jesus Christ."[167] In the Presbyterian Confes-

---

[165] Calvin, *Institutes,* III, 11, 2; *CCC* 1701.
[166] Calvin, *Institutes,* III, 23.
[167] *The Book of Common Prayer* (New York: Oxford University Press, 1944), 605.

sion of Faith, justification is defined as "an act of God's free grace, wherein He pardoneth all our sins, and accepteth us as righteous in His sight, only for the righteousness of Christ imputed to us, and received by faith alone."[168]

This concept of imputed justice has been forthrightly described in Karl Barth, whose devotion to Calvin appears in every page of his eleven volume *Die Kirchliche Dogmatik.* Barth is examining the notion of the pardon of man, and asks himself, "What does the forgiveness of sins mean?" What is meant by the often-repeated Scripture assurance that our past has been cancelled?

> The man who received forgiveness does not cease to be the man whose past (and his present as it derives from his past) bears the stain of his sins. The act of the divine forgiveness is that God sees and knows this stain infinitely better than the man himself, and abhors it infinitely more than he does even in his deepest penitence—yet He does not take it into consideration, He overlooks it, He covers it up, He passes it by, He puts it behind Him, He does not charge it to the man, He does not "impute" it, He does not sustain the accusation to which the man has exposed himself, He does not press the debt with which he has burdened himself, He does not allow to take place the destruction to which he has inevitably fallen victim.[169]

It would be impossible to improve on the foregoing description of what classic Protestantism calls justification, whose quintessence is the merciful attribution of righteousness to man whose inner being remains objectively sinful.

---

[168] *Constitution of the Presbyterian Church U.S.A.* (Philadelphia: Board of Christian Education of the Presbyterian Church in the U.S.A., 1955), 214–15.

[169] Karl Barth, *Church Dogmatics* (Edinburgh: T. & T. Clark, 1956), 4:597.

It is not easy for a Catholic to understand what this means. None of his categories of thought allows for this idea, in the words of the Formula of Concord, that "The word 'justification signifies the *declaring* anyone just, on account of the justice of Christ, which is by God *imputed* to faith," so that "our justice is not of us."[170]

Perhaps the best explanation is to conceive this justification as a judicial act of God, whereby the believing (trustful) sinner is delivered from the punishments of sin, but not from the sin itself. The great difference, therefore, between the Catholic and Protestant doctrines is that according to Catholic principles the justice of Christ is immediately appropriated by the believer to become part of his inward self and changes his whole moral existence;[171] whereas by Protestant norms the justice remains in Christ, does not pass into the sinner's inward life and stays in a purely outward relation to him. His injustice is indeed covered, but has not been removed, since his will has not been healed.

Seen from another viewpoint, the Protestant theory pictures Christ casting only His shadow on the believer, so that the latter's continued sinfulness is merely not observed by God. Hence the explicit dogma of the Formula of Concord that "the just are pronounced and reputed such on account of faith, through the obedience of Christ. But because of their corrupt nature they still are and remain sinners as long as they bear this mortal body."[172] It may be added that the Formula of Concord is the most definitive confession of Evangelical (Lutheran) faith, drafted in 1577 as the last of the so-called symbolical (creedal) documents of continental Protestantism. Its authority is incontestable in all Lutheran Churches.

---

[170] *Formula of Concord*, III, "On Justifying Faith," (n.p.: Evangelical Lutheran Synod of Missouri, Ohio, and Other States, 1986), 11.
[171] *CCC* 1266.
[172] *Formula of Concord*, 15.

If we look for a basis for the theory of imputation, we find it in the Protestant identification of original sin and concupiscence. Where Catholics admit that concupiscence remains after a man if justified, but he is not *per se* stained by this inherent drive, Protestants represent concupiscence as sin in itself, and in fact as the yet subsisting original sin. They dismiss as unimportant and untrue the distinction between the mere feeling of that incitement to sin and the consent to the same. It is precisely on this ground that they rest their assertion that justification consists in the mere declaration of the remission of sin; but not in the purification from sin itself, because original sin (painfully recognized by everyone in the risings of concupiscence) still continues after baptism, and no amount of prayer or grace from God will just make it go away forever.

However, it would be a mistake to suppose that such radical departure from traditional Christian teaching remained long unchallenged, or that all Protestants always held and still profess this doctrine. Within the ranks of Protestantism is a strain of Arminian theology on grace that deserves closer study among Catholics than it has so far received. As an attempted compromise with Catholic doctrine it offers prospects for ecumenical discussion that are impossible with orthodox Calvinism or modern Barthianism.

Jacob Arminius (1560–1609) was a Dutch Reformed theologian whose studies of St. Paul led him to question Calvin's theories on predestination, justification and grace. He was charged with heresy and, though his efforts to liberalize Dutch Calvinism quite failed, he exercised a great modifying influence on subsequent generations of Protestants, notably in English-speaking countries. The Arminians, as his followers were called, insisted that the divine sovereignty was compatible with a real free will in man; that God's predestination to salvation rests upon His foreknowledge that certain people will believe in Christ and persevere in this belief to the end; that Christ died for the whole human race and performed atonement for all men, though only believers share in His benefits; that the grace of God is not irresistible, for man can resist the Spirit of God; that it is not certain that a man cannot fall from grace once he has received it.

Arminians went still further. They traced five stages in the history of a sinner who has already obeyed the divine call, been converted to faith, and, under the assistance of grace, is obeying the divine precepts. The first stage is election, by which true believers, whom God marks as His own, are separated from the profane crowd of those who perish. After election comes adoption, whereby the elect are received into the family of God and admitted to the rights of a heavenly destiny, which they will finally achieve. The third is justification, which they described as the gracious absolution from all sin, by means of a faith "working by charity" in Christ Jesus and by His merits. Sanctification goes beyond justification to effect a perfect, inward separation of the sons of God from the children of this world. And lastly, the sealing through the Holy Spirit is a firm and solid confirmation of a person in true confidence, in the hope of eternal glory, and in the assurance of divine grace.

Though remarkably close to Catholic doctrine Arminianism is still Protestant in several ways. Justification is taken as only a step in the process of man's restoration to grace, whereas there are no partial justifications. A man is either wholly restored to God's friendship or not. Moreover justification itself is considered only a judicial act on the part of God; only later, through sanctification and the sealing, does the soul approach what Catholics believe is a unitary effect, occurring at the moment when sanctifying grace is infused. There may be growth in holiness, of course, but this means a development *ab esse ad bene esse,* from good to better, and not a drawn out *fieri* that finally terminates in what we would call "the state of grace." Equally un-Catholic was the Arminian insistence that all of this movement from sin to grace happens under the unique impulse of trustful confidence (faith) and independent of good dispositions in the believer. They were inconsistent in making this concession to Reformed theology, but the inconsistency is part of their system.

We can get some idea of how influential Arminianism has been over the centuries if we read John Wesley (1703–1791), founder of the Methodist Church and the greatest figure in post-reformation Protestantism. Reared in the Anglican Church and steeped in its teaching on grace, he sought to reform the prevalent theory of justification by adopting a type of Arminian theology that has since become known as perfectionism. In 1764 he made a review of the subject in *A Plain Account of Christian Perfection,* which stands poles apart from orthodox Protestantism and that has incalculably affected the lives and conduct of a large segment of non-Catholic Christianity. He described what he means by "rising above justification" in a series of short propositions.

> There is such a thing as perfection; for it is again and again mentioned in Scripture.
>
> It is not so early as justification; for justified persons are to "go on unto perfection" (Hebrews 6:1).
>
> It is not so late as death; for St. Paul speaks of living men that were perfect (Philippians 3:15).
>
> It is not absolute. Absolute perfection belongs not to man, nor to angels, but to God alone.
>
> It does not make a man infallible; none is infallible while he remains in the body.
>
> Is it sinless? It is not worthwhile to contend for a term. It is "salvation from sin."

It is "perfect love" (I John 4:18). This is the essence of it: its properties, or inseparable fruits, are, rejoicing evermore, praying without ceasing, and in everything giving thanks (I Thessalonians 5:16).

It is improvable. It is so far from lying in an indivisible point, from being incapable of increase, that one perfected in love may grow in grace far swifter than he did before.

It is amissible, capable of being lost; of which we have numerous instances.[173]

Wesley was convinced of his position and so critical of the opposition he urged that "all our preachers should make a point of preaching perfection to believers constantly, strongly, and explicitly; and all believers should mind this one thing, and continually agonize for it."[174] His urgings produced results that have been far-reaching. It is a safe estimate that—except for Arminianism on the continent and Methodism in England and America—Protestantism would not have survived as a system to the present time. As it was, though, its compromise with the Catholic doctrine on sanctifying grace and growth in holiness has both kept the system alive and given it vigor that the negative theory of "extrinsic imputation" could never have supplied.

SPIRITUAL REBIRTH

In meeting the challenge of the Reformed teaching on justification, the Council of Trent ranged through both Testaments of Sacred Scripture as well as Western and Eastern patristic traditions. It took more than passing cognizance of the scholastic developments incorporated in the writings of St. Thomas, and used the corpus of ecclesiastical

---

[173] John Wesley, *A Plain Account of Christian Perfection* (London: Epworth Press, 1952), 106; *CCC* 1709.

[174] John Wesley, *A Plain Account of Christian Perfection* (London: Epworth Press, 1952), 107–8.

documentation, conciliar and papal, to an extent previously unknown in any Council of the Church.

Decree on Justification

Preparatory to its sixth session, which opened in January 1547, the Council impressed upon the assembled bishops and theologians the importance of studying the problem of justification from both sides, i.e., from the side of the Reformers and of Catholic tradition. The delegates were instructed to read Protestant writers with impartiality so that they could censure what they considered erroneous and approve what deserved approbation. After private conferences, the theologians were to submit their opinions to the Fathers of the Council, who would discuss what was submitted and individually state their judgments. Finally a preliminary set of decrees was drafted, which underwent numerous revisions before voting. To the very end there were changes in wording, deletions and additions to produce the masterful *Decretum De Justificatione,* whose Proemium, Chapters, and Canons are the most authoritative declaration of Catholic thought we have on the subject.

The cardinal issue on the nature of justification was the familiar Protestant theory that when a man is justified two things happen to him. His sins are forgiven in the sense that they are covered over and not imputed to him, while internally he remains a sinner. And the justice he "acquires" is not his own as something inhering in his soul, but the alien justice of Christ or of God which is credited to him without being really his.

Trent defined justification as "a passing from the state in which man is born a son of the first Adam, to the state of grace and adoption as sons of God (Romans 8:15), through the second Adam, Jesus Christ our Savior."[175]

---

[175] *DS* 1524; *CCC* 1996.

There is no doubt, therefore, that justification implies the remission of sins, as a true, internal, and unequivocal removal, and not a mere covering-over. The year before, and four months after Luther's death, Trent had defined that through the grace of baptism "everything having the true and proper nature of sin is taken away," and not "only brushed over (*radi*) or not imputed."[176] This is not to say, as Barth insinuated, that forgiveness means "to make what has happened not to have happened."[177] It means that the guilt and stain of soul contracted by sin are completely taken away. There is also a sense in which our sins are no longer imputed to us, once we receive grace, for the good reason that the sins are gone, which is quite otherwise than the nonimputation of guilt for a sinful condition that still perdures.

What sins are removed by justification? If baptism is received, all sins are deleted: original and personal, mortal and venial. If remission takes place through the sacrament of penance or by an act of perfect love, the amount of venial guilt remitted depends on a person's dispositions.

However, this is only the beginning. Besides remission of sins, when a person receives sanctifying grace there is also "sanctification and renovation of the interior man."[178] No doubt the forgiveness of sins is also a kind of renewal, which theologians call negative or moral, since a defect is cleared away and the person becomes morally clean. And there is more. Renovation in the Tridentine sense means a positive and physical change in the soul "through the voluntary reception of grace and gifts."[179]

It may seem like theological hairsplitting to insist there is no middle ground between intrinsic and extrinsic justification, except that the question was one of the most heatedly discussed at the Council of

---

[176] *DS* 1515; *CCC* 997–98, 1987.
[177] Barth, *op. cit.*, 597.
[178] *DS* 1528; *CCC* 1266.
[179] *DS* 1528.

Trent and is currently of major importance in the ecumenical move-ment, where some sort of compromise is sought between Catholic and Protestant theologies of grace.

Among the proponents of the *via media* were Martin Bucer (1491–1551) among the Protestants and Cardinal Seripando, Master General and zealous reformer of the Augustinians. Seripando ardently advocated his theory before the Council of Trent in the laudable effort to meet, if possible, the Reformers halfway. He said there were two kinds of justice: intrinsic and extrinsic. In virtue of the former we pass from the state of sinners to that of children of God, and are enabled to practice good works with the help of divine grace. The latter is not intrinsic to us but belongs to Christ alone. It consists of His justice and merits, which He imputes to us as though they were ours, according to His own good pleasure. He felt the first without the second is imper-fect and insufficient to make us reach heaven.

Only a handful of theologians (five to be exact) approved Seri-pando's theory that to obtain eternal glory the justice of Jesus Christ must be imputed to us. Everyone else was against the idea, particularly James Lainez of the Society of Jesus, who produced a long reply. Seri-pando's critics explained there are two kinds of causes: one type produces an effect but is not needed to keep the effect in existence and operation, like the father whose son can live quite independently of his parent. Another kind is continually required to preserve what it produces, as light is constantly dependent on the sun. Our need of God belongs to the second class, since we depend on Him absolutely in every aspect of life, whether in the temporal or supernatural order. Accordingly there is no call for imputing the merits of Christ to us, over and above the intrinsic effect produced in the soul when grace enters. The same intrinsic justice which is the effect of Christ's merits makes us rise from sin and gives us power to perform acts of virtue that are meritorious of heaven. All of this follows on the strength of God's promise in consequence of the passion and death of the Savior.

Briefly stated, therefore, the sanctifying grace which God infuses into our souls perfectly applies to us the merits of Christ through a constant and perennial inflow in our favor. Hence the Tridentine declaration that "the one and only (*unica*) formal cause" of justification "is the justice of God, not by which He is Himself just, but the justice by which He makes us just, namely, the justice which we have as a gift from Him, and by which we are renewed in the spirit of our mind."[180] Any compromise with this intrinsic rebirth would deprive us of merit in the spiritual life, make satisfaction and reparation for sins impossible, and subvert a cardinal principle of Catholicism, which holds that we have been truly elevated to a supernatural order of reality which is physically inherent to our being and is not a mere putative declaration.

Protestant theologians sincerely concerned with bridging the gap with the Catholic Church feel that we misunderstand them when, in spite of their readiness to admit some kind of internal righteousness, they refuse to let go of the idea of imputation. K. E. Skydsgaard, for example, is an outstanding Danish Lutheran who did yeoman work in the ecumenical movement, but who was bewildered by Catholic intransigence.

> Roman theology often misunderstood the Evangelical point of view. The accusation is made that, according to the Evangelicals, righteousness is nothing more than an "imputed" righteousness, which does not penetrate into the person but only clothes the man as a coat. It is laid upon him without the slightest consequence in him.
>
> This cannot possibly be accepted as a correct description of the Evangelical position. God forgives sinners. This must be understood absolutely literally, and if this were not true, then

---

[180] *DS* 1529.

everything else would be vain. This forgiveness has its root and its power in God's mercy alone, in His grace. That man whose sins are forgiven by God remains a sinner as long as he is on earth.[181]

The last sentence is the "giveaway." It reveals that no matter what protestations are made that righteousness means forgiveness and does not mean only imputation, in the last analysis Evangelical theory leaves the justified man still in his sins and does not renew him to the marrow of his spiritual being.

There is no mistaking what Trent had in mind by this intrinsic change. Those who are justified are sanctified "through the voluntary reception of grace and gifts."[182] No one can be just unless he shares in the merits of Christ's passion, whereby "the charity of God is poured forth by the Holy Spirit into the hearts of those who are justified and remains (*inhaeret*) in them." So that, at the same time as his sins are remitted, "a man receives through Jesus Christ to whom he is joined, the infused gifts of faith, hope and charity."[183] Consequently the justice we possess "is said to be ours because it inheres in us," and because God "has poured it into us through the merit of Christ."[184] Then the Council Fathers summarily censure anyone who says that "men are justified either through the imputation of Christ's justice alone, or through the remission of sins alone, excluding grace and charity which is poured forth in our hearts by the Holy Spirit and inheres in them, or also that the grace which justifies us is only the good will of God."[185]

---

[181] K.E. Skydsgaard, *One in Christ* (Philadelphia: Muhlenberg Press, 1957), 141–42.
[182] *DS* 1528.
[183] *DS* 1530; *CCC* 1266.
[184] *DS* 1547.
[185] *DS* 1561.

Commenting on this doctrine, Barth sadly observed that "the Roman Church adopted an official attitude to the Reformation teaching in the decree of the Council of Trent on justification. And, unfortunately, we have to admit that in this decree it laid down its attitude for all time. The decree itself is theologically a clever and in many respects a not unsympathetic document, which has caused superficial Protestant readers to ask whether there might not be something to say for it."[186] But that is wishful thinking, which Barth spends over two volumes to dissipate.

Pauline Theology

The Tridentine decree on justification was almost a tessera of citations from St. Paul, whose letters are the wellspring of Catholic doctrine on the "new man" reborn in Christ Jesus.

The men justified are said to be regenerated. From having them unwise, unbelieving, going astray, and slaves to lust and pleasure, "when the goodness and kindness of God our Savior appeared," all this was changed. "He saved us through the bath of regeneration and renewal by the Holy Spirit; whom He has abundantly poured out upon us through Jesus Christ our Savior, in order that, justified by His grace, we may be heirs in the hope of life everlasting."[187] If we are regenerated, this implies we have received a new principle of life, for as generation means the communication of nature from one person to another, so rebirth, by definition, signifies that a new *principium vitae* has been received, whose nature is in the same order of reality as the generator, who in this case is God. That is why Paul could keep coming back to the same theme, that, "you are now dead (to the world), and your life is hidden with Christ in God"; and that "we are

---

[186] Barth, *op. cit.*, 624.
[187] Titus 3:4; *CCC* 1215.

buried with Him by means of baptism into death, in order that, just as Christ has arisen from the dead through the glory of His Father, so we also may walk in newness of life."[188]

The roots of Pauline thought on regeneration are, of course, found in the teaching of Christ, recorded in St. John. Unless a man be born again of water and the Holy Spirit, Christ told Nicodemus, he cannot see the kingdom of God. As interpreted by Nicodemus himself, the Savior must have spoken of second birth, other than one's first natural birth, to justify our rendering *anôthen* by "again," which is not only the Latin version but also the Coptic, Syriac, Arminian, Ethiopic and Georgian.[189] Without this second birth that is "from above," a man cannot belong to the kingdom of God. Christ spoke of *seeing* the kingdom, which has the sense of *experience* or *enjoyment* in Scriptural language. Strangely, the term "kingdom of God" occurs only once in St. John, in this particular text, though frequently in the Synoptics. It corresponds broadly to the word *life* in Joannine terminology and to *justice* in St. Paul.

Justification is also called renovation. "Be renewed in the spirit of your mind," Paul told the Ephesians, "and put on the new man, which has been created according to God in justice and holiness of truth."[190] Renovation means nothing less than a restoration of that justice which was lost by man's fall through original sin. If the sin was intrinsic to man's nature and deeply penetrated in his soul, his deliverance from sin must be at least equally intrinsic to the spirit in which it inheres. "How can we be said to be renovated," St. Augustine asked, "unless we receive that which the first man (Adam) lost, in whom we have all died? Clearly there is something we receive and something we do not. We do not get immortality of a spiritual body, which man did not have yet (when he

---

[188] Colossians 3:3; Romans 6:4; *CCC* 654, 1003.
[189] John 3:1–15.
[190] Ephesians 4:23.

sinned); but we do get the justice from which he fell by his sin. We are therefore renewed in the spirit of our mind, according to the image of Him who created us, which Adam had lost when he sinned."[191]

Augustine is most helpful in untangling the sense in which Christ's justice is received by those in His grace, that what we obtain is truly ours and no mere judicial attribution. Commenting on the text in Romans which speaks of "the justice of God through the faith of Jesus Christ upon all who believe," he explains that "just as this faith is said to be Christ's, not because Christ believed (since He enjoyed the beatific vision), so also this justice is of God, but not that by which He is just. For both are our own; yet they are called God's and Christ's because we received them of His bounty."[192]

In order to stress the utter newness of this life of grace, St. Paul frequently calls it a creation and those who receive it "a new creature in Christ." The letters to the Corinthians, Ephesians, and Galatians emphasize this notion.[193] It was impossible to use a stronger term to show how complete a change takes place within the soul through justification, where the two termini, by analogy with God's creative act, are as far distant from each other as "nothing" and "something," wherein God exercises His infinite power to bring "existence" out of "nonexistence."

A final Pauline figure to describe the proprietorship of sanctifying grace is taken from contemporary Greek and Latin life, where the terms "seal" and "pledge" were the ultimate expressions signifying ownership and personal right. The Corinthians are told that Christ has "stamped us with His seal, and gave us the Spirit as a pledge in our hearts."[194] The seal (*sphragis*) was used to mark something as a man's property, so that God has marked the faithful as His own by the indelible character of

---

[191] St. Augustine, "De Genesi ad Litteram" 6:24, *MPL* 34, 353.
[192] St. Augustine, "De Spiritu et Littera" 9, *MPL* 44, 209.
[193] 2 Corinthians 5:17; Ephesians 2:10; Galatians 6:15.
[194] 2 Corinthians 1:22; *CCC* 698, 1296.

baptism. Moreover the presence of the Spirit, which we denominate as grace, is the pledge (*arrabona*) or security of eternal life.

PERMANENT GIFT

According to St. John, grace is the very life of Christ. Its origins begin at baptism and its development spans the whole of man's earthly existence. Christ communicates this life to us by giving us His Spirit, who abides in our hearts and by whose inspiration we are enabled to live the new life of God. St. Paul complements this doctrine by stressing the function of the Holy Spirit who takes up abode in the souls of the just.

This raises two problems. Is this gift of God's love something created, or is it not rather the Holy Spirit and God Himself, according to the statement of St. John, that "God is love, and he who abides in love abides in God, and God in him"?[195] And whether this gift is uncreated or not, is it something physically permanent in the soul, or only a moral quality comparable to the moral perdurance of guilt after a person sins?

The common teaching of theology drawn from the authoritative documents of the Church is that sanctifying grace is not the Holy Spirit Himself but a created gift of God which inheres in the soul as a perduring reality that perfects the spirit of man, not unlike the way his body is informed by the rational soul.

Created Grace

Patristic tradition among the Greek Fathers uniformly elaborated the concept of grace as a communication of the life of Christ by the Holy Spirit, who comes to us and takes up His abode in our souls. During the Middle Ages, a number of scholastics, notably Peter Lombard

---

[195] 1 John 4:16.

(1100–1160), went a step beyond the Greek Fathers to claim that justifying grace is identical with charity, and charity is the person of the Holy Spirit.

There was quite a difference, however, between Lombard and the Fathers. The latter distinguished two gifts in sanctifying grace, one was uncreated, namely, the three persons of the Trinity, the other a created gift, which is the effect produced in the soul by the Holy Spirit, to whom the work of sanctification is specially attributed. Peter Lombard seems not to have sufficiently dwelt on this distinction. Together with others, like Hugh of St. Victor, he made grace identical with charity, charity with the Third Person, and the only source of acts of charity is the Spirit of God Himself, and not infused habits, as with faith, hope, and other virtues.

This raised a storm of protest. No one questioned that the Holy Spirit, along with the Father and the Son, dwells in the souls of the just; but to say that this Spirit was literally the *forma informans animam*, giving supernatural life to the soul which is *materia informata,* provoked strong criticism. The divine indwelling was admitted, but always on the supposition that in some mysterious way the Third Person was united to the soul through some created *forma* of unique character. There were two gifts, it was argued: the Holy Trinity as the uncreated *donum Dei,* and the created form which results from the presence and action of the Spirit in the justified soul.

It is to the lasting credit of St. Thomas that although he taught Lombard for years and used him as his principle guide, he did not hesitate to depart radically from his former preceptor in the interests of theological clarity and truth. His treatment of sanctifying grace as a created gift is a case in point.

> Peter Lombard held that charity was not a created reality,
> but the Holy Spirit dwelling in the soul. He did not mean that

the Holy Spirit was identified with our movement of love, but that charity, unlike the other virtues, such as faith and hope, was not elicited from a habit which was really ours. He was trying to enhance charity.

Ponder well, that this opinion tends rather to discredit charity. It would mean that active charity rises from the Holy Spirit so moving the mind that we are merely passive, and not responsible for our loving or otherwise. This militates against the character of a voluntary act. Charity would not then be a voluntary act. There is a snag here, for our loving is very much our own.

Nor is the situation eased by the additional qualification that the Holy Spirit moves the will as a principal cause moves an instrumental cause. An instrument, of course, is a principle, but not of the kind which decides its own activity or inactivity. The implication would be that the voluntary character of charity was made away with, and merit banished.

No, the Holy Spirit moves the will to love, but in such a way that we are principal causes.[196]

Relying on the authority of the ancient Fathers, St. Thomas argued that sanctifying grace must be a created gift because of the universal norm of Providence, which implants in creatures forms and powers that are principles of action for the natures in question. Consequently it would be unthinkable that on the supernatural plane God would act in any other way. Those whom He is leading to the everlasting mansions, "He infuses into them certain forms or supernatural qualities, through which they are gently and promptly directed by Him in order to obtain the eternal supernatural good" to which they are destined.[197]

---

[196] St. Thomas Aquinas, *Summa,* II–II, 23, 2; *CCC* 798, 1813.
[197] Ibid., I–II, 110, 2.

Physical Reality

St. Thomas and scholastic theologians after him have further refined the precise nature of sanctifying grace. It is, first of all, not a substance but an accident. For, as Thomas explained, "every substance is either the very nature of a thing whose substance it is, or it is part of the nature, as matter and form are called substances. Now since grace is above human nature, it cannot be a substance or a substantial form; but it is an accidental form of the soul itself. For what is substantially in God, becomes accidentally present in the soul which participates in the divine goodness, as is evident with knowledge."[198]

Moreover sanctifying grace is an absolute, and not merely relative or modal, accident. It is therefore not a simple relation or pure mode, but has its own proper entity, and becomes the foundation for other supernatural relations with God. It is capable of growth and decline, of strength and weakness, in a manner similar to other spiritual accidents. It is a quality, since it makes the soul qualitatively different than it was or would be without such modification; and it is also really distinct from the soul, as logically follows from its absolute and supernatural property.

Most important, sanctifying grace is a habit. This means a permanent and not transient quality, as would be single acts, by which the soul is disposed for a supernatural life. Spiritual habits in general are those abiding qualities which perfect the very substance of the soul or its faculties, enabling them to respond to the qualitative perfection they possess. There are two kinds of habits, one that perfects the soul in its being, and the other perfecting the soul's faculties in order to assist them in the performance of their proper actions.[199]

Sanctifying grace is a unique kind of habit, which St. Thomas called entitative, as distinct from operative. The difference between the two

---

[198] Ibid.; *CCC* 1997.
[199] *CCC* 2000.

species is subtle. An entitative or existential habit disposes a thing *in ordine ad ipsam naturam,* i.e., in the order of its very nature; it may be described as an inherent quality by which a substance is rendered inherently good or bad, like beauty, health or disease. An operative habit, on the other hand, gives not only the power to act, but also a certain ease or facility, which in turn may be good, bad, or morally indifferent, like the habit of honesty, prudence, or an artistic ability to paint.

Strictly speaking Aristotelian philosophy has no category for a purely entitative habit, namely one which imparts no facility to act but merely a disposition to certain forms of being. The nearest approximations are such things as beauty or health, noted above. Hence St. Thomas observed that "grace belongs to the first species of quality (entitative), though it cannot properly be called a habit, because it is not immediately ordained to action, but to a kind of spiritual being which it produces in the soul."[200]

Still another reason why grace is not a habit in the ordinary philosophical sense is the fact that it supplies no acquired facility to act. Suarez was so impressed by this, he avoided speaking of grace as habit, and seems to have induced Bellarmine to describe sanctifying grace as a quality *per modum habitus* (like a habit), to accentuate that grace is *sui generis* among habits; it imparts a supernatural perfection of being rather than a facility to action. The Council of Trent was aware of these difficulties, and as a consequence defined sanctifying grace simply as a permanent quality.

In scientific theology, however, there is no choice but to use the categories at our disposal. Moreover sanctifying grace does bear a relation to activity, which is common to habits in general, although it imparts no facility. It gives the power to perform supernaturally meritorious acts, so

---

[200] St. Thomas Aquinas, *De Veritate,* XXVII, 2, 7.

that it is more than just an entitative habit; it is also remotely an opera-tive habit whose terminal effects are acts deserving of reward.[201]

One more familiar distinction in philosophy breaks down in connec-tion with grace. In psychology we speak of native and acquired habits, where the first are part of man's nature and the second are cultivated by practice. Supernatural habits cannot be a part of nature or an acquisi-tion of mere natural effort. Consequently supernatural habits of what-ever type, whether entitative (like sanctifying grace) or operative (like the virtues), can be imparted to the soul only by infusion from God Himself. For this reason they are called infused habits, which the Holy Spirit pours into the human spirit. When He infuses sanctifying grace, the result is an existential quality which gives the soul a supernatural principle of being. When He infuses the virtues, He confers on the soul supernatural powers that by faithful cooperation with actual grace can develop into facilities for performing salutary acts.

In Aristotelian terminology, then, sanctifying grace is a kind of enti-tative habit because it lays the foundation for permanent righteous-ness, holiness and divine sonship. It is also an infused habit because a person is not conceived or born with it, nor can it be acquired by sheer natural practice. All the terms used in Scripture to describe grace warrant this classification: it is a *re*-creation, a *re*generation, a life from above (*anôthen*), and, most graphically, in the words of St. John, "whoever is born of God does not commit sin, because His seed abides in him."[202] Those who are justified have a new life, which stems not from nature but from the generative powers of God Himself.

Distinct from Charity

A practical question has been raised since before the Council of Trent, as to whether sanctifying grace is really distinct from the

[201] *CCC* 2008, 2009, 2011.
[202] 1 John 3:9.

infused habit of charity. The problem would not even be raised if we took sanctifying grace in the broad sense of a complexus of all the gifts we receive in justification, and by which we are internally sanctified. But sanctifying grace can also be taken in a more restricted sense as that specific *donum* which is distinguished from the theological virtues and the gifts of the Holy Spirit. Understood thus, we reasonably ask if sanctifying grace is a distinct entity or not. We know, for instance, that when a person sins mortally he loses sanctifying grace and infused charity, but may retain faith and hope. But sanctifying grace and charity are never thus separable; they are always together, either both present or both absent. So we ask: Are they really distinguishable, or should they be objectively identified, while allowing for a purely rational distinction between them?

Most theologians follow St. Thomas to say the two are really distinct. They reason from the numerous statements of the Church, like the Council of Trent, where the terms *grace* and *charity* are separately described, and from the writings of the Popes, where similar disjunctions occur. Thus Pius XII said that "men may lose charity and divine grace through sin, and yet not be deprived of all life, if they hold on to faith and hope," and he urged the faithful to "advance generously in grace and virtue."[203] Why disjoin the two concepts in speaking of them if the realities they express are not objectively different?

St. Thomas' own explanation is so lucid it deserves citation in full, especially because of the practical consequences that follow on distinguishing sanctifying grace from the infused virtue of charity.[204]

During his lectures in Paris (1256–1259), which grew into the *De Veritate,* Aquinas said there were two schools of thought on the subject: on one side were Peter Lombard, Alexander of Hales, and

---

[203] *Mystici Corporis* 87.
[204] *CCC* 1813, 1999–2000.

Bonaventure, and on the other was his former teacher, Albertus. The first school said that grace is essentially the same as virtue in reality, though it differs conceptually, so that virtue is often spoken of insofar as it perfects an act, and grace insofar as it makes man and his act acceptable to God; and among the virtues they especially identify charity with grace. The second school, which he favored, held that grace and charity differ essentially, so that no virtue is essentially grace.

The reasoning behind this conclusion begins with the premise that different natures have different ends, and that there are three prerequisites for obtaining any end among natural things: a nature proportioned to that end, inclination which is a natural appetite for that end, and a movement toward the end. In the natural order, man is proportioned to a certain end for which he has a natural appetite and for which he can work by his natural powers. That end, Thomas declared, is a contemplation of divine things such as is possible to man according to the capacities of his nature. Philosophers like Plato, Aristotle, Philo, Avicenna and Averroes have placed man's ultimate happiness in this kind of natural contemplation.

> But there is an end for which man is prepared by God which surpasses the proportion of human nature, that is, eternal life, which consists in the vision of God by His essence. That vision is not proportioned to any creature whatsoever, being connatural only to God.

> It is therefore necessary that there be given to man not only something by which his appetite should be inclined to that end, but also something by which man's very nature should be raised to a dignity which would make such an end suited to him. For this, grace is given him. But to incline his will to this end, charity is given; and for carrying out the works by which that end is acquired, the other virtues are given.

Accordingly, just as in natural things the nature itself is distinct from the inclination of the nature and its motion or operation, in the same way in man's gratuitous gifts, grace is distinct from charity and the other virtues.[205]

St. Thomas concludes by saying that no one can have a spiritual operation, in this case a supernatural one, unless he first receives a spiritual existence, just as he cannot perform the actions of a particular nature unless he first has existence in that nature. An animal must first have a rational nature before it can act rationally. Even so a man must first have a *super*nature before he can act supernaturally.[206]

The functional value of this idea is incalculable. Once we see that sanctifying grace has an entity all its own, it becomes the foundation for the whole theological edifice of our deiform nature, whose transcendent qualities we can understand by comparison with human nature without grace.[207]

Both nature and supernature have an ultimate operative principle of activity, the soul in one and sanctifying grace in the other. Both have proximate principles of operation, the sensitive and spiritual faculties in one case, and the infused virtues in the other. Both have immediate responsive principles, instincts in nature and the gifts of the Holy Spirit in nature deified. Finally both have their proper effects, which are human acts for us as human beings and deiform acts produced by men who have been elevated to a share in the very life of God.

In a later context we shall examine the implications of this relationship more closely. For the present it was necessary to have seen the metaphysical basis on which the relationship rests, namely, the divine consistency between the two orders of reality.

---

[205] St. Thomas Aquinas, *De Veritate*, XXVII, 2 (corpus).
[206] *CCC* 260, 356, 1998.
[207] *CCC* 1999.

SUPERNATURAL LIFE

Before entering on a dogmatic analysis of the supernatural life, it is well to recall that the Church has given us the principles by which the mysteries of faith can be understood, however dimly, by the aid of divine grace. In treating the relation between faith and reason, the First Vatican Council stated that although divine mysteries can never be comprehended by reason alone, nevertheless, when enlightened by faith "reason attains some, and that a very fruitful understanding of mysteries, from the analogy of those things which it naturally knows."[208]

Accordingly, though revealed truths like the Trinity, Incarnation, and the supernatural life are beyond the capacity of the human mind to comprehend directly until the beatific vision, we can, by means of comparisons and similarities with known things in nature, penetrate ever more deeply into the mysteries of religion.[209] The foundation for the comparison must be derived from Scripture or revealed tradition. The process should be guided by the Church's teaching, telling us how far the correlation may go. Within these limits, however, the method of analogy is not only useful but imperative for understanding and communicating the truths of revelation.

The most fruitful analogy that revelation gives us for sanctifying grace and the state of righteousness is the concept of life, which the Greek authors of the New Testament regularly rendered by the word *zôê*, in preference to two other terms they might have used, *bios* and *psuche*.

Where English and Latin have only one word, life and *vita*, Greek has three; and the choice of one of these to describe the divine life we receive through grace must be significant. The true antithesis of *zôê* is *thanatos* (death), and means life taken intensively, as contrasted with *bios*, which refers to life extensively, or its duration, and with *psuche*, the breath that in animated beings is a sign of life.

---

[208] *DS* 3016; *CCC* 286.
[209] *CCC* 40, 41.

The term *zôê* is used selectively and exclusively to designate the supernatural life which God communicates to us through Christ; indeed, He is our life and its Author. Most often the combination, *zôê aiônios* (eternal life), is found in the Gospels and St. Paul; yet the same *zôê* that we possess on earth will continue into eternity. This is the divine life that was in the Word from the beginning, "and the life was the light of men."[210] It is also the life that the Persons of the Trinity have in common. "For the Father has life in Himself, even as He has given to the Son to have life in Himself."[211] It is a participation in this life that those who believe in Christ have received.

Nature and Origins

In order to appreciate what our sharing in the divine life means, we should begin by inquiring what life itself is. As explained by St. Thomas Aquinas, the higher a nature is, the more intimate to the nature is that which comes from it, for its inwardness of activity corresponds to its rank in being.[212] Inanimate bodies hold the lowest place of all; because nothing emanates from them except by the action of one thing on another.

Above inanimate bodies are plants, in which there is an issuing from within, since they can grow and reproduce themselves. They represent the first degree of life, for living things are those that set themselves into activity, whereas things that are in motion only inasmuch as they are acted upon from the outside are lifeless. This is the index of life in plants, that within them is a principle of motion.

Yet plant life is very imperfect, for though the emanation is from within at the beginning, that which comes forth gradually becomes wholly extraneous in the end. The blossoms change into fruit distinct

---

[210] Colossians 3:4; Acts 3:15; John 1:4.
[211] John 5:26.
[212] St. Thomas Aquinas, *Summa Contra Gentiles*, IV, 11.

from the boughs on which they grow, and presently these, when ripe, fall to the ground and become other plants. Scrutiny shows that the principle of this process is extrinsic to the plant.

Above plants there is a higher grade of being, that of sensitive things. Otherwise than with plants, their process, though initiated from without, terminates within the animal; and the more perfect the animal the more interior this result. A sensibly perceptible object impinges on the external senses; the impression goes into the imagination and then deeper into the store of memory. So that which began from the outside is thus worked up within, for the sensitive powers are conscious within themselves. Consequently the vital process in animals is superior to that in plants, because of its greater immanence. However it is not wholly perfect, since the emanation is always from one thing to another.

Only in the mind do we reach the highest and perfect grade of life, where a person reflects on himself and understands himself. Yet there are various degrees of intelligence. At the lowest rung is the human intellect, which can know itself but must start from outside objects and cannot know these without accompanying sense-images. Above the human level are angels or pure spirits, whose mind does not proceed from outside things to know itself, but knows itself by itself, without prior dependence on phenomena outside.

Even angelic knowledge is not the highest form of life. Though the ideas that angels have are deeply immanent, they are not identical with the substance of their minds, since the being is not the same thing as the understanding in spiritual creatures. The highest perfection of life is in God, where activity is not distinct from being, and where knowledge *is* the divine essence.

By His infinite goodness and in a way that "eye has not seen nor ear heard, nor has it entered into the heart of man," God has made possible a participation in this divine life by His rational creatures, to be had in faith and hope on earth and through sight and possession in heaven.

As defined by Benedict XII, the angels and blessed in heaven "see the divine essence with an intuitive and even face-to-face vision, without the interposition of any creature in the function of object seen; rather the divine essence manifests itself to them plainly, clearly, openly."[213] The possession of sanctifying grace on earth is on the same level of reality as the vision of God in heaven; objectively the same participated divine life is had by the soul in grace as by the souls in glory. Only the subjective effects are different, although even these tend to merge in the mystical experiences of some of the saints, where something approximating the beatific vision may be enjoyed even before eternity. A person in the state of grace, therefore, is already living the deiform life that elevates him to the divine family, and has only to wait until heaven to enter its glorious fruition.

Following the basic analogy of grace as a form of life, we find that it, like other types of life, has a beginning. There is such a thing as being born into the supernatural life of grace.[214] As our natural life comes to us through generation, so deiform life begins through the spiritual birth of baptism, according to the words of Christ, that unless a man be born again of water and the Holy Spirit, he cannot enter the kingdom of God.

The Council of Trent described justification as a passing from the state in which a man is born a son of the first Adam, to the state of grace and adoption as sons of God, through the second Adam, Jesus Christ our Savior. "Since the Gospel was promulgated, this passing cannot take place without the water of regeneration or the desire for it."[215] In the Church's liturgy, the role of baptism as the *lavacrum regenerationis,* the source of a new life, is forcefully brought home to the faithful. During

---

[213] *DS* 1000; *CCC* 1023.
[214] *CCC* 168.
[215] *DS* 1524; *CCC* 1265, 1266.

the blessing of the baptismal water, the priest asks God to "send forth the Spirit of adoption to re-create a new race whom the font of baptism will bear to Thee." He asks that it "may be a living fountain, a water that gives rebirth," and that every man who enters this sacrament of regeneration be born again in a new childhood of true innocence." And in the actual ceremony of baptism, after the rite is performed, comes an invocation to "almighty God, the Father of our Lord Jesus Christ, who has given you a new birth by means of water and the Holy Spirit."

However, baptism is only the normal sacramental agency for conferring the life of grace. It presupposes the profession of faith, personally in adults and vicariously in those responsible for the baptism of infants. This presses the analogy with natural life a stage further, since no one comes to the Christian faith (except by a miracle) unless someone who already believed had first brought him the message of salvation. Just as it is in the natural order, no one brings himself into the world. He depends absolutely on the previous and loving cooperation of others, his parents in the flesh, to make his conception and eventual birth possible.

St. Paul had this law of communication in mind when he told the Romans that "with the heart a man believes unto justice," i.e., unto supernatural life, which rests on belief in the Lord, and calling upon His name.

> How then are they to call upon Him in whom they have not believed? But how are they to believe Him whom they have not heard? And how are they to hear, if no one preaches? And how are men to preach unless they be sent?[216]

The duty of communicating the supernatural life to those who do not yet have it rests not only on the successors of the apostles, the bish-

---

[216] Romans 10:14–15; *CCC* 875.

ops and priests of the Church, but on all members of the Mystical Body. "Christ before His ascension into heaven," wrote Pius XII, "confided to His apostles, and through them to His whole Church, the responsibility of evangelizing the whole world in His name. Every Christian ought, therefore, to be persuaded that a part of this responsibility rests on his shoulders and that no one can relieve him of this responsibility."[217]

Perseverance and Growth

Since the deiform life is eminently vital, it requires the proper nourishment, atmosphere, and exercise to remain alive and to grow. The indispensable means for this perseverance and development is grace, which Christ has promised to furnish us by the sacramental system, through prayer and the practice of virtue.

St. Thomas summarizes the function of the sacraments, spanning the whole of the supernatural (already seen or to be seen), by comparing the two courses of the physical and spiritual life that run parallel, and that "the sacramental elements correspond to the provision of bodily needs." They fall into two groups, affecting, respectively, the life-receivers and the life-givers.

> The first group covers three essential phases in human development. A man must be born to begin with, afterwards he must reach his proper stature, and in order to be sustained and grow he must eat. These three correspond to the three vegetative functions of reproduction, growth and nourishment. They are matched in the life of the spirit. Baptism is a spiritual birth, confirmation a setting up in full strength, and the Eucharist a special food. Then there is the case of sickness, an incidental

---

[217] Pius XII, *Discorsi e Radiomessaggi* (Vatican City: Tip. Polyglotta Vaticana, 1940–1959), 19:438; *CCC* 905.

phase. For our healing Penance cures our soul only, but the effects of Extreme Unction (anointing of the sick) may well spread from the soul to the body.[218]

Of the people who give and govern life, some are responsible for its natural origin, namely parents, others for its civilized and peaceful continuance, namely rulers and leaders. Matrimony is for a man and a woman to beget children and bring them up in God's service; they bear them physically and rear them spiritually. Holy Orders are for those who kindle and keep the life of the spirit through their spiritual ministrations.[219]

Among the sacraments, the Eucharist is *par excellence* the nourishment of the supernatural life. The two "unity" councils (Florence for the Greeks and Trent for the Protestants) dealt at length with the absolute need we have of the Blessed Sacrament to retain and grow in the life of grace. Its immediate effect "in the soul of a person who receives it worthily, is to unite him with Christ. Since it is by grace that a man is incorporated into Christ and united to Christ's members, it follows that those who receive this sacrament worthily, receive an increase of grace. And all the effects which material food and drink have on the life of our body—maintaining and increasing life, restoring health and bringing pleasure—all these effects this sacrament has on our spiritual life."[220]

To meet the widespread neglect of the Eucharist in Reformation times, and its denial by the Reformers, the Council of Trent further delineated the fruits of Holy Communion. Our Savior instituted this sacrament just before leaving the world to return to His Father. He poured out the riches of His love by its institution, and ordered us to receive it for the preservation of His memory.

---

[218] *CCC* 1212, 1420–21.
[219] St. Thomas Aquinas, *Summa Contra Gentiles,* IV, 58; *CCC* 1581, 1641; cf. *Lumen Gentium* 11§2.
[220] *DS* 1322; *CCC* 1392.

It was His will that this sacrament be received as the soul's spiritual food, to sustain and build up those who live with His life, as He said, "He who eats me, he also shall live because of me." This sacrament is also to be a remedy to free us from our daily defects and to keep us from mortal sin. It was Christ's will, moreover, that this sacrament be a pledge of our future glory and our everlasting happiness and, likewise, a symbol of that one Body of which He is the head.[221]

The unitive purpose of the Eucharist is more than symbolic. Our physical lives are not only individual but social, and we should expect Christ to provide for the corporate dimension of our life of grace by giving us the means to cultivate that God-like charity which joins the members of His Mystical Body.[222]

Illustrated in the liturgical prayer that has come down to us from the first century, "as this broken Bread was scattered over the hills and then, when gathered became one mass, so may Thy Church be gathered from the ends of the earth into Thy kingdom. For Thine is the glory and the power through Jesus Christ for evermore."[223] The unitive power of the Eucharist is contained in the person of the Savior, the Author of grace and Head of the Mystical Body, who is offered in the Mass and received in Holy Communion. Receiving our Lord in Holy Communion is to receive His love which enables us to live beyond ourselves by loving Christ in His Mystical Body.

Similar to the necessity of the sacraments, especially the Eucharist, to retain and grow in the supernatural life, is the need of constant prayer, of which St. Robert Southwell wrote in a set of verses prefixed to his *Short Rules of Good Life,* shortly before his martyrdom in 1595.

---

[221] *DS* 1638; *CCC* 1393–96.
[222] *CCC* 1331, 1396, 1398.
[223] *The Didache,* Chap. 9.

"Nothing more grateful in the highest eyes, nothing more firm in danger to protect us, nothing more forcible to pierce the skies, and not depart till mercy do respect us: and as the soul life to the body gives, so prayer revives the soul, by prayer it lives."[224]

It is not by chance that the Pelagians opposed prayer on philosophical grounds, on the logical supposition that if a man's native powers are enough to make him reach his destiny, why should he pray? St. Augustine pointed out that not the least effect of Pelagianism would be to erase all the prayers of petition in the Church of God. He explained that while there are certain blessings of grace which God gives without request on our part, like the gift of baptism for those baptized in infancy, others He will not grant except in answer to fervent prayer. This includes the grace of perseverance in the supernatural life.

The range of efficacy through prayer is all but infinite. For "as God created all things by His word, so man by prayer obtains whatever he wills. Nothing has so great a power to obtain grace for us as prayer when rightly made; for it contains the motives by which God easily allows Himself to be appeased and inclined to mercy."[225]

Hidden in the mystery of prayer is the supernatural providence by which God had predetermined from eternity to bestow the graces which He foresaw we would pray for. Bellarmine showed that here, too, the order of grace is fully consistent with the order of nature. In both cases the ultimate effective agent is the almighty power of the First Cause; and equally in both cases, secondary causes must be cooperative, at the risk of not obtaining the effect desired. In the natural order, God has decreed to give us food and drink, and all that we need to sustain the life of the body. "He has also ordained to give us these necessities through human effort, by which the fields and vines are cultivated. Would anyone deny

---

[224] St. Robert Southwell, *Verses Prefixed to Short Rules of Good Life* (Charlottesville: Folger Shakespeare Library, University Press of Virginia, 1973).
[225] Leo XIII, *On the Right Order of Christian Life* [*Exenunte Iam Anno*], (1888), 12.

the need of plowing and sowing, of planting and digging, and or other like labors, if we want to reap and gather in the harvest?"[226] The same is true in the realm of grace. Prayer corresponds to the secondary cause in nature; in the providence of God, it is the ordinary means of obtaining sustenance for the supernatural life.

Law of Conflict and Struggle

The reason for this necessity of constant prayer is the inevitability of conflict which the deiform life must face, not unlike the struggle for survival that is common to all living things, from the lowest among the animal species to the physical well-being of man.

There are few things on which Christ was more insistent than the universal visitation of trials to be experienced by those who follow Him and live by His Spirit. The eight beatitudes are a summary of the difficulties and obstacles to be overcome by the faithful Christian. He spoke of persecution for justice' sake; of being brought before tribunals and put to death for belief in His name; of the inner struggle within men's hearts when they are torn between fidelity to Him and to their relatives, friends, and all natural loves; of the need His disciples would have of patience under duress, in which alone they would "possess their souls". His parable of the seed which fell amid thorns and briars was to stress that faithfulness to the Gospel brings conflict with the world, the flesh and the evil spirit. In the Lord's Prayer, He epitomized this *militia Christiana* by bidding us pray not to be led into temptation but to be delivered from evil. In a word, He came, as He said, to bring not peace but the sword.

Christianity is quite unique in recognizing the element of trial at the heart of man's religion, and that "it seems to have been determined in the designs of God that there would be no salvation for men without

---

[226] St. Robert Bellarmine, "De Oratione", *De Bonis Operibus in Particulari,* I, 3.

struggle and pain." The very redemption of the human race was conditioned on the Lord's becoming man and expiating sin to the last degree. Though Christ might have satisfied the divine justice in other ways, He chose to do so by enduring the worst kind of suffering and the sacrifice of His very life.

> Therefore He has imposed it upon His followers as a law signed with His blood, that their life should be an endless strife with the vices of their age. What made the apostles unconquerable in their mission of teaching truth to the world? What strengthened our countless martyrs in bearing witness by their blood to the Christian faith? Their more than readiness to obey fearlessly this law. All who have taken heed to live a Christian life and to seek after virtue have trodden the same path. We, too, must walk along this road if we desire to assure our own salvation or that of others.[227]

But man's powers alone are unequal to the responsibility of so many and varied contest. Consequently, "as we must ask God for our daily sustenance of the body, so we must pray to Him for strength of soul that we may be sustained in virtue."[228] Hence that universal condition and law of our supernatural life, which is a perpetual warfare; and the correlative indispensability of prayer.

Among the writers who urged the need of praying for help, St. Alphonsus Liguori (universal patron of moral theologians) was, perhaps, the most outspoken. What disturbed him, he said, was to see preachers and confessors paying so little attention to telling their listeners and penitents about constant petition for aid.

---

[227] Pope Leo XIII, *Exenunte Iam Anno* 11. English trans.: *Letter of Our Holy Father by Divine Providence Pope Leo XIII. On the Closing Year of his Sacerdotal Jubilee* (London: "Tablet" Off., 1888).
[228] Ibid.

The spiritual books which presently circulate among the faithful also do not speak of it; when all preachers and confessors and books should insist on nothing with so much urgency and ardor as this prayer. Well do they inculcate the many excellent means given to the soul to keep itself in the grace of God, as fleeing occasions, frequenting the sacraments, resisting temptations, hearing the word of God, and meditating on eternal truths, all most useful, no doubt. But to what purpose, I ask, are sermons, meditations and all other means, except to produce spiritual harm, without prayer, when the Lord has declared that He does not will to give graces except to one who prays?

To actually do good, to overcome temptation, to exercise virtue, in a word, entirely to keep the divine precepts, it is not enough to receive lights and make reflections and resolutions. We still need the actual help of God. And the Lord does not grant this actual aid except to one who prays and prays with perseverance. The lights received, the reflections and good resolutions conceived serve this purpose, that, in the dangers and temptations of transgressing the divine law, we actually pray; and with prayer we obtain the divine help which preserves us then from sin. But if at the time we do not pray, we are overcome.[229]

Since the whole of life is a probation, the constancy of prayer for help is a revealed necessity. It ends only with death, which itself should be the special object of supplication, to persevere in God's friendship in spite of the assaults of fallen nature and the enemy of the human race.

---

[229] St. Alphonsus Liguori, *Opere Ascetiche* (Turin: Marietti, 1845), 2:576; *CCC* 2744.

Intensity and Variety

We saw that the biblical term for the life of grace communicated to souls is *zôê* whose characteristic feature is life taken intensively. The principle of analogy with living things in nature allows us to speak of degrees of intensity and variety in the supernatural life, since no two people are equally vibrant with physical energy, and no two are perfectly alike. Even so there are modes of supernatural vitality and varieties of form that the divine life may take in the soul.

The number of factors which determine the variations of sanctifying grace is myriad. According to the divine will, "each one has his own gift from God, one in this way, and another in that."[230] It would be an impertinence to inquire why St. Paul did not have the grace of Peter, why Augustine was not Jerome, or Ignatius not a Francis of Assisi. The best we can say is that God is mysteriously glorified by this diversity, and His infinite perfections more manifest as we see them participated in so many different ways.

But if Providence ultimately determines the degree and variety of spiritual vitality, our cooperation with graces offered is also a large determining factor. The supernatural life is capable of increase and depth, depending on the frequency and fervor with which the sacraments are received. Devotion to prayer and, in fact, the whole gamut of good works performed, helps to merit growth in sanctifying grace and advancement in the soul's nearness to God.

It was not a passing remark when the Council of Trent described justification as a "renovation of the interior man through the *voluntary* reception of grace," since our free wills have much to do with setting limits to divine generosity. St. Francis de Sales observed that in the measure to which we divest ourselves of self-love, so that our heart does not refuse consent to the divine mercy, God "ever pours forth and cease-

---

[230] 1 Corinthians 7:7.

lessly spreads His sacred inspirations, which ever increase and make us increase more and more in heavenly love." He then asks how it happens that we are not so advanced in the love of God as some of the saints.

> It is because God has not given us the grace. But why has He not given us the grace? Because we did not correspond with His inspirations as we should have. And why did we not correspond? Because being free we have herein abused our liberty. But why did we abuse our liberty?
>
> We must stop there for, as St. Augustine says, the ill-use of our will proceeds from no cause, but from some deficiency in the agent who commits the sin. And we must not expect to give a reason for the fault that occurs in sin, because it would not be a sin if it were not without reason.[231]

The same principle was enunciated by St. Ignatius Loyola in his Constitutions for the Society of Jesus. "Generally speaking," he said, "the more closely a person binds himself to God and the more generous he is in dealing with His sovereign Majesty, the more generous will he find God towards him. He will also become daily better disposed to receive graces and richer spiritual gifts (*dona spiritualia uberiora*)."[232] Living the deiform life, therefore, is a vital process from the divine side and from ours. God is free to confer this life and to confer it in the degree that pleases His unfathomable will. We are free to receive what He offers and to receive as much as we choose according to our generosity.

One aspect of this subject which may be overlooked, however is that when God wishes to communicate His graces to souls He normally

---

[231] St. Francis de Sales, *The Love of God,* II, Chap. 11, third ed., trans. Rev. Henry Benedict Mackey, O.S.B. (Rockford, IL: Tan Books, 1997).

[232] *Constitutiones Societatis Iesu* (Rome: In Collegio Eiusdem Societatis, 1583), III, 1, 22.

uses human instruments that are possessed of the kind of divine life He intends to give. Again Ignatius points out how philosophy and experience teach us that in the generation of man or animals a cause or agent of the same species is required which possess the same form as that which is to be transmitted. "In like manner, to transmit the *form* of humility, patience, charity, and so forth, to others, God wills that the immediate cause which He uses as instruments, such as the preacher, or confessor, be humble, charitable, patient."[233] The implications of this principle for the apostolate are self-explanatory.

Weakness, Death, and Resurrection

The natural life of the body is liable to sickness and debility arising from alien forces or weakness from within. In similar fashion the spiritual life of the soul may be injured and debilitated through conflict with temptations and yielding to what are called venial sins. Moreover, as the physical body may be not only ill or suffer injury, but cease to retain its principle of life; so the soul can lose sanctifying grace through mortal sin and supernaturally cease to live.

Scholastic theology explains the difference between mortal and venial sin in terms of a soul's proper orientation to its last end, the triune God, by analogy with the respective conditions in a human body.

> The degrees of disorder may be marked. One turns the whole order upside down; the other leaves the principles intact, but muddles the details and subordinate pattern. The balance of health may be so utterly wrecked that life is destroyed; or it may be upset so as to cause sickness, but not death. The final purpose of life is the key to the moral order. When our acts are so deranged that we turn away from our last end, namely God,

---

233 *Letters of St. Ignatius Loyola,* trans. William John Young, S.J. (Chicago: Loyola University Press, 1959), 129.

to whom we should be united by charity, then the sin is mortal. Short of that, the sin is venial.[234]

This means that a soul in grave sin is spiritually dead because it is no longer united with God who gives it supernatural life, even as a body is dead on separation from its animating principle, which is the soul. While still on earth, this union with God is both a possession and a movement. We possess Him by grace and in faith, and we are moving towards Him in the beatific vision of glory. When a man sins mortally, he is dead twice over—once because he loses the gift of divine life he formerly had, and once again because he is no longer moving towards the consummation of that life in heaven.

St. Thomas further compares the two types of sin in terms of their curability. "Bodily death is incurable by nature, but for sickness remedies may be found." The same thing holds true in the supernatural order. "Turn away from your last end, then of itself your sin is mortal and beyond repair, with everlasting penal effects. But venial sin can be repaired, and is undeserving of interminable punishment.[235]

This difference explains why grave sins are called mortal, and light sins venial. The former are not remissible through any intrinsic power within the soul itself, much as the human body, once dead, cannot be brought back to life except by a special intervention of God. But venial faults are venial (from *venia*, pardon) precisely because the soul still has the vital principle that allows a cure *ab intrinseco,* just as in the healing of a sick or diseased body, whose source of animation (the soul) is still present, the ailing bodily function is restored to health.

Both kinds of sin are detrimental, but in vastly different ways. Deliberate venial guilt is a disease that slackens the spiritual powers, lowers a man's resistance to evil, and causes him to deviate from the

---

[234] St. Thomas Aquinas, *Summa* I–II, 72, 5; CCC 1854–55.
[235] Ibid.; *CCC* 1863.

path which leads to glory. It places obstacles in the way of virtue and reduces fervor for the things of God. "Can this be of little consequence?" asked Teresa of Avila. Yet the person who sins venially, even through inveterate habit, is supernaturally alive. Not so the man estranged from God. He is spiritually dead, and in patristic literature the restoration is compared to the resuscitation of Lazarus from the grave. The exercise of almighty power in either case is the same. "Every one who sins dies," said St. Augustine. Only the Lord, "by His great grace and great mercy raises souls to life again, that we may not die eternally."[236] It is only the frequency of this wonder that makes people forget the divine love and condescension it implies.

---

[236] St. Augustine, "In Joannis Evangelium Tractatus," 49, *MPL,* 35, 1747.

5

SHARING THE DIVINE NATURE

All religion is somehow based on the recognition of a superhuman Reality of which man is at least vaguely conscious and towards which he strives to orientate his life. This orientation may take on extreme forms, or it may be so simple as almost to elude inquiry, but its driving spirit is always the desire to communicate with the divine and, so far as possible, to share in the attributes of the one who is God.

It is the glory of Christianity that its faith and worship not only satisfy this profound hunger for union with the divine, but sublimate its appetite to a degree incomprehensible to the human mind; at the same time protecting it from those aberrations into which other religious systems have invariably fallen. Indeed nowhere else does the wisdom of Catholicism appear more evident than in its teaching on the effects of sanctifying grace. It is here that the infinite distance between the Creator and creature is carefully secured, while at the same time the highest aspirations of the will for communion with God are gratified.

The Church's teaching on the formal effects of justifying grace will be better appreciated when seen against the background of the faltering efforts made by those who are not Christians to explain what it means to be joined with the Deity. This becomes more clear especially when viewed in the context of errors that were either propagated in Catholic circles or threatened the integrity of Catholic doctrine from outside. In fact, not to have understood something of this aspect of divine grace is to miss the full perspective of what St. Augustine meant when he defined the true religion as "that by which the soul in united to God."

QUEST FOR DIVINE UNITY

It was Tertullian who coined the phrase, "the soul is Christian by natural instinct" (*anima est naturaliter Christiana*), partially to explain why the pagan religions of Greece and Rome placed so much emphasis on communion and even identification with the divine. His point was that alongside the divinized men and humanized gods are to be found numerous signs of belief which explain these transmutations as the natural desire of the human heart for some kind of communication with God.

Classic and Oriental Religion

At one extreme we meet such complaints as that voiced by Achilles in the *Iliad*, that "the eternal gods have assigned to us unhappy mortals hardship enough, while they enjoy bliss idly without end."[237] At the other extreme we find what has been rightly called the culmination of Greek genius and the peak of natural religion, expressed by Plato as the hopeful destiny of man. "What shall we think," he asked, "if it should befall anyone to perceive very Beauty itself, simple, pure and undefiled—not infected with flesh of men or human embellishment, or other such perishable folly, but absolute divine Beauty in its simplicity."[238]

Although destined only for the highest minds and conceived only as possible, Plato speculated on what this vision of Beauty would effect in the human soul.

---

[237] Homer, *Iliad*, 26, 526.
[238] Plato, *Platonis Opera*, II, "Symposium" (Oxford: Clarendon, 1957), 210; *CCC* 2519.

Do you think it would be a mean sort of life for a man, if his gaze were directed on that goal, and he not only beheld it in all its perfection but associated himself with the same? Do you not suppose that there alone, contemplating the Fair as best it may be seen, it will be his privilege to produce not mere images of virtue but true virtues themselves, since it is Truth which he embraces. And after rearing true virtue which he begot, shall he not become dear to the gods and immortal—if ever this lot may befall a man?[239]

Between these extremes, with varying degrees of clarity, the poets and philosophers among the Greeks and Latins voiced the common thirst of their people to partake in some way of the good things that were enjoyed by the gods. The gods would never die, so they pictured their heroes and great men as taken up to the heavenly regions to receive the elixir of life which gave them immortality. The gods were very powerful, so on occasion a deity came down to earth to beget an offspring of superhuman strength, as in the case of Hercules. The gods were very wise, so at times they joined in marriage with mortal women to produce such men as Plato, who was deified. The gods were handsome and the goddesses beautiful, so, in the case of Pandora, Vulcan made her of clay, but Venus gave her beauty. The art of captivating men was bestowed on her by the Graces.

If we examine the living religions of the East, notably Hinduism and Buddhism, we find the same eager longing for divine communion, only now projected into monistic extremes.

Among the sacred books of the Hindus, the most subtle for speculative insight are the *Upanishads,* which date back to at least the sixth century before the Christian era. The master idea of the *Upanishads* is

---

[239] Ibid., 211–12; *CCC* 2784 (quote from St. Gregory of Nyssa).

the doctrine taught by previous sages and expanded into a means of redemption from the burden of life and the wearisome trials of reincarnation. This mystery of salvation is expressed by the equation: Atman equals the Brahman, in which Brahman stands for the transcendent yet immanent supreme deity and Atman for that eternal portion of Brahman which abides in every living being.

If the main theme of the *Upanishads* is that Brahman and Atman are the same, that the reality of the world outside is identical with the reality of the self within, then this final secret is found only as the crowning discovery of a long and painful search. On the way towards that solution many alternative suggestions are made and rejected. But when the ultimate revelation has been fully grasped, it can only be repeated again and again in a sort of rapture—"I am Brahman" and "You are That,"—the key words of the Hindu religion which unlock all beatitude.

In Zen Buddhism there is no dualism of heaven and earth, natural and supernatural, man and God, mortal and immortal, present existence and future destiny. "Buddhism," the Zen monks declare, "places the center of the universe in the subjectivity of the individual mind, whereas other religions put it in the objectivity outside the individual mind." In reply to the question, what is the first cause of all things, they say: "Some religions answer God, Allah, Brahman, or something outside the individual. Buddhism sweeps aside your idle speculation and tells you to find the answer in your own realization."[240] Yet the same monks who sweep aside the "idle fancies" about God's existence specialize in meditation beyond anything comparable in the Western world, and their purpose is to establish contact with ultimate reality.

---

[240] Senzaki, Nyogen, *Buddhism and Zen* (New York: Philosophical Library, 1953), 11.

Extremes in Christian History

A remarkable feature of Catholic Christianity is the fact that for centuries and up to the Middle Ages there was no occasion for a major ecclesiastical declaration about man's union with God through grace. This is all the more striking if we consider the prevalent notions outside the Church during the whole patristic age, along with the variety of opinions on which the general councils passed definitive judgment in the field of grace, Christology, and the mystery of the Trinity.

The first significant exception occurred in the early fourteenth century, when the German mystic and preacher Meister Eckhart (1260–1327) began teaching his doctrine on the spiritual life. Eckhart has been the subject of extensive research and recently several of his previously unedited writings have appeared. A benign interpretation suggests that ambiguities arose from his attempt to express the inexpressible, and the fact that he was first rediscovered by romantic poets and philosophers out of sympathy with the theological tradition in which he stood. But this was not the judgment of the Holy See which condemns seventeen propositions excerpted from his works as heretical and eleven others as suspect of heresy.

In 1329, John XXII published the Constitution, *In Agro Dominico,* in which Eckhart was formally censured.[241] The Pope ordered the Archbishop of Cologne to issue the condemnation, lest the errors "should take deeper root in the hearts of those simple-minded persons to whom he had preached." He also stated that before his death Eckhart had retracted twenty-six of the articles in question and everything that was capable of leading to error in his works "as far as it can be so understood." He submitted formally to the Church's authority. As he had declared before the Inquisition, he was "capable of error,

---

[241] *DS* 951–79.

but not of heresy, because the one depends on the understanding, the other on the will."

Throughout his sermons and formal treatises runs the insistence on the nearness of a devout soul to God, such nearness that it becomes one with Him. Eckhart allows the just man to apply to himself the words of Wisdom in the Book of Ecclesiasticus, "Before the world, was I created," which he changes to read, "Before the created world, I am." The man of virtue, he said, "is raised up above time into eternity. He works there one work with God." Such a man "works with God what God worked a thousand years ago and what He will work a thousand years hence. And this is for wise people a matter of knowledge, and for the ignorant a matter of belief."[242]

Elsewhere he exclaims that "God performs such wonders in some people, (that) they become transfigured by the Divine Being and it is God who works in them and not they themselves."[243] And in a closely reasoned exposition of St. Paul's statement, how "he that cleaves to God is one spirit," he simply identifies a justified man with God, on the grounds that both have the same mind.

> Intellect properly speaking belongs to God, and "God is one." To the extent therefore that each thing possesses intellect or intellectual power, to that extent it possesses God and the one, and to that extent it is one with God. For the one God is intellect and the intellect is one God. Hence God is never and nowhere as God save in the intellect.
>
> To ascend to the intellect therefore and to be subjected to it is to be united to God. To be united, to be one, is to be one with God for "God is one."[244]

---

[242] *Treatises and Sermons of Meister Eckhart,* trans. James Clark and John V. Skinner (New York: Octagon Books, 1958), 55.
[243] Ibid., 107.
[244] Ibid., 212.

If it was possible to be still more explicit, Eckhart clarified what he meant in his commentary on the Gospel according to St. John. He is speaking of the just man, whom he describes as being "in justice itself, for how could he be just, if he were outside justice, if he stood without, separated from justice." His exposition left nothing unclear, to prove that the justified person is literally and physically of one nature with the Father, even as Christ.

> It is obvious from this that the just man is the offspring and son of justice. He is called, and actually is, the son because he becomes different in person but not in nature. "I and my Father are one." We "are," that is to say, distinct in person, since nothing begets itself, but "one" in nature, because otherwise justice would not beget the just man, nor the Father the Son, to become other than Himself.
>
> Now if the Father and the Son, justice and the just man, are one and the same in nature, it follows that the just man is equal to, not less than justice, and similarly with the Son in relationship to the Father. This is expressed by "the word was with God." The term "with" signifies equality.[245]

Eckhart has been acclaimed the forerunner of Martin Luther's emphasis on faith, of Immanuel Kant's critical idealism, and of Hegel's evolutionary pantheism. Although Hegel's acquaintance with Eckhart was superficial, it is certain that he regarded him as a predecessor and a kindred spirit.[246] Schopenhauer was also an admirer of Eckhart, whom he quoted more than once with approval.

The link between Eckhart and the Reformation is Martin Luther who read the Dominican mystic and was specially influenced by

---

[245] Ibid., 238.
[246] Hegel, *Werke,* Vol. XII, 1925, 257.

Eckhart's fellow-religious, Johann Tauler (1300–1361). Tauler's orthodoxy is unimpeachable but he never tired of repeating Eckhart's injunction that God must be born in the soul. He was careful to add (as Eckhart had not been) that the soul is not God, that the Creator and creature are distinct, that they are of a different nature, and that in this life we can only be united with God as a result of divine grace.[247]

During the critical years 1515 to 1518, Luther read Tauler with enthusiasm and not without profit. Without distinguishing the genuine from the spurious writings of the preacher, he thought he saw in Tauler a support for the new doctrines that were developing in his mind. He felt that Tauler stood for an "evangelical Christianity," without any adulteration of papistry. Four ideas are known to have attracted him particularly: the notion that we should completely resign ourselves to the will of God, the ostensible attacks on outer works as useless in themselves, the graphic description of the trials undergone by a devout soul, and the critical attitude towards Scholasticism.

No doubt Tauler occasionally urged the renunciation of external works if these stand in the way of communion with God, but he was never in favor of passivity or quietism. He held that even a sinner can do good and prepare himself for sanctification. Also at times Tauler departed from strict Scholastic teaching, but only in incidentals. And the "dark night of the soul" he described as a passing phase of spiritual loneliness, common to all the mystics. It was not Tauler but Pseudo–Tauler who had the most drastic effect on Luther. Both writers furnished the Reformer with an approach to religion that had partial validity in the limited sphere of mystical experience but that proved radically disruptive to the Catholic tradition of man's relationship with God, when interpreted in the light of Luther's theory of justification.

---

[247] *CCC* 1997.

As we read through the writings of Luther and Calvin, it may seem surprising that the Council of Trent went to such great lengths to teach the extraordinary effects of sanctifying grace in the soul. Superficially it would seem the Reformers never questioned the fact, and even dwelt on the difference between themselves and those who could not grasp the idea of salvation by trust alone. Calvin quoted the words of Christ against his opponents: "My Spirit was unknown to the world; he is recognized only by those among whom he abides."[248] In reality, however, whatever participation in the divine nature the Reformers admitted, they did not admit an intrinsic perfection abiding in the soul. Their premise was that justification itself meant only the external imputation of Christ's merits.

If they spoke of the "indwelling Spirit," His union with the soul may have been interior, but it was not due to any permanent physical reality which raised the soul to a share in the very life of God. It was either a moral connection arising from the sinner's acceptance by God, or a literal substitution of the Spirit for that cooperative effort which became impossible on the hypothesis of an utterly depraved will.

Protestant scholarship has shown conclusively what a gulf divides the Catholic from the Reformation doctrine on the effects of justification. The acute change from Indeterminism to religious Determinism took place in Luther (and through him in Calvin) under the direct influence of German mysticism. In the *Servo Arbitrio* (Enslaved Will) it attained its extremest limit. This is not explained, as some have thought, by Occamism, but by German Mysticism. After his period of mysticism, in which he replaced human freedom with the all-doing Spirit, Luther took leave altogether of what he called the "Semi-Pelagianism and Indeterminism" of the Scholastics. "Any concurrence between free will and its faculties and grace, or any kind of preparation

---

[248] John 14:17.

for grace, is completely done away with. God's grace alone works for salvation, and predestination is the only cause of salvation in those who are justified."[249]

In this as in so many other areas, Baius and the Jansenists clarified Protestant theology by expressing it in terms familiar to Catholicism. Two propositions of Michael de Bay which Pius V censured deal specifically with the doctrine of partaking in the divine nature. "The raising of human nature," said Baius, "to a participation of the divine nature was due to the integrity of man in his first state and for that reason should be called natural, not supernatural."[250] And more pertinently, "The justice by which a sinner is justified through faith consists formally in obedience to the commandments, which is the justice of works. It does not consist in any kind of habitual grace infused in the soul, by which a man is adopted as a son of God, renewed according to the inner man and made a sharer in the divine nature, so that, renovated through the Holy Spirit he can thereby live a holy life and fulfill the precepts of God."[251]

If the same position was less clear in the Reformers, this was not because of any basic difference from Bainism but because the Reformation principles had become more refined and their formulation more precise under the scrutiny of sympathetic theologians who sought to bridge the gap between Catholic and Protestant theologies of grace.

An extreme form of Quietism troubled the Church in the late seventeenth century, with the publication in 1675 of *The Spiritual Guide* by Michael Molinos, a Spanish priest then living in Rome. Although dangerous, the book was susceptible to an orthodox interpretation. The

---

[249] "Luther und die deutsche Mystik," *Neue Kirchliche Zeitschrift*, 19 (1908), 985–88; *CCC* 1993, 2002.
[250] *DS* 1921.
[251] *DS* 1942.

letters of spiritual direction which Molinos wrote, however, presented total passivity as the Christian ideal of perfection. After several years of sifting this correspondence, which amounted to twenty thousand pieces of mail sent to persons in every walk of life and rank in the Church, Molinos was finally arrested and found guilty of teaching erroneous doctrine. On September 3, 1687, he made a solemn abjuration, after which he was taken back to prison, where he died towards the end of 1696.

Originally two hundred and sixty-three propositions were extracted from Molinos's letters, and acknowledged by him as his in their objectionable sense. These were later reduced to sixty-eight, and condemned by Innocent XI on November 20, 1687.

For Molinos, perfection of the interior life consisted in a perfect passivity of soul. This is the secret of peace, union with God and sanctification. One's own activities or thoughts are the great enemies of the divine life. Whoever puts this doctrine into practice simplifies not only his prayer but the whole conduct of his life. To resist temptations, gain indulgences, recite vocal prayers, all of this is useless in the state of perfection, once God takes complete possession of man's spirit.

A man must learn to annihilate his own powers, according to Molinos, and this is the true interior way. "To wish to do anything actively is to offend God, who alone desires to be agent, and "natural activity is hostile to grace, impedes the operations of God and true perfection, because God desires to work within us but without us."[252]

The foundation of this Quietism was a not-unfamiliar idea that might have been quoted from the sermons of Eckhart. "By doing nothing, the soul annihilates itself and returns to its first principle and origin, which is the essence of God, in which it is transformed and divinized, and God then abides in Himself. As a result there are

---

[252] *DS* 2204.

no longer two realities united one to the other, but only one, so that God lives and reigns in us, while the soul ceases to be in its operative existence."[253]

In Quietist spirituality, therefore, the ideal towards which a person must strive is self-annihilation to the passive condition of a "dead body," which offers no resistance to whatever urges may arise, on the supposition that now God and not the will must do all the activity. Molinos began by commending devotion to the Church and progressing to devotion to Christ, who was *deiformis non Deus,* finally rising superior to both in devotion to God alone. Hence the state of perfection was to be reached by the total annihilation of the will. Following this doctrine, priests and religious whom Molinos directed began to refuse to say their office and to go to confession, they discarded their external forms of piety, made no effort to be rid of temptations, and communicated without confession, even when they had every reason to fear they had committed grievous sin.

Some idea of the extremes to which Quietists were led, appears from the direction they received about going to Holy Communion.

> Neither before nor after Communion is there required any other preparation or thanksgiving than to remain in one's customary passive resignation. This passivity more perfectly supplies for all the acts of virtue which can be and are produced in the ordinary way. Moreover, if at the time of Communion there arise feelings of humiliation, petition, or gratitude, they should be suppressed, unless recognized as coming by a special impulse of God. Otherwise they are movements of a nature which is not yet dead.[254]

---

[253] *DS* 2205.
[254] *DS* 2232.

Though bizarre, Quietism was consistent with itself, since it assumed that the more perfect a man becomes the less active his own contribution to the spiritual life needs to be. The resulting complete perfection means complete divinization to the point of absolute domination by the Spirit of God.[255] Implicit always was the notion that man's will is capable only of evil, and true virtue consists in the suppression of human volition.[256]

Far removed from spiritual direction but yet within the same general tradition as Quietism was a philosophy of religion that went the "whole way" in its theory of man's communion with God. Modern pantheism in the Western world was born of German idealism under Immanuel Kant and has since penetrated into every form of religious thought.

European writers immediately after Kant tended to an extreme idealism that he personally never professed but which derived very logically from the principles he laid down. On the one hand he credited the mind with a unique power regarding external phenomena. It determined what features of reality are to constitute our phenomenal world. According to Kant, phenomena owe their fundamental patterns to the *a priori* categories which inspire all human thinking. Without the categories the objects of knowledge might well be given in experience, but they would never be known. From this point it was no great step to the idea that the world of external phenomena is in some way produced by the mind, not perhaps mine or yours, but a cosmic mind, perhaps a sort of pantheistic deity. Thus the very existence and the full structure of phenomena might be thought to depend upon the activity of consciousness which in this case is not merely selective and interpretative in function but actually creative. It was

---

[255] Paul Dudon, *Le Quietiste Espagnol Michel Molinos* (Paris: Gabriel Beauchesne, 1921), 91–92.
[256] *CCC* 1749.

left to the post-Kantian idealists to take this final step and deify the human intellect.

The first of three philosophers who derived a form of pantheism from Kantian ideas was Johann Gottlieb Fichte (1762–1814). His starting point was the disunity in Kantianism which he tried to reduce to a single principle. Kant was aware he had failed to coordinate the dualism of the moral and speculative orders, or reconcile the dichotomy of a world of phenomena with things-in-themselves. Fichte discovered a basis of unity in the Ego, which replaces the essences of things as the ultimate reality, and becomes the ultimate criterion in the practical and speculative order.

In Fichte's theory, all thought and all being, including the noumena of things, are derived from the Ego. The resulting system is a type of subjective idealism or pan-egoism, although Fichte protested against identifying the Ego with individual consciousness. It has been called "substantial pantheism," where the only substance whose existence is admitted is the eternal Ego.

From his study of theology at the universities of Jena and Leipzig, Fichte retained enough theological vocabulary to give a new meaning to the *sola fide* doctrine of the Reformation. "I have found the organ by which to apprehend reality," he wrote. "It is faith. It is not knowledge, but a resolution of the will. So has it been with all men who have ever seen the light of the world. Without being conscious of it, they apprehend all the reality which has an existence for them, through faith alone; and this faith forces itself on them simultaneously with their existence. It is born with them."[257]

Like Kant, Fichte had to defend himself against the charge of undermining the Christian religion. His defense was anything but concilia-

---

[257] Johann Fichte, *The Vocation of Man* (New York: Liberal Arts Press, 1956), 99–101.

tory. "No one who reflects a moment," he maintained, "and honestly avows the result of his reflection, can doubt that the notion of God as a particular substance is impossible and contradictory. It is right candidly to say this, to silence the babbling of the schools, so that the true religion of cheerful virtue may be established in its place."[258] It was no wonder the University of Jena dismissed him in 1799 for atheism; but soon after he was appointed to the newly founded University of Berlin.

Friedrich Schelling (1755–1854) was a disciple of Fichte, who later modified the latter's subjective idealism by combining it with the theories of Spinoza into the System of Identity. Object and subject, the real and ideal, nature and spirit were made identical in the Absolute, which Schelling denominated as God. He made complete this identification of all things with the Absolute, not in the qualified sense that the Absolute has power to develop and produce all things, but because the Absolute indeterminately *is* all things.

Later Schelling changed his system to explain the origin of the universe as a "breaking away" or "falling off" from the Absolute. In his own words, "there is no continuous transition from the Absolute to the actual; the origin of the sensible world is conceivable only as a complete falling off from absoluteness, by a leap. The Absolute is what alone is real; finite things, on the other hand, are not real."[259]

Schelling's philosophy has been called "essential pantheism," because it affirms the identity in essence of all things, notwithstanding his curious explanation of the world as "fall" from the Absolute.

The third and greatest post-Kantian thinker who tried to synthesize ultimate being was Georg Hegel (1770–1831), who reversed Schelling's theory of the world as proceeding from the Absolute by postulating that the Absolute becomes successively matter and spirit

---

[258] Johann Fichte, *Popular Works* (London: Trübner, 1873), 1:122–23.
[259] Friedrich Schelling, *Werke* (Augsburg: J.G. Cotta, 1856), 6:38.

and all things. Both made the Absolute the only principle of reality, but where Schelling called it a genetic source, Hegel believed it was a continuous process.

The essence of Hegel's dynamic Absolute was the Idea, which continues to develop by successive stages—thesis, antithesis, and synthesis—into all the varieties of being. This idea is something present in all things, not only in those which are, but also in those which are not. It is simultaneously being and nonbeing, the negation of being and universal being, determined being and undetermined being. In a word, the foundation of Hegel's philosophy was a denial of the principle of contradiction. His concept of universal being postulated a deity that is not yet but is becoming.

Unlike Fichte and Schelling, Hegel wrote so much on the subject of religion that some writers believe he was primarily a theologian and a philosopher only to support his theology. His preoccupation has earned him the title of "God intoxicated."

Hegel's influence on the sacred sciences has been immense. The modern study of ecclesiastical history began with the Tubingen School, which drew its inspiration directly from Hegel. Its outstanding figure, David Strauss (1808–1874), projected a theory of the Incarnation that has entered the stream of modern rationalism and was one of the main reasons for the condemnation of pantheism by the First Vatican Council. Where Hegel and others had stopped short of injecting their ideas into the Christian faith, the theologian Strauss used Hegelianism to explain man's union with the divine in terms that represent the *ne plus ultra* of radical Western thought.

It is elementary Hegelianism that the initial figure in any historical development, here it is the Christian religion, cannot be the greatest in the series. It is also basic with Hegel that true reality is the fusion of the human and divine, in successive stages, until final perfection of the deity is achieved. Strauss applied these principles to the Christian Incarnation.

> If reality is ascribed to the idea of the unity of the divine and human natures, is this equivalent to the admission that this unity must actually have been once manifested, as it never had been, and never more will be, in one individual? This is indeed not the manner in which the (Hegelian) Idea realizes itself. It is not wont to lavish all its fulness on one exemplar, and be niggardly towards all others—to express itself perfectly in that one individual, and imperfectly in all the rest. It rather loves to distribute its riches among a multiplicity of exemplars which reciprocally complete each other—in the alternate appearance and suppression of a series of individuals.
>
> Is this not the true realization of the Idea? Is not the concept of the unity of the divine and human natures a real one in a far higher sense, when I regard the whole human race as its realization, than when I single out one man as such a realization? Is not an incarnation of God from eternity a truer one than an incarnation limited to a particular point of time?[260]

This was no passing observation, but the key to a right understanding of Christianity. "As subject of the predicate which the Church assigns to Christ, we place instead of an individual, an idea; but an idea which has an existence in reality, not in the mind only." Therefore "humanity is the unity of the two natures, God become man, the infinite spirit remembering its infinitude. It is Humanity that dies, rises, and ascends to heaven, for from the negation of its phenomenal life ever proceeds a higher spiritual life."[261]

---

[260] David Strauss, *The Life of Jesus* (London: Sonnenschein, 1892), 3:437.
[261] Ibid., 437–38.

Strauss's work, which exercised a profound influence on subsequent German Protestant theology, roused a storm of indignation and led to his dismissal from Tubingen. Yet the principle on which he built was nothing new. It had already been seen in the off-guarded statements of Eckhart. "If God and man are in themselves one," Strauss observed, "and if religion is the human side of this unity: then must this unity be made evident to man in religion," which he proceeded to do.[262]

From the proceedings of the First Vatican Council we know that the main adversaries that the council had in mind when drafting the definitions on God's nature and His real distinction from the world were the pantheists then current in Germany. The familiar declarations of Vatican I take on new meaning when seen in the light of the errors against which they are aimed: the conception of a deity who was somehow confused with the universe and who needed the world and man in order to fulfill his own nature.

There can be no question whether God needs man or anything outside Himself since He is "all powerful, eternal, unmeasurable, incomprehensible, and limitless in intellect and will and in every perfection." Since He is one unique and spiritual substance, absolutely unchangeable, "He must be declared really and essentially distinct from the world."[263]

This is also to say that God did not create the world "to intensify His happiness nor to acquire any perfection," since He is infinitely happy and perfect in Himself. He created "by a complete free decision" and "in order to manifest His perfection through the benefits which He bestows on creatures."[264]

---

[262] Ibid., 433.
[263] DS 3001; CCC 293.
[264] DS 3002.

Accordingly the union which Christian revelation tells us God desires to establish and perfect between Him and the souls He justifies must begin with the antecedent axiom that God is infinite. Even the highest of creatures is a finite being. Therefore God never ceases to be God and creatures never cease to be creatures no matter how closely He unites Himself with them. In only one case, in the Person of Christ, is the union substantial or hypostatic, where the human nature of the Savior was wholly assumed by the divinity to become the exemplar and meritorious cause of our participation in the Godhead.

PARTICIPATION IN THE GODHEAD

Before examining the Catholic doctrine on how we share divine nature, it will be useful to place the matter in focus. We have already seen that justification means the infusion of sanctifying grace in the soul as a permanent, physical reality that inheres in the soul's substance as a qualitative habit that perfects the human spirit and gives it supernatural life. We now ask what are the formal effects of this sanctifying grace or, in other words, what are the "built-in" consequences that logically and necessarily flow from the mere fact that the soul has been animated by its form of life.

Theologians commonly recognize five such effects consequent on the reception of sanctifying grace: supernatural justice or righteousness, which includes the remission of sins; participation in the divine nature; adopted divine sonship, with its correlative right to the inheritance of heaven; divine friendship; and the indwelling of the Holy Spirit. While there is still some discussion about which of these are primary and which secondary, the fundamental effect is generally considered to be sharing in the divine nature, and serves as basis for all the others.[265]

---

[265] *CCC* 654.

Sharing in the Divinity

It is no exaggeration to say that a correct knowledge of how we partake of God's nature by grace is the key to a right understanding of the supernatural order. Evidently the operative word is "participation," which means to have a part of, to share in, to partake of what someone else possesses. When we participate we receive from another what before had belonged only to the person who gave us a share in his own possession.

In quantitative terms, to participate means to divide, as when a man shares his wealth with another and is consequently poorer because of his benefaction. Spiritual things can also be shared, as when a teacher communicates knowledge to his students, or a mother gives her affection to a child. The object of communication—wisdom, love, skill—is in no way lessened because it is shared, since spiritual realities cannot be divided or broken into parts. The giver still retains what he had, and the receiver is enriched by what he obtained. This is a mystery that we cannot fully explain and yet know as a matter of experience.

As we approach the immensity of God, we see immediately that the divine perfections can be viewed from different aspects, and on a clear distinction here largely depends a true appreciation of what sharing God's nature by sanctifying grace really means.

There are perfections in God that by their essence constitute the Divinity. Thus self-subsistence, pure act, absolute and perfect self-sufficiency are perfections that cannot be predicated of any creature in their strict and formal implication, not even analogously. Every creature is essentially dependent, essentially composed of act and potency, and essentially a contingent being. It is impossible formally (and intelligibly) to speak of a creature partaking of God's self-existence, because its essence is to have a dependent existence and God cannot contradict Himself by "sharing" what uniquely makes Him God.

At the other extreme are divine perfections that by their formality prescind from the Divinity, and that are naturally communicated to creatures by their very creation. Thus God communicates to others outside Himself the properties of being, substantiality, life, knowledge, volition and a myriad of other perfections that run the gamut of natural participation in the attributes of God.

However, there are still other perfections in God which do not formally include the concept of Divinity, and yet are so properly divine that no creature has or can have any claim upon them. They are the ability to see and actually to see the divine essence *intuitively* in itself, with no creature between as a means of having this knowledge; to have the very "quiddity" of God, namely, that which makes God what He is in Himself as the object and source of beatitude. Whatever perfections by their nature belong to such beatitude, whether they constitute or derive from it—all these may be communicated to rational creatures supernaturally and, in fact, are what God allows us to share with Himself by reason of sanctifying grace.

If we ask why the intuitive vision of the divine essence belongs by right to God alone, and why only He has a natural claim on the happiness which is consequent on such intuition, we have a dimly analogous answer from human life. In a very true sense, no one except a person himself can literally "see himself" by direct insight into his own soul and operations. No one else can have the knowledge that comes only from "self-intuition," as no one else can love himself in the way that follows on such immediate self-cognition. We admit, of course, that this self-knowledge is not strictly intuitive and that even here we have to reflect on the soul's activity and reason to certain conclusions. The difference between how a man knows himself and how he knows anything else is so profound that nothing can bridge the gap. It is a part of his personality and proper to no one but the man himself.

Continuing the analogy, knowledge of self has a depth and intimacy for which there is no counterpart. It has extension and a variety of detail that cannot be acquired about another person. It has penetration into meaning and a personal character which find reflection in the autobiographies of men, Augustine and Rousseau, but can never be fully expressed. It has a breadth of perception which suffuses the whole man and a distinctiveness that sets us apart as individuals with a personality all our own. If experience is the mother of wisdom, then self-experience is the parent of the self-knowledge which psychologically makes us what we are.

As we transfer this pale comparison to God, we begin to see both how truly the intuitive vision of His essence is properly divine, and what happiness must be the fruit of such intuition. For the degree of joy that the will derives from a loveable object is proportioned to the goodness it finds in that which it loves. When this object is nothing less than the ocean of infinite bounty, the beatitude takes on immeasurable dimensions.

Among the meditations of Cardinal Newman is one on the prospects of heaven that brings out the meaning of what God has prepared for those who die in His grace.

My God it was Thy supreme blessedness in the eternity past, as it is Thy blessedness in all eternities, to know Thyself, as Thou alone canst know Thee. It was by seeing Thyself in Thy co-equal Son and Thy coeternal Spirit, and in Their seeing Thee, that Father, Son, and Holy Ghost, Three Persons, One God, was infinitely blessed. My God, what am I that Thou shouldst make my blessedness to consist in that which is Thy own! That Thou shouldst grant me to have not only the sight of Thee, but to share in Thy very own joy! Prepare me for it, teach me to thirst for it.[266]

Through justification a soul is elevated to that high nature which is destined to enjoy this intuitive vision of God. He alone has the connatural power of seeing His own divine essence; yet by the condescension of His love those who live the supernatural life are made capable of the same intuition and the same resulting beatitude—by reason of the sanctifying grace they possess.[267]

Divine Sonship by Adoption

Closely associated with sharing in the divine nature is the gift of divine filiation effected in those who are justified. The precise nature of this filiation has been the shoals on which more than one theological speculation has been wrecked. The same biblical texts which Chalcedon used to establish Christ's divinity, Arius quoted to bolster his theory to the contrary, and Eckhart, to illustrate our oneness with God.

Scriptural terminology is fluid, since the expression "Son of God" may refer to any one of a broad variety of divine relationships.[268] At the lowest scale all rational creatures, whether angels or men, are sons of God. All have come from His creative hands and are made to His image and likeness in having an intellect and a will. On the highest level is "the only-begotten Son, who is in the bosom of the Father," who is generated by the Father from all eternity and became man for our salvation. There is finally a spiritual generation, of which St. John

---

[266] John Henry Newman, *Meditations and Devotions* (London: Longmans, Green, 1893), 425.
[267] *CCC* 1028.
[268] *CCC* 441.

says that "to as many as received Him, He gave the power of becoming sons of God, to those who believe in His name."[269] This is the adopted filiation which divine grace produces in the souls of the just.

In order to recognize the dignity of our adopted divine filiation we should view it by comparison with the other two. "Man is made to the image of God," says St. Thomas, "because he is created with an intelligence. Only intelligent beings are said to be made in His image; they alone can be called His sons, and can be adopted through grace." However, adoption goes further than natural creation, for a right to inheritance is implied. "God's heritage is His own happiness, of which only intelligent creatures are capable, though they have no strict title to it from the fact of their creation. Such happiness is a gift, the gift of the Spirit. Sharing of possessions is not enough; there must be a sharing of heritage. And so the adoption of creatures mean their communion in the divine happiness."[270]

In contrast with us, Christ should not be termed God's Son by adoption because He is begotten eternally by the Father. His divine nature has the heritage of beatitude by natural right, not by additional concession, since, as He declared of Himself, "all things that the Father has are mine."[271]

Adoption therefore means the gratuitous acceptance of another person into sonship with the right of inheritance. In human relations it is a free choice made by the adopting parent. A person other than one's own flesh and blood is acknowledged as son in name and dignity, with the title to receiving the paternal heritage. By transfer to the supernatural plane, the heritage in store for us comes due to us at the end of mortal life. Then we may enter into possession of the infinite riches which are intrinsic to God, namely His consummate beatitude.

---

[269] John 1:12, 18; *CCC* 1692.
[270] St. Thomas Aquinas, III *Sententiarum,* 10, 2, 2.
[271] John 16:15; *CCC* 423, 454.

There is this difference between natural and adopted filiation that the latter is analogous to the former. In natural sonship the father communicates his own nature to the child and thereby gives him a right to the paternal inheritance. In adopted filiation this communication of nature occurs by an act of the will, by which the one adopted is accepted as a son and, in a sense, reborn by this act of charity. Thus the normal connection between father and child is established by procreation. It is supplied by effective love in the case of adoption.

The difference is still greater between human and divine adoption. When a child is adopted by human parents, this presupposes a certain fitness in the child, mainly that he has the same nature as the people who receive him into their family. Once adopted, nothing intrinsic changes in the child. He remains essentially the same, except for the moral and civil ties that now bind him to his legal parent. He has a claim on their love and a title to sharing in their possessions.

In divine adoption, on the other hand, God does not presuppose our fitness for the role of adopted sons but effects it. Mysteriously but truly God communicates His divine nature to us, making ours deiform through the infusion of sanctifying grace. What He confers is no mere moral acceptance as His children, but the physical principle of a new life and a supernatural reality that makes us like to Himself. We could never say of a child adopted by human parents that he was born of them, in the way that we may and must say that those adopted by God are born of Him.

The dogmatic ground for both these mysteries, of sharing the divine nature and adopted filiation, is the recurrent teaching of the New Testament. St. Peter began his second epistle by urging Christians to the practice of virtue because Christ "has granted us the very great and precious promises, so that through them you may become partakers of the divine nature, having escaped from the corruption of that lust which is in the world."[272] The apostle does not here specify in what this partaking of the Godhead consists, but the rest of Scripture supplies the answer.

We are sharers in God's nature because we have been reborn to a new life through grace, having been given "the power to become sons of God," because we "were born not of blood, nor of the will of the flesh, nor of the will of man, but of God."[273] This on the word of Christ that unless a man be reborn of water and the Holy Spirit, he cannot enter into the kingdom of God. For we have received "the spirit of adoption as sons, by virtue of which we cry, 'Abba! Father!' The Spirit Himself gives testimony to our spirit that we are sons of God. But if we are sons, we are heirs also; heirs indeed of God and joint heirs with Christ."[274]

For ages the world had been enslaved in sin. "But when the fulness of time came, God sent His Son, born of a woman" in order that "He might redeem those who were under the Law, that we might receive the adoption of sons."[275] Twice St. Paul repeated the tautology "Abba, Father," which the Spirit bids the justified address to God, because he wished to stress the central importance of this supernatural Father-and-son relationship in the Christian faith. The word *Abba* is an emphatic statement of the Aramaic term *Ab* and corresponds to the vocative expression, "My Father!" Christ used it regularly to describe His relation to the First Person of the Trinity, since He spoke in Aramaic. Once only do the evangelists give the interpretative combination, when Mark quotes the Savior's prayer, "Abba, Father, all things are possible to Thee."[276] St. Paul does the

---

[272] 2 Peter 1:4.
[273] John 1:13.
[274] Romans 8:15; *CCC* 1265.
[275] Galatians 4:4.
[276] Mark 14:36.

same in writing to the Romans and Galatians, who would not be expected to understand Aramaic. And since they would not be much impressed if he gave the Greek alone, he added the Aramaic to make sure they understood that the mystery and its expression came from Christ Himself.

The Council of Trent crystallized the doctrine in a series of statements declaring that the justified are "reborn" and "regenerated by the Holy Spirit," that they are "created according to God, are made beloved sons of God, heirs, indeed, of God and co-heirs with Christ." Justification itself is called "the state of grace and adoption as sons of God."[277] Shortly after Trent, Baius was condemned for denying that elevation to a share in the divine nature was supernatural and claiming it consisted in nothing more than obedience to God's commands.[278]

However, the most elaborate teaching on the subject in the Church's *magisterium* came from Leo XIII, at the very time that rationalism was in its heyday and Adolph Harnack was saying that the essence of Christianity is the purely naturalistic recognition of the Fatherhood of God.[279] "No one can express the greatness of this work of divine grace in the souls of men," the Pope explained. "Wherefore, both in Holy Scripture and in the writings of the Fathers, men are styled regenerated, new creatures, partakers of the divine nature, godlike and the children of God." If physical procreation arises from the love of parents for their offspring, "spiritual generation proceeds from love that is infinitely more noble, coming from the uncreated Love" of God for His creatures.[280]

As we might expect, there is a close connection between our own adopted filiation and the natural filiation of the Son of God. Ours is at once a likeness to His, and intends for us to become more and more

---

[277] *DS* 1514–15, 1523–24, 1528–29.
[278] *DS* 1921, 1942; *CCC* 1998.
[279] Adolph Harnack, *What is Christianity?* (New York: G.P. Putnam's Sons, 1908).
[280] Leo XIII, *On the Holy Spirit* [*Divinum Illud Munus*] (1897), 8.

like the divine exemplar. In terms of the Mystical Body, there can be no relation of Head and members unless both share in the same nature. This conformity is an accomplished fact on the side of Christ, since He assumed our nature in all its perfection, along with its limitations except sin. Having once become man, Jesus remains the God-man for eternity, in a substantial union of our humanity with His divinity. But on our side the divinization depends on the grace of God and our effort to become assimilated to the Word Incarnate.

"It is the will of Jesus Christ," therefore, "that the whole body of the Church, no less than the individual members, should resemble Him."[281] Another name for this call to resemblance is the imitation of Christ, as found in the Gospels and Christian tradition. "Learn of me," is the Master's invitation to His followers. St. Paul exhorted the Corinthians to "be imitators of me, as I am of Christ," and Ignatius of Antioch, "be imitators of Jesus Christ, as He is of the Father."[282] According to St. Augustine, a man is perfect if he follows Christ perfectly, and to follow perfectly is to imitate.

We may legitimately ask why the imitation of Christ should be so essential to Christian perfection. The reason is that this was one of the motives for God becoming man. Since mankind needed to be taught the way to God, "it had to be formed after some model. The first thing necessary was that some norm or pattern of discipline be demonstrated. This was done by the divinely appointed method of the Incarnation, in order that from it should follow our knowledge, through the Son, of the Father."[283]

Accordingly we become more like our divine Head as we more closely imitate His practice of virtue during His visible stay on earth, and more faithfully conform to the pattern He daily shows us through

---

[281] *Mystici Corporis* 47.
[282] 1 Cor. 11:1; St. Ignatius of Antioch, "Epistle to the Philadelphians," 7.
[283] St. Augustine, "Sermo 142," *MPL* 38:783–84.

His infallible Church. Viewed in this double aspect, the imitation of Christ becomes more than prayerful reflection on the biography of the Gospels. It includes a responsiveness to the norms of holiness presented by the Mystical Christ through His appointed teachers and through the members of His Body who approached nearest to the sanctity of their Head.

Divine Friendship and Righteousness

In a special way, sanctifying grace also makes us the friends of God, endowing with spiritual rectitude or righteousness as defined by the Council of Trent and derived from the constant teaching of the Church. "The justified become both friends of God and members of His household." And when Faith operates along with other works, "the justified increase in the very righteousness which they received through the grace of Christ and are justified the more."[284]

What does it mean to become a friend of God through the infusion of His grace? Negatively it means the removal of sin which stands at enmity with God, and positively it stands for all the evidences of divine love that only the justified enjoy. Friendship has been defined as the mutual and manifest benevolence, which is not hid but outwardly shown and that shows itself by an exchange of what the friends possess. Each element is significant in the analysis of divine friendship through grace.

When I love a person with benevolence, my motive is not selfish advantage but the sheer excellence of the person loved.[285] His goodness in and of itself impels me to love him, not merely gratitude for what I may have received in the past, and still less what I hope to get in the future. From the divine side God cannot love in any other way

---

[284] *DS* 1535; *CCC* 277.
[285] *CCC* 1767.

than benevolently, since He never seeks (or could possibly desire) any benefit from His creatures. But from our side we are quite capable of loving God from motives lower than His infinite goodness; in fact the virtues of hope and fear are directly motivated by self-concern, either of receiving what is good or avoiding what is evil. These virtues are good and demand cultivation, but they are not yet that pure form of love of which we are supernaturally capable through justification.

True friendship does not hide its affection. There is a self-revelation of one to the other, without which the love would be suspect. In the words of Christ, "No longer do I call you servants, because the servant does not know what his master does. But I have called you friends, because all things that I have heard from my Father I have made known to you."[286] The consequent intimacy is bilateral. The soul is self-revealing to God in a way that may surprise the natural man and, in the lives of the saints, may seem almost extreme. God reveals Himself with manifestations that are commonplace in hagiography and familiar to all Christians in the degree of their nearness to Him.

But most important, friendship is communicative. It presupposes a certain equality between the two who love, either natural, as among man, or of dignity, as happens when God raises man to a level comparable to His own nature. It also presupposes a certain agreement of mind and will, which in human society may be as trivial as two people having the same taste in sports. But divine friendship is a consensus of ultimate purpose—the glory of God and our beatitudes. Divine friendship presupposes, especially, that the parties mutually exchange what they possess—which prompts the soul to give itself and all it has to God for the advancement of His honor; while God more than requites the generosity by giving Himself. He does this as man in the person of Christ, as the God-man in the Eucharist, as the

---

[286] John 15:15; *CCC* 1972.

indwelling Spirit who abides in the soul, and, in heaven, as the object of eternal happiness.

Correlative with friendship, sanctifying grace confers a righteousness that gives the soul power and facility to direct its actions rightly, i.e., to that proper end to which humanity is destined in the beatific vision.[287]

This orientation is the bedrock of the supernatural order, since order is the right use of means to a given end. A man in grace is thus directed from within to employ his faculties and whatever enters his life to the attainment of the heavenly goal to which his deiform nature is spontaneously impelled. From the side of God, there is a special providence in favor of the justified, a protection and guidance that follow logically on adopted filiation and divine friendship and that were promised in both the Old and New Laws. "Can a woman forget her child," the Lord asked, "so as not to have pity on the son of her womb? And if she should forget, yet I will not forget you," He promised to those whom He chose.[288] Nothing is excepted from the scope of this provident care, since "we know that for those who love God all things work together unto good, for those who, according to His purpose, are saints through His call," that is, are made holy through the grace to which He invited them.[289]

THE INDWELLING SPIRIT

Few doctrines of the Catholic faith are more personally satisfying than the mystery of divine inhabitation, assured us by Christ at the Last Supper. "I will ask the Father," He promised, "and He will give you another Advocate to dwell with you forever, the Spirit of truth whom the world cannot receive, because it neither sees Him nor knows Him. But you shall know Him, because He will dwell with you and be with

---

[287] *CCC* 1266.
[288] Isaiah 49:15; *CCC* 219.
[289] Romans 8:28; *CCC* 313.

you." Then to clarify the Trinitarian nature of this indwelling, He added, "If anyone love me, he will keep my word, and my Father will love him, and we will come and make our abode with him."[290]

For the earliest Christian tradition, the faithful reflected on the love which prompted God to give the souls in grace not only the created gift of supernatural life but the uncreated gift of Himself. "We believe in the Holy Spirit," the Credo of Epiphanius read, "who dwells in the saints."[291] St. Augustine summarized the patristic tradition at the beginning of the fifth century.

> Although God is everywhere wholly present, He does not dwell in everyone. It is not possible to say to all what the apostle says, "Know you not that you are the temple of God and that the Spirit of God dwells in you?"
>
> Who would dare to think, unless he were completely ignorant of the inseparability of the Trinity, that the Father or the Son could dwell in someone in whom the Holy Spirit does not dwell, or that the Holy Spirit could be present in someone in whom the Father and the Son were not present? Hence it must be admitted that God is everywhere by the presence of His divinity, but not everywhere by the grace of His indwelling.
>
> He that is everywhere does not dwell in all, and He does not dwell equally in those in whom He does dwell. It is (moreover) remarkable how God dwells in some souls who do not yet know Him and does not dwell in others who do. We say, then, that the Holy Spirit dwells in baptized children although they do not know it. They are unconscious of Him although He is in them. He is said to dwell in such as these because He works in them secretly that they may be His temple, and He

---

[290] John 14:23, *CCC* 260.
[291] *DS* 44; *CCC* 1197.

perfects His work in them as they advance in virtue and persevere in their progress.[292]

The Council of Trent made several references to the indwelling
Spirit, for example in speaking of those who fall into mortal sin after
having been justified. Their sin is more serious who, "after they have
received the gift of the Holy Spirit, have not been afraid to destroy
knowingly the temple of God and grieve the Holy Spirit."[293] But the
most detailed authoritative exposition was given by Leo XIII, in the
Encyclical *Divinum Illud,* written, as the pontiff said, to remind
"preachers and those having care of souls that it is their duty to instruct
the people more diligently and more fully about the Holy Spirit." His
analysis is the best single dogmatic source on that presence of God in
the soul which differs only in degrees and fruition from His union with
the saints in glory.

Mode of Presence

We begin with the established fact, universally taught by faith, that
God is present in a special manner in the justified, other than in
sinners, unbelievers, or the unbaptized. The precise mode of this presence, called inhabitation, has not yet been determined. However
certain features of it must be verified.

> There is question here of a hidden mystery, which during
> this earthly exile can only be dimly seen through a veil, and
> which no human words can express. The Divine Persons are
> said to indwell inasmuch as they are present to beings
> endowed with intelligence in a way that lies beyond human
> comprehension, and in a unique and very intimate manner,

---

[292] St. Augustine, "Epistola ad Dardanum," *MPL* 33:837–38.
[293] *DS* 1690.

which transcends all created nature, these creatures enter into relationship with Them through knowledge and love.[294]

Theologians agree that whatever the indwelling is, it must be more than the ordinary presence of God everywhere by His immensity, which is common to all creatures and without which they would not exist. However it cannot be a substantial union between the soul and God to coalesce into one nature or one person: because God cannot be fused with a creature to form one nature with it, and because revelation tells us that there is only the one hypostatic (personal) union in Jesus Christ. Hence the warning of the Church "to reject every kind of mystic union by which the faithful of Christ should in any way pass beyond the sphere of creatures and wrongly enter the divine, were it only to the extent of appropriating to themselves as their own but one single attribute of the eternal Godhead."[295]

One theory of inhabitation explains it as a presence of production, which conceives God dwelling in the just man by affecting in him something entirely new and above his nature, namely sanctifying grace with all its concomitants. The principle behind the theory is the familiar one that God becomes present to me in the first place by producing me, which is the presence of His operation or immensity. Taking this as a general norm, any subsequent and higher "presence" should be explained in the same way. When I receive sanctifying grace, God produces something entirely different and essentially superior to the human nature I already possess. He gives me the deiformity of a life comparable to His own divine Son, with whom I become a joint heir of heaven.

Another explanation goes further, saying that if inhabitation were only a kind of higher production in the soul the result would not be

---

[294] *Mystici Corporis* 79.
[295] Ibid., 78.

radically different from God's omnipresence but only a matter of degree. The real newness of the indwelling should be sought in God's presence as the *object* of a special knowledge and love, which need not be actual here and now but has at least the capacity for realization, in varying stages. These stages take us from the dawn of reason (and the exercise of faith), through spiritual growth, to the beatific vision.

Some theologians stress the element of quasi-experimental knowledge, others of loving friendship, in which God becomes the new object for the soul. Regarding knowledge, this might be illustrated from human experience in the vastly different ways that people can know one another. In a broad sense I can say that I know every person in the world to the extent that I understand what human nature is; therefore everyone who answers this basic definition is "known" to me. But people in my own country, or city, or neighborhood are better known still. If we continue refining these kinds of knowledge we finally come to the members of our own family, and to the *alter ego* whom I feel I know almost as well as myself. Something comparable to this is suggested as taking place through the divine inhabitation, where the soul is enabled to "know God" with a depth and intimacy that beggar description and yet are as real as a man's own existence.

Part of this intimate knowledge of God is an insight into divine Truth, which the mind acquires quite without effort and with a clarity that no amount of natural reflection could provide. In the lives of the mystics this may reach extraordinary proportions, as happened to St. Ignatius in his famous vision at the river Cardoner.

> The eyes of his understanding were open. He beheld no vision, but he saw and understood many things, spiritual as well as those concerning faith and learning. This took place

with so great an illumination that these things appeared to be something altogether new. He cannot point out the particulars of what he then understood, although they were many, except that he received a great illumination in his understanding. This was so great that in the whole course of his past life right up to his sixty-second year, if he were to gather together all the helps he had received from God and all that he knew, and add them together, he does not think they would equal all that he received at that one time.[296]

What is most distinctive, however, about the knowledge that some would identify with the indwelling is not only its intensity but its span of perception of divine objects, accepted now by faith but which one day will be seen in vision. No mystical experience is needed to recognize the chasm that separates the believing from the unbelieving mind, the one having the Spirit of Truth and the other (perhaps naturally much superior) operating on its own. "This is eternal life," Christ defined, "that they may know You, the only true God," on which St. Thomas commented that "this supernatural knowledge is now entered by faith, which believes, through infused light, truths exceeding our natural understanding."[297] Mysteries like the Incarnation and Real Presence, the solidarity of the faithful in the Mystical Body and the Church's power of forgiving sins, doctrines like papal infallibility and the Catholic teaching on divorce and birth control are believed with a conviction that scandalizes those who do not have the Light of the abiding Spirit.

This special knowledge is associated with a love for the things of God, i.e., the coextensive object of the divine indwelling. Again the

---

[296] *St. Ignatius' Own Story,* trans. W.J. Young, S.J. (Chicago: Regnery Co., 1956), 23–24.

[297] John 17:3; *De Veritate* XIV, 2.

same serial analogy can be made, starting from the generic sort of love we have for "the human race," on through the various persons who have more and more intimately entered our lives, until we come to the one person above all others whom we love the most. In comparable fashion the soul in whom the Trinity dwells has the capacity for loving God in a way that as far exceeds the native power of the will as the supernatural is above nature. Once again the mystics give us an insight into the extremes of this love, as in the famous passage where Teresa of Avila describes the rapture of having her heart pierced through with a long spear of gold. When the angel of the vision "drew it out, he seemed to draw out my very entrails also, and to leave me all on fire with a great love of God." She writes in her autobiography—

> The pain was so sharp that it made me utter several moans, and so excessive was the sweetness caused me by this intense pain that one can never wish to lose it, nor will one's soul be content with anything less than God. It is not bodily pain, but spiritual, though the body has a share in it—indeed, a great share. So sweet are the colloquies of love which pass between the soul and God that if anyone thinks I am lying I beseech God, in His Goodness, to give him the same experience.
>
> During the days that this continued, I went about as if in a stupor. I had no wish to see or speak with anyone, but only to hug my pain, which caused me greater bliss than any that can come from the whole of creation.[298]

As before with knowledge, so with the love that comes from the Spirit of God, its experimental character is not limited to certain saints, whose raptures (according to the norms set down in canonical

---

[298] St. Teresa of Avila, *Autobiography,* trans. E. Allison Peers. *Complete Works of Saint Teresa of Jesus*, Vol. I (NY: Sheed & Ward, 1957), 192–193.

processes) do not prove sanctity. This love is the common experience of all believers, graded from the lowest to the highest, depending on the measure of God's presence in the soul.[299]

Still another explanation of the divine indwelling does not deny the preceding but seeks to combine the two theories of God's presence as agent and object of knowledge and love, and to place the ensemble on metaphysical grounds.

According to this theory, God is aid to "actuate" the essence of the soul, without informing it, i.e., without being its form, which would make God depend upon the soul as upon a material cause. He unites Himself to the soul by giving Himself to it. Actuation here means a "joining with" the human spirit in the way God will unite and give Himself to our minds in the beatific vision. The souls of the just are considered actuated in the sense of a previously existing substance, having its own rational life, made live under the influence of an added divine life stemming from a vital, uncreated principle which is God Himself. This principle communicates itself to the soul, without becoming its formal cause, and by this communication gives it the fundamental capacity to fulfill the functions of a new life whose plen-itude is the face-to-face intuition of God.

Sanctifying grace thus becomes the created communication of the Spirit of life to the essence of the soul, even as the light of glory is the created communication of divine Truth to the faculty of the mind. In both cases God dwells within us, through grace, in the whole substance of our spirit and through the light of glory in the intellect of the blessed.

Once more the principle of analogy will help to explain. The indwelling may be compared to the interpenetration of our body by the soul, which is whole and entire in every part of the body and not less in one portion than in another. Analogously God compenetrates every

---

[299] *CCC* 2093.

portion of the soul, to the very depths of its being. He is united with the soul by permeating its essence, yet always by a union which is only accidental and not substantial, albeit permanent and habitual and destined to continue for eternity.

The supernatural union consequent on the indwelling is also a possession of God. He gives Himself personally so that He is not only in the soul but belongs to the soul. The soul of the just man possesses Him as its property, since "by the gift of sanctifying grace the rational creature becomes capable of enjoying not only the created gift but even the divine Person."[300] Our having God is ontologically the same by grace as it will be in glory. In this life the enjoyment is through a mirror, darkly, but in heaven there will be no created medium between the soul and God.

Nevertheless already by grace God's abiding union with the soul can effect supernatural happiness that faith tells us is a foretaste of final beatitude. "Whoever possesses God is happy," wrote St. Augustine.[301] In the *City of God* he expanded on the principle that underlies this concept of the indwelling as an inchoate beatific vision. There are two kinds of persons, those who seek their happiness in God and those who look for it in themselves; the first have the Spirit of the Lord within, the second are dwelling alone. "If it is asked why the ones are happy, the right answer is, because they cleave to God. If it be asked why the others are miserable, the right answer is, because they do not cleave to God. There is no good capable of making any rational intellectual creature happy except God."[302]

Accordingly in the measure that God, who alone can satisfy the heart of man, is present in the soul, and the soul responds to His presence, *true* happiness will result. For there are two kinds of happiness

---

[300] St. Thomas Aquinas, *Summa Theologica,* I, 43, 3, 1.
[301] St. Augustine, *De Vita Beata,* IV, 35; *CCC* 1718.
[302] St. Augustine, *City of God,* XII, 1; *CCC* 2548.

for mortal men: that which is carnal and earthly and hangs on the changing circumstances of life, and that which is spiritually perfect, which depends on the possession of God.

Appropriation to the Holy Spirit

Although we normally speak of the Third Person inhabiting the souls of the just, there is a real problem if we take the ascription literally. At the Last Supper, when Christ foretold the mystery, He affirmed that all three Persons would come and make their abode in the faithful. Interpreted by tradition, this means that "God the Trinity, Father, Son and Holy Spirit come to us, as we come to them; they come to assist and we to obey; they to illuminate and we to behold; they to supply and we to receive that our vision of them be not external but deeply within; that their dwelling in us should not be for time but for ever."[303]

We are further led to the same conclusion by the fact that all the divine operations outside of God, except the hypostatic union, are performed by the whole Trinity.[304] Certainly the union of the soul with the Holy Spirit through sanctifying grace is not hypostatic, otherwise He would be assuming each soul into a substantial union of person—which cannot be held because the only hypostatic union admissible is that of the Incarnate Word.

Nevertheless there is a peculiar fitness if we appropriate the indwelling to the Third Person in preference to the other two. To appropriate means to apply to one Person some action common to all three. Of course this is not to say that one of the Persons is more active in producing a certain effect, since that would destroy their absolute equality of nature. It is simply a human way of saying that

---

[303] St. Augustine, *In Joannem* 76, 7; *CCC* 260.
[304] *CCC* 258.

some effect outside of God (*ad extra*) bears a greater resemblance to an operation within God (*ad intra*), which pertains to one divine Person rather than another. In this way goodness may fitly be ascribed to what is proper to the Holy Spirit who proceeds from the Father because power, as such, is a kind of principle or source, and it is proper that the First Person be the principle of the *whole* Divinity. By the same token whatever involves wisdom in creation can be referred to as the Son because it is characteristic of Him who proceeds from the Father as the Word of God by means of intellectual generation.

Since the manifestations of divine love in the world are analogous to the Holy Spirit who is the hypostatic love, proceeding from the Father and Son, they are rightly attributed to Him in the workings of grace consequent on the divine indwelling. Hence the statement of St. Paul, that "the charity of God is poured forth in our hearts by the Holy Spirit, who has been given to us."[305]

It is also proper to the Third Person to proceed from the other two by way of sanctity, since the essence of divine sanctity is the infinite love of an infinite good, so that the two processions by way of love and sanctity are really the same. For this reason, "because the divine Person proceeds through the love by which God is loved, it is properly called the *Holy* Spirit."[306] Consequently though all three Persons are essentially holy, holiness is specially applied to the Holy Spirit, and the indwelling which makes us holy is likewise ascribed to Him.

Finally we may speak of the Holy Spirit as the nature of a personal gift, since love carries the connotation of a primary gift through which all other gifts are freely granted. "A gift is freely given, and expects nor

---

[305] Romans 5:5.
[306] St. Thomas Aqiunas, *Summa Theologica,* I, 36,1.

return. Its reason is love. What is first given is love; that is the first gift. The Holy Spirit comes forth as the substance of love, and Gift is His name."[307] Among the blessings of divine generosity none ranks higher than the personal dwelling of the Trinity in the just, which the Church therefore attributes to the Holy Spirit, whom we invoke as "the Giver of gifts" and "the Gift of God most high."

---

[307] Ibid., I, 38, 2.

6

Actual Graces

Our dependence upon God and His supernatural communication affects every aspect of our being. Through sanctifying grace we are given a new life that raises us to the divine family and makes us partakers in the very nature of God. This corresponds to the vital principle in the physical order, enabling us to perform actions that are meritorious of heaven. Just as, naturally speaking, we receive from God both our nature and the constant influx of His general concursus; so supernaturally He gives to His elect not only the wellspring of deiform vitality but also the special assistance we need to guide the mind and inspire the will in our pathway to glory. Another name for this transitory light and inspiration is actual grace.[308]

The precise term "actual grace" is relatively new, and seems to have been used for the first time in its technical sense by the Dominican theologian John Capreolus (1380–1446), surnamed *Thomistarum princeps,* whose stout defense of St. Thomas did much to establish Aquinas's reputation in Catholic thought. It was more than coincidence that Capreolus had to defend Thomas against such men as William of Occam, whom Luther was later to call "my teacher," praising him above all the Scholastics.

HISTORICAL DEVELOPMENT

If the specific name was a medieval innovation, the concept of actual grace is rooted firmly in the Scriptures. Already in the Psalms

---

[308] *CCC* 2000, 2024.

we find the recurring theme of God's providential care. He gives His light and strength to those who ask Him, and man has a corresponding need to pray for this help at the risk of falling prey to his enemies. "Enlighten my eyes, or I shall fall asleep in death," the Psalmist begs, "turn my darkness into light. Train me to observe Your law, and I will cherish it with all my heart."[309]

The evangelist St. John, with his preference for the symbolism of light, tells how God comes to illumine every man born into this world, and quotes the words of Christ about the divine call to the mind that must precede any following of the Master. "No one can come to me unless the Father who sent me draw him," so that "everyone who has listened to the Father, and has learned, comes to me."[310] And in the same strain, the author of the Acts describes the conversion of Lydia, the seller of purple, who worshipped God and, as she listened to the preaching, "the Lord touched her heart to give heed to what was being said by Paul."[311]

St. John again, in the Apocalypse, pictorially speaks of divine grace operating on the will. Christ orders him in vision to write to the luke-warm bishop of Laodicea that "those whom I love I rebuke and chastise. Be earnest therefore and repent. Behold, I stand at the door and knock. If any man listens to my voice and opens the door to me, I will come in to him."[312] The Corinthians are reminded to the same effect that "I have planted, Apollo watered, but God has given the growth."[313] Paul and Apollo, who preach the Gospel, are only the external instruments of the word; but unless the Lord cooperates within by His grace, all their ministrations are in vain.

There was no serious challenge to this specialized assistance from God until the time of Pelagius. The British monk and his followers

---

[309] Psalm 118:34.
[310] John 6:44–46; *CCC* 259.
[311] Acts 16:14.
[312] Apocalypse 3:19–20.
[313] 1 Corinthians 3:6.

perverted the concept of actual grace by their intransigent position on the native capacities of man. Having denied his real elevation to the supernatural order, they logically reduced whatever help he does obtain to mere external assistance. They admitted that we may benefit from the life and works of Christ, but not so as to receive internal grace supernaturally infused into our souls. "There was a help to keep the law and doctrine," wrote Pelagius, already in the time of the prophets. "But the help of grace, which is grace properly so-called, comes to us from the example of Christ." Its function is "to show us the way we must walk, although we possess in our own free wills the power not to stray from the right path and therefore do not really need any aid outside of ourselves."[314] At most this auxiliary grace was to make the practice of virtue easier. It was not strictly necessary.

In the anti-Pelagian writings of St. Augustine we have the first detailed exposition of the nature of actual grace. "It is God," he quoted St. Paul, "who of His good pleasure works in you both the will and the performance. Wherein the apostle clearly shows that even our good will is performed in us by the operation of God. Indeed, unless the will have something occur to it by which it is attracted and invited, it can never be moved; this occurrence is not in the power of man" but only of God.[315]

The same limitation applies to the mind. "Let us understand this if we can. Sometimes God so deals even with His holy ones as not to give them either the assured knowledge or the conquering delight for performing a certain good work, to make them realize that they receive what light they need to illumine their darkness not of themselves but from Him. He is the one who bestows the serenity that causes the earth of their souls to bear fruit. When we plead with Him to grant us help to practice and perfect our justice, what else are we

---

[314] Pelagius, quoted by St. Augustine, "De Gratia Christi," *MPL* 44:361, 381.
[315] Philippians 2:13; St., Augustine, "De Diversis Quaestionibus," *MPL* 40:118, 128; *CCC* 2001.

asking but to have opened what is closed, and to make pleasant what is not to our taste?"[316]

Church councils during the fifth and sixth centuries further clarified and stamped with their authority the teachings of Augustine, Jerome, Prosper, and others who defended the existence and necessity of actual grace. At the Council of Carthage (A.D. 418), later confirmed by Pope Zosimus, it was decreed that "knowledge of what we ought to do and love for doing it are both gifts of God."[317] In the catalogue of papal pronouncements, published shortly after the death of St. Augustine, Pelagian naturalism is condemned since "God so works in the hearts of men and in free will itself that the holy thought, the gentle counsel, and every movement of a good will is from God, because it is through Him that we can do any good, and without Him we can do nothing."[318]

Still more explicitly, the Council of Orange (A.D. 529) declared how helpless man is to do anything on the road to salvation without the prior assistance of God, "Without the illumination and inspiration of the Holy Spirit."[319] This terminology has since become technical to define actual grace as the internal enlightening of mind and inspiration of will that God supernaturally infuses in the respective faculties.

During the whole patristic period and into the Middle Ages, there was no particular effort to distinguish actual from habitual grace, although the early councils were clear enough about the existence of the two kinds of benefits to the soul. With the advent of Scholasticism, however, the familiar Aristotelian categories of habit and action were pressed into the service of theology, with the result that by the time of St. Thomas the difference between a "habitual gift" and "the

---

[316] St. Augustine, "De Peccatorum Meritis et Remissione," *MPL* 44:170.
[317] *DS* 226.
[318] *DS* 244.
[319] *DS* 377.

divine help for willing and doing well" was fully established.[320] Capreolus then added the terms *habitual* and *actual* that are still current today.

Consistent with their ideas of justification, the sixteenth-century Reformers paid little attention to what Catholics called actual grace, since they questioned the existence of a supernatural order that implied an elevation of man above his natural powers of being and operation. They allowed for neither habitual nor actual grace in their Catholic sense. Sanctifying grace for them meant the merciful favor of God, who does impute (without conferring) the holiness of Christ to the justified man. Actual grace would mean a kind of direct assistance which affects the soul, in the absence of true human freedom, moving it to perform good actions for which God alone is fully responsible.

Since the principal kind of actual grace denied by the Reformers was that which precedes man's justification, the Council of Trent stressed its absolute need and utility. The justification of adults must begin with God's call, by which "God touches the heart of man with the illumination of the Holy Spirit; if a man receives that inspiration, he can also reject it."[321] Moreover the same kind of assistance is available after a person has sinned gravely and finds himself urged to repent from salutary fear. This is "a gift of God and an inspiration of the Holy Spirit, not, indeed, as already dwelling in the soul, but as merely giving the impulse that helps the penitent make his way towards justice."[322]

Under the aegis of Protestantism, Baius and the Jansenists had no more sympathy with the Catholic idea of actual than of habitual grace. According to Baius, "we should reject both terms of the distinction

---

[320] St. Thomas Aquinas, *Summa Theologica* I–II, 109, 6; 111, 2; *CCC* 2000.
[321] *DS* 1525; CCC 2001.
[322] *DS* 1678; *CCC* 1433; cf. John Paul II, *On the Holy Spirit in the Life of the Church and the World* [*Dominum et Vivificantem*] (1986), 28–33.

between two kinds of justice, one of which takes place through the indwelling Spirit of charity, and the other which occurs by the inspiration of the Holy Spirit urging the heart of penance."[323] Or, more positively, in the words of Quesnel, "Grace is the work of the hand of the omnipotent God, which nothing can hinder or retard"; it is "nothing more than God's omnipotent will commanding and doing what He commands."[324] Thus the vital quality of actual grace was reduced to an immanent divine power that no human will can resist.

From the seventeenth century on, the most debated issue about actual grace has been the domestic one of its relation to human conduct and, especially to the free cooperation by man. The long and sometimes acrimonious controversies between Thomists and Molinists were partly stimulated by the earlier conflict with Jansenism. If they contributed somewhat to clarifying the speculative meaning of actual grace, they had the practical effect of obscuring the importance of habitual righteousness and the sublimity of the indwelling Trinity. A new impulse to study the implications of God's transitory operation on the faculties has come from the modern interest in applied psychology, notably in the area of motivation and the development (or conquest) of moral habits.

THEOLOGICAL ANALYSIS

Catholic theology commonly defines actual graces as internal and immediate illuminations of the intellect and inspirations of the human will. They are internal because they are conferred on either of the two spiritual faculties, that alone can perform salutary actions that positively lead a person towards the beatific vision. Later we shall examine in detail the much neglected external graces, whose number and vari-

---

[323] *DS* 1963.
[324] *DS* 2410–11.

ety are myriad but which are either not internal because they originate outside the intellect and will or, though internal to the spiritual faculties, they are not strictly graces but the native movements of the soul.

The immediacy of actual graces is an elusive concept. It does not mean that whenever God gives an actual grace, He dispenses with such external media as preaching, spiritual reading, exhortation, or good example. On the contrary, He normally uses such means as the occasion for conferring internal light or strength. The grace is called immediate because it does not arise by means of purely natural causation, such as would be inherent in the native powers of the soul or as God supplies by the general concursus He gives to all secondary causes. God enters the faculty in a special and gratuitous manner, so that the mind or will are now able to produce acts that are essentially superior to anything a man could perform naturally and without such divine influx.

While insisting on the existence of immediate actual graces in the intellect, we do not question there are also mediate graces for the mind. Such would be any one of a countless number of ways that God may enlighten us, in keeping with His supernatural providence. In other words the mental image or operation arises spontaneously and naturally according to the laws of psychology, even though God may have generously directed certain factors outside the mind in our favor.

Similarly we may speak of mediate inspirations of the will, that follow naturally on a previous mental illumination which the mind presents to the appetitive faculty. God may also have arranged things so that the antecedent knowledge was not the bare fruit of our own thinking but supernaturally infused, or at least we came by this knowledge with providential help. Unless the essence of the inspiration is itself supernatural, it is still mediate and not an actual grace in the strict theological sense. It is interesting to note that a few older theologians, who did not deny there were immediate inspirations, questioned their necessity once a man received an immediate divine illumination, which then *sua sponte* produced supernatural affections in the will.[325] Their theory is generally frowned upon as hard to reconcile with the sources of revelation.

What are these actual graces concretely? In the mind they can be supernaturally infused judgments, whether practical or speculative, which patristic literature variously calls divine exhortations, vocations, or simply divine knowledge. They can also be single ideas, especially when so strongly impressive as almost to constitute a positive judgment. Inspirations of the will may be movements of charity or of any other virtue, like hope, temperance, penance, or fear of God's justice.

Before we examine more closely the nature of actual grace, we should clearly distinguish between what are styled *gratiae excitantes* (prevenient graces), also known as the grace which calls (*vocans*), and their antithesis, the *gratiae adjuvantes* (helping graces), sometimes known as the grace that cooperates (*cooperans*). The distinction is not abstruse, since the vital acts of the soul are either spontaneous impulses or free acts of the will. Regarding the will, grace may either precede the exercise of freedom or cooperate with it. When actual graces precede the free determination of our will they are called prevenient (coming before). When they accompany or coincide with the will's determination and merely cooperate with the will they are considered cooperating (working with).

There are two theories on the ultimate analysis of actual grace, each with a different explanation of the two general kinds of grace—the prevenient and the cooperating. Briefly stated, the first (Molinist) is based on the idea of God's *simultaneous* action, along with the vital

---

[325] Thus Denis Petavius (1583–1652), who wrote against the Jansenist Arnauld, and Gabriel Vazquez (1549–1604), a Spanish moralist.

activity of man's faculties. The second (Thomist) postulates a divine *previous* action, in the nature of a premotion that God applies to the mind and will before they exercise their vital function.

According to the Molinist theory, prevenient grace is explained by identifying it with the respective illuminations and inspirations by which God immediately affects the spiritual faculties. Of course the latter must be raised in order to perform (elicit) actions that are truly (entitatively) supernatural; but to do this we need no recourse to a new entity that has somehow been previously received in the faculty.

The postulate in Molinist terms is for an elevation that is not intrinsic but extrinsic. In other words, God comes to the assistance of the mind or will. He personally and immediately supplies what these powers naturally lack to produce supernatural acts. Thus the first supernatural reality which the faculty gets is not some divine movement prior to the act, but the indeliberate act itself, the whole of which proceeds from God and simultaneously from the faculty. Both God and the faculty together are responsible for the totality of the effect, but separately and partially regarding the cause, since the act is vital relative to the human faculty but supernatural in that it comes from God.

Underlying this solution of the problem is the premise that our natural powers of cognition and will are taken over by God to produce supernatural effects, in virtue of an obedience potency that is strictly active. Our spiritual faculties are endowed with some potency mysteriously subject to the influence of an almighty power, which can activate it to operate in a way that is higher, more noble and absolutely not due to our nature—in a word, to effectuate in us indeliberate and vital acts that are intrinsically supernatural.

Much the same is explained to take place in the case of helping graces. They are said to consist in something very vital, i.e., something in which the mind and will of man vitally participate, and require neither a special divine influx over and above that received from the prevenient grace nor a new physical premotion from God. It is a motion because through it God moves a creature to action. It is a *pre*-motion because it logically precedes the action of the secondary cause, namely the exercise of its native activity. It is physical and not moral because it does not operate objectively by means of knowledge and attraction, but subjectively as a physical cause that flows into the faculty. In fact the two species of grace (*excitans* and *adjuvans*) are said to be really the same grace, only looked at from different view-points: the one preceding and the other assisting the free exercise of our wills.

In the Thomist explanation the essence of prevenient grace is found in some sort of movement or physical reality whose effect is the mental enlightenment and volitional impulse. There must be an antecedent supernatural help given to the faculties in order to enable them to act in a supernatural way. This elevation is strictly intrinsic to the faculties. The divine aid comes logically before the act which they produce. It is a physical entity, not vital, because it is not produced by the mind or will but only by God. It is not, as we say, in the intentional order because it does not move the faculties as an object to which they respond but as a physical impulse moving them to action.

Consistent with this theory, it is held that helping grace is also a non-vital reality which God infuses into the soul. The reality is a new physical premotion, divinely conferred in addition to the previous actual grace. This time the help is not to stimulate the will to action but to enable it to perform a free supernatural act.

The complex nuances involved in these speculations are considerable, as will be seen in a later, detailed analysis of the rival theories on the relation of grace and free will.

EXTERNAL GRACES

One of the most practical aspects of actual grace is the function of external graces in the spiritual life. Ascetical writers often describe the providential disposition of life with all its elements as a series of divine graces. They see all creation unified in this divine operation and consequently regard every creature, in its way, as a predestined means to lead men to their appointed end, that is, as a grace of God.[326] The order established by God, we are told, the good pleasure of God, the will of God, the action of God, grace—all are the same thing in this life. They are evidence of God laboring to make the soul like to Himself. Perfection is nothing else than the soul's faithful cooperation with this labor of God.

It is not the business of spiritual writers to offer subtle theological distinctions, not to explain in technical language the valid insights they give to their readers. Yet some clarification of this important phase of ascetical literature is necessary. It is certainly useful to understand what we mean when we say that all creatures have been made "for man to help him in attaining the end for which he was created," and thereby verify their claim to being somehow divine graces offered us on the road to heaven.

Although writers seldom distinguish between internal and external graces, but consider everything in some way as a grace of God, it is not difficult to trace such a distinction in their writings. In fact, precisely this distinction gives us the only sound basis for universalizing the concept of grace and applying the term, analogously, to all the other things on the face of the earth.

External grace in this context is every creature which is not an internal grace of God. It is called external because it is not internal in the strict sense of a special and direct illumination or inspiration that God directly produces in the human mind and will. Perhaps a better word

---

[326] *CCC* 358; cf. *Gaudium et Spes* 12§1; 24§3; 39§1.

would be "extrinsic" to distinguish such graces from the intrinsically supernatural lights and impulses we have previously analyzed. They may be internal experiences of the soul, in its spiritual or sensible powers; external experiences received through the bodily organs; persons or events that enter our lives, living or inanimate objects that affect us; words spoken or heard, ideas communicated or received; circumstances of time and place; in a word, no creature is excepted from the possible ambit of things which the divine Intelligence may intend to use as an instrument of our salvation.

In what sense are these myriad things graces? They are such primarily because the providence of God, in the existing supernatural order in which we live, is absolutely universal. As defined by the First Vatican Council, "by His providence God watches over and governs all the things that He made, reaching from end to end with might and disposing all things with gentleness. For all things are naked and open to His eyes, even those that are going to occur by the free action of creatures."[327] Put into ascetical terms, the divine order gives to all things, in favor of the soul which conforms to it, a supernatural and God-given value. Whatever this order imposes, whatever it comprehends, and all objects to which it extends, may become the instruments of holiness and the means of reaching God.

Furthermore the ordinary way that God infuses graces is through the instrumentality of external ones. We recall the words of St. Paul about the necessity of preaching. How will people believe, he asks, unless they have heard the Gospel taught? And how will they hear without someone to preach to them? The issue here is profound. For not unlike in the natural order, the mind is determined to act by some extrinsic object, supernaturally God has established innumerable extrinsic media, by which men are to be led to their eternal end.

---

[327] *DS* 3003; *CCC* 302.

Consequently, when a pious thought or a good impulse naturally arises from any of these sources, whether seen, or heard, or no matter how produced, God as it were interposes Himself in the process and then by a supernatural concursus evokes an internal actual grace. His entrance into the sequence raises an otherwise natural activity of mind or will to the salutary level of a means that leads to heavenly glory.

There is still another way in which external graces warrant the title of "grace," besides their instrumental function of leading *to* internal illuminations and inspirations from God. They are also the normal way *by* which these internal graces find expression or embodiment. After all, the internal graces are given for a purpose, which is to fructify an act. They are directed to having a man perform some good actions, whether interior, as in mental prayer, or exterior, as in the practice of fraternal charity. In either case the terminal effect is obviously not the internal grace itself but something beyond it, to which it gives rise. This something outside and beyond the internal supernatural light or impulse also partakes of the supernatural as the means by which strictly internal graces "take on flesh." The material aspect of what I do under a divine impulse may be quite natural—giving money to the poor or assisting a man with advice—but the soul of the action is more than natural, since it comes from the special operation of God.

Varieties and Forms

An exhaustive tabulation of the various types of external grace is impossible. They are too numerous and varied to allow strict classification, and too complex to describe except in the most generic way. Yet certain broad lines of emphasis appear regularly in ascetical literature, which goes back to the homilies of Origen and Augustine, and may be found in all the classic writers on the spiritual life.

As a general principle, the love of God transforms into grace everything which is good, and does not limit the transformation only to things that appear good to us. For divine love is present in all creatures, with the sole exception of those that are sinful and contrary to the law of God.

God uses temporal afflictions and adversities to convert and sanctify souls.[328] No matter how painful, sickness and physical suffering are in reality external graces, always intended as such for the one suffering and sometimes used by Him for the conversion and sanctification of others. We know from experience, however, that sickness and adversity often can be more easily accepted as coming from God than to recognize His gift in the negative conditions of mind and emotions: distaste for spiritual things, worry, anxiety, strong passions, or fears. No doubt these may be due partially to past negligence, but that is not the point. They are also species of grace. St. John of the Cross observed that just as God converts, reproves, and sanctifies ordinary people through temporal afflictions and trials so He normally converts to Himself, rebukes and leads to sanctity those on whom He has higher designs by means of spiritual trials and interior crosses that are many times more grievous than material or bodily pains.

In the same way, God uses the actions of other people as graces for our sanctification. Their ordinary words, conduct, and gestures are intended to produce supernatural effects in our souls. This is particularly hard to see where the actions are offensive and the offender is personally not wicked, and may even be quite virtuous. Hence an exclamation coined by the saints—"Blessed be the God of all things for sanctifying His elect through one another." Unless we look beyond the petty (or grave) offenses caused us by others, we shall not see their providential purpose of refining our souls and making us daily more fit to receive greater divine blessings.

---

[328] *CCC* 385, 1502.

It is of special value to see God operating in the persecution or perhaps criminal actions of others. He permits these things in order to draw good out of them. St. Paul's panegyric on the great believers of the Old Law—Noe, Abraham, Moses, Isaac, Jacob, and Joseph—is an application of this principle.[329] God tries His chosen servants by sending them trial and opposition. Their sanctification is determined by the measure of faith which recognizes in these human obstacles the workings of divine grace. This was the spirit in which David accepted the cursing of Semei, as a just punishment ordained by God for his spiritual welfare. St. Augustine tells us to "marvel at the way God uses even the malice of those who are wicked, in order to help and elevate those who are good."

The same with temptations. When they come from the devil, their diabolical intent is to destroy our souls. But from the viewpoint of God's permissive will, which never allows a man to be tried beyond his strength, they are true graces. Comparably the revolt of the passions or other signs of our fallen nature, no matter how strong, are so far from sinful that they are one of the main instruments of sanctification.[330]

Sins at least might seem to be excluded from the category of external graces. Evidently God does not want anyone to offend Him; and yet, without willing sin, He uses it as a most powerful means of drawing souls to Himself. The humility they engender and the self-depreciation they induce are the bedrock on which God intends to build. Speaking of Peter's denial of Christ, St. Augustine declared this was permitted to teach the apostle not to trust himself but to rely entirely on his Master. The experience he gained was a lesson for all of us on the relation between sin and the acquisition of virtue.

---

[329] Hebrews 11; *CCC* 164–65.
[330] *CCC* 2847.

Sanctifying Effect

The salutary purpose of external graces was familiar to the Fathers, and was explained by St. Thomas who recognized that God exercises a special providence over souls living in His friendship. It is special not only in the broad sense of God's solicitude for rational beings as distinct from His interest in all creatures, but in the very particular sense that persons in the state of grace have a claim to God's love and the promise of His care that no one else is assured. This was the basis for St. Paul's astounding statement that "for those who love God *all* things work together unto good, for those who, according to His purpose, are saints through His call."[331]

Though external graces are sanctifying in countless ways, we can reduce these modes to the three familiar ones of purification, illumination, and union with God; without implying that only these effects take place, that they occur in any particular sequence, or least of all that the terminal results can take place without the correlative presence of internal grace to purify, enlighten, and unite the soul with God.

A great deal of spiritual literature centers on the purifying aspect of external grace, achieved through detachment from creatures and stripping of self-love. Repeatedly the axiom is stated that "a person cannot be united with God, source of all purity, except through detachment from everything created" that tends to draw a man to himself and away from the Creator. The stress may be so great it may seem exaggerated or misplaced; yet properly understood, detachment is the *sine qua non* condition for sanctity.

The normal way that God effects detachment in souls is through suffering. He appears to measure it out according to the perfection He has in store and the degree of holiness to which He had destined a

---

[331] Romans 8:28; *CCC* 313, 395.

man. As a general rule, "suffering makes wicked souls miserable, but borne with fortitude it purifies souls that are good."[332] There is a more subtle difference in His way of acting with different persons. Those already advanced in the spiritual life, He is accustomed to despoil of spiritual gifts and sensible fervor, which in the saints may reach the "dark night of the soul." With less perfect individuals, He may deprive them of temporal possessions and secular goods in order to detach their hearts from this world.

Throughout Christian tradition we find the same basic theme: God purifies by suffering and trial. Not only are just men tried by affliction as gold is tried in the fire, but crosses and tribulations are said to be such great graces that generally sinners are not converted except through them, and good persons are not made perfect except by the same means.

Following the analogy used by Augustine, God is a compared to a doctor who administers bitter medicine to restore health to a soul and removes with the scalpel of suffering whatever stands in the way of spiritual progress. In those whom God loves, like a wise physician, He cuts away the tumor of self-confidence.

This law of purification is universal. It applies as well to the worldly minded as to the saintly; it affects temporal goods as well as spiritual attachments; and it is proportionately more intense as the degree of union with Himself to which God intends to raise a soul is greater. According to the proportion of its purity will also be the degree of enlightenment, illumination, and union with God—either more or less according to its quality of self-detachment. We may therefore conclude that the more God retrenches self-love through purifying trials, the more He bestows the supernatural.

External graces also enlighten the soul to recognize the will of God. We may look upon this manifestation of the divine will as the spiritual

---

[332] St. Augustine, "De Agone Christiano," *MPL* 40:295.

direction of God. One of the surest means of sanctification is to use whatever God, the supreme director of souls, places before us moment by moment, to either do or suffer. Souls who thus search for God's will find evidence everywhere of what He wants. They are directed by the intermittent actions of a thousand creatures, which serve, without study, as so many illuminating graces of instruction.

Consequently God leads us not only by the internal light He infuses in the mind but by all the events and circumstances of life. He "speaks" to us in the book we are reading, in the counsel given by a friend, in the misunderstanding that befalls us, in the success or failure we experience, in the passing trial we have. Too often people look upon these things as only a matter of chance, or caprice, or natural coincidence, forgetting that with God there is no chance; that His providence embraces every last detail of what ostensibly just "happens" in our lives.

The illuminating function of external grace is particularly useful when the obstacle to recognizing God's lesson is not that we mistake it for chance or coincidence, but fail to see His will because a certain effect was the result of sin, our own or someone else's. Yet there is divine pedagogy also, and emphatically, in the sinful actions of men.

Faith tells us that nothing happens unless the Omnipotent wills it to happen. He either permits it to happen, or He brings it about Himself. Therefore we may not doubt that God does well, or wants us to learn from the fact, even when He permits evil.

> He does not permit this except for a just reason, and all that is just is good. Although, therefore, what is evil, in so far as it is evil, is not good. Nevertheless it is well that not only good but also evil should exist. Were it not a good that evil things should also exist, the Omnipotent God would most certainly

not allow evil to be, since beyond doubt it is just as easy for Him not to allow what He does not will, as it is for Him to do what He wills. Unless we believe this, the very first sentence of our profession of faith is endangered, wherein we profess to believe in God the Father almighty. He is called almighty for no other reason than that He can do whatever He wills, and because the effectiveness of His almighty will cannot be thwarted by the will of any creature whatsoever.[333]

Unless we steel ourselves against the natural evidence to the contrary, we may fail to see the supernatural workings of Providence, whose purposes are often brought about through the sins and even malice of men. It was by the good will of the Father, working through the envy of the high priests and the cowardice of Pilate, that Jesus Christ was slain. The result was so beneficial that when Peter protested that this should not be allowed, he was called Satan by the soon to be slain Savior. We are told in the Book of Acts how earnestly the faithful begged Paul not to go on to Jerusalem, for fear he would suffer the evils foretold by a local prophet. Yet it was God's will that the apostle too should suffer for the preaching of Christ and prepare himself for martyrdom. He carried out His ulterior purpose not through the good intentions of the Christians but through the evil ones of the Jews. Both God and His enemies brought about the same effect; He through them for a good end, and they against Him with their evil designs.

The same thing occurs, on a lesser plane, in the lives of all men. The genius of faith is to see behind the veils of external (humanly mistaken or malicious) circumstances and recognize in them the hidden objectives of God.

---

[333] St. Augustine, *Enchiridion* 96; *CCC* 311–12.

Every situation of daily life, then, is somehow an expression of the divine will for us at that moment: of something to be done or avoided, accepted or refused, enjoyed or sacrificed, continued or abandoned, depending on the circumstances and conditioned by the dictates of right reason and faith.

On the same illuminative plane, external graces afford us a convenient way to learn by experimental knowledge of God's dealings with us, and give us what no books or spiritual direction could supply. In the realm of the spirit, real knowledge as distinct from notional cognition can be acquired only by action and suffering. No one understands God's mercy the way a forgiven sinner can, or the value of kindness as the man to whom some great favor was done, or the meaning of humility if he has never been humiliated.

An important element in this knowledge is the experience it gives of our weakness and imperfection in the face of trial and temptation. These occasions—external graces of tribulation—show us how impotent we are to do any good without the help of God. They teach us to turn to Him instead of depending on ourself. It is a hard lesson to learn, that our misery is the cause of the weaknesses we have, and that God permits them by His mercy. Without such realization we might never be cured of secret presumption and self-complacent pride. Naturally speaking we should scarcely understand that all the evil comes from ourselves, and all supernatural good from God. A thousand experiences are needed to help us acquire this twofold knowledge as an abiding habit; and the more deep-rooted the urge to self-complacency, the more necessary is the experiential cure.

The most important effect of external graces is the love of God which they develop in the soul, to which detachment and illumination are only contributing means. It is the common teaching of spiritual masters that awareness of the divine benefits is necessary to grow in the love of God. In St. Ignatius's words, a person is told to strive "for an intimate knowledge of the many blessings received, that, filled with gratitude for everything, I may in all things love and serve the Divine Majesty."[334] And according to St. Thomas, the first condition required to attain to perfect charity is "the recollection of God's benefits, since all that we have, in body and soul and external possessions, has come from Him. Consequently to love Him with a perfect heart, we must earnestly reflect on everything He has given to us."[335]

In the ordinary disposition of Providence, unless there is a previous consideration of God's goodness in my regard, I will not rise to that love of Him that is true friendship. At this point a whole panorama of prospects opens, to see that every good thing I possess, or satisfying experience I have, is a divine invitation to be recognized as a token of God's love. The number of these good things and pleasant satisfactions is past counting. They are a stream of benefits that impinge on my consciousness daily and many times a day. Yet each one is a quasi-sacramental sign of the mysterious reality which God need not have communicated outside Himself, yet chose to do so in the multitudinous ways we call creatures—beginning with myself and including every least blessing that crosses my path.

From gratitude we rise spontaneously to love the One from whom the benefits proceed. But then we go a step further. The creatures that enter our lives do not only foster divine love and lead us through knowledge to perfect charity, they are ready instruments for putting that charity into action.

The ultimate goal of external graces, therefore, is to have them serve as channels for the practice of the virtues to which Christian

---

[334] "Contemplation to Attain the Love of God", *Spiritual Exercises of St. Ignatius*, trans. Louis J. Puhl, S.J. (Chicago: Loyola Press, 1951), 233.

[335] St. Thomas Aquinas, "De Duobus Praeceptis Caritatis", *Opuscula Omnia* (Paris: P. Lethielleux, 1927), 4:420.

charity gives rise. They help us give expression to the sentiments that strictly interior graces inspire. The expression may take the form of laboring at our own sanctification, or of furthering the interests of the Church; it will always partake of some kind of charity for the neighbor which is the language of our love for God.

7

GRACE AND FREE WILL

God's loving care extends to all His creatures, with a special predilection for man. In keeping with His providence, which is the world-plan in the mind of God, we believe He is directing us at every moment to our ultimate destiny in the possession of him for eternity.

But does He seriously desire all men to reach heaven? What of the evident difficulties that everyone experiences in the service of God and what seem to be insurmountable obstacles to salvation for many people? Though we answer in the affirmative,[336] we know the issue is filled with mystery and not fully soluble by human speculation. We do not know why some people will not realize the goal of their existence in spite of the fact that God wants all mankind to be saved.

We know that somehow man's destiny involves two kinds of freedom: his own and that of God. In examining the dialectic between the two, we keep in mind that from the divine side God "will have all men to be saved and come to the knowledge of truth," but from man's side there is power to follow or resist the loving intentions of God.

UNIVERSAL SALVIFIC WILL OF GOD

Our immediate purpose is to examine whether and in what sense God offers ample grace of salvation to all persons who have reached the age of reason, on whose acceptance or rejection depends their heavenly lot. However, an antecedent problem must first be cleared,

[336] *CCC* 74.

regarding God's purposes towards the millions of children who die before reaching mental maturity and without the saving waters of Baptism. It is common teaching in Catholic theology that the divine salvific will includes also infants, even though they are not the direct object of actual grace offered to them for cooperation.

Infants

If we ask how God may be said to desire the salvation, of infants, the explanation must be that He offers them the possibility of justification by wanting them to be baptized. This is beyond question since He instituted the sacrament of regeneration as the necessary means of salvation for all people, and prescribed its reception as the channel of sanctifying grace. Since He wants the merits of Christ to be applied to all infants through baptism of water (or blood),[337] God surely desires all of them to enter heaven.

Many children die without Baptism, which implies that the divine salvific will towards them is not absolute but conditional; it depends on a variety of secondary causes that can either negatively or positively stand in the way of a child's being baptized. Consequent on the divine prevision of these factors, whether physical or free, which culpably or inculpably prevent Baptism, God does not will their salvation; His salvific will in their favor is antecedent to the foreknowledge of such obstacles. A minority school holds that no child dies without Baptism except through someone's negligence or fault; certainly the element of culpability need not be found in those immediately responsible for a child's welfare. Once we get into the huge arena of the non-Christian world with its high rates of infant mortality, the question of assigning guilt becomes impossible, except on the broadest and least tangible terms.

---

[337] *CCC* 1250.

Might not God have given the children who die without Baptism some other means of obtaining sanctifying grace, which would not be dependent on the conduct of adults? He might have. He was not obligated to do so. And children are not responsible for their conduct. The supernatural life of grace is gratuitous by definition, and when adults die without sanctifying grace, they suffer positive eternal punishments. Infants are merely deprived of a higher kind of beatitude but without undergoing any pain. "They are unaware of their deprivation and therefore experience no sorrow on that account."[338]

Catholics believe as a matter of faith that after the Gospel has been promulgated Baptism is the unique remedy of original sin, necessary for the salvation of infants and adults by a necessity of means, i.e., strict necessity determined by the will of Christ.[339] No one can be saved unless he receives this sacrament in reality or desire.[340] The solemn promulgation of the New Law was made on Pentecost Sunday the days after the Ascension of the Lord. However it is still an open question whether the Gospel has been sufficiently diffused throughout the world to make the law absolutely binding on all members of the human race.

Most theologians believe that sufficient diffusion has been made to invoke the general law, which then binds everyone in Christian and non-Christian lands. The few who think otherwise appeal to the facts of history and point out how oblivious of Christian revelation are the peoples of China, India, and Japan, except for a small fraction who have had the Gospel preached to them.

If Christian revelation has not yet been fully diffused, a "sacrament of nature" is postulated as a substitute. This so-called sacrament is the kind of *remedium naturae* we attribute to the Old Law for the Gentiles who had not received the Mosaic Covenant. It might be a sensible

---

[338] St. Thomas, *De Malo*, 5, 3; *CCC* 1261.
[339] *CCC* 1257.
[340] *CCC* 1258–59.

sign, some sort of religious rite by which parents (or others) manifest their faith in God and their desire of salvation for the child. The ritual could be an act of oblation, an invocation, a blessing or purification.

Similar, and less satisfactory, theories have been formed to avoid the painful consequences of saying that all children, whether in Christian countries or not, must be baptized to obtain sanctifying grace. Some have proposed the illumination theory, according to which dying children receive a sudden enlightenment that enables them to receive Baptism of desire by making an act of perfect love. The classic exponent of another theory was Cajetan (1469–1534), who said that infants dying in the mother's womb may be justified by the prayers of the parents. A blessing of the unborn child in the name of the Trinity, he thought, would secure salvation. Disapproved at the Council of Trent, the opinion was ordered by St. Pius V to be expunged from the writings of Cajetan.

Another effort was the opinion that when children die before the age of reason, they suffer a type of martyrdom and are saved in virtue of this "Baptism of Blood," because their death is a faint imitation of the passion of Christ. This theory was condemned by a Roman decree in 1898, which called it "a bold and temerarious manner of speaking." A compromise opinion would have it that while children do not, indeed, receive sanctifying grace if they die before Baptism of water, the original sin on their souls is somehow removed at death and their condition in eternity is that of our first parents before the fall, in the state of innocence and corresponding happiness. While more ingenious than probable, the theory is not untenable since it does not question the necessity of Baptism for infants to attain the beatific vision.

The accepted teaching has been stated by Pius XII, when he declared that a child receives the supernatural life "When it is baptized." He explained that "under the present economy there is no other way of

giving this life to the child who is still without the use of reason. The
state of grace at the moment of death is absolutely necessary for salvation; without it, no one can attain to supernatural happiness, the beatific
vision of God. In the case of a grown-up person, an act of love may
suffice for obtaining sanctifying grace and making up for the lack of
Baptism. To the child still unborn or the child just born this path is not
open."[341] Accordingly the cooperation of human freedom with divine
grace for infants must be a vicarious act on the part of adults whose
faith in the necessity of Baptism prompts them to confer the sacrament
of regeneration on a physically helpless child.

Sinners

We have already seen that God is solicitous for the salvation of
those in His friendship, surrounding them with helps of all kinds to
sustain their supernatural life, tiding them over difficulties, and finally
(provided they do their part) giving them the gift of final perseverance.

At first sight it would seem that people living in personal mortal sin
would be excluded from a comparable salutary providence. We read in
Scripture how God blinds the sinner and hardens the heart of those
who despise His law. On the other hand, all that we know of God's
mercy assures us that the Lord does not withdraw His grace
completely even from the most obdurate. When He is said to confirm
the evil man in his ways, the fault lies always with the sinner, who
obstinately resists the call of grace. No doubt the greater and stronger
graces are withheld from those who persistently reject the divine
mercy, as a punishment for their malice—but even they are not
completely deprived of all supernatural aid.

Time and again in the Bible, sinners are urged by God to repent and
are assured of His pardon. "As I live, says the Lord God, I desire not

---

[341] Pius XII, *Acta Apostolicae Sedis*, 43 (1952), 84.

the death of the wicked, but that he should turn from his way and live."[342] And according to St. Peter, "The Lord does not delay in His promises, but for your sake is long-suffering, not wishing that any should perish, but that all should turn to repentance."[343] The parables of the prodigal son, the Good Shepherd, the Pharisee and publican; the story of Mary Magdalen and the good thief; in fact the whole message of Christ's life on earth is a thematic affirmation that no sinner, no matter how abandoned by human calculations, is ever truly abandoned by God.

Christian tradition clearly distinguishes between ordinary sinners and the obdurate. The former are living in grave sin but also aware of their condition and have some desire to get out of this state; while the latter have become inured to estrangement from God, are oblivious of their plight and only with the greatest difficulty could be recalled back to virtue. Yet even in these extreme cases, the situation is not hopeless and grace is still available. "God gave them over to a reprobate mind," St. Augustine quotes the Scriptures, "for such is the blindness of the mind. Whosoever is given over to it is shut out from the interior light of God; but not wholly as yet, while he is still in this life. For their is an 'outer darkness,' which is understood to belong rather to the day of judgment; so that only he is entirely without God who, while there is time, refuses correction."[344]

The kind of actual grace that sinners are offered is at least remotely sufficient to bring them justification. It would be proximately sufficient if the internal light or inspiration directly and without any other means led the sinner to make his peace with God. Persons in grave sin can expect remotely sufficient grace from God, because they are urged by supernatural impulse to pray or perform some equivalent action

---

[342] Ezechiel 33:11; also Wisdom 11:24.
[343] 2 Peter 3:9; also 1 Timothy 4:10 and 1 John 2:2; *CCC* 1037.
[344] St. Augustine, *Enarrationes in Psalmos*, 6, 8; *CCC* 1859.

that at least implicitly calls upon the divine help. Fidelity to this primary impulse, which Augustine called the "initial or little grace," will insure the "great grace" that brings infusion of supernatural life.

Two principles underlie this assurance, and both derive from the justice and goodness of God. He does not enjoin impossibilities, but in His injunctions counsels us both to do what we can and to beg His assistance in what we cannot do. Every divine law, we may be sure, carries with it the grace by which it may be observed.

Of course we have the sobering reminder that God may permit a man to be tempted to the limit of his powers. He may do this to prove to us our deficiency. Yet He always gives the grace to pray for the help to observe what, without such prayer, would be above endurance. "When man has not sufficient strength to overcome temptation, he has at least the common grace of prayer to obtain the additional help that he needs."[345] St. Bernard asked, "Who are we, or what strength have we? But God wished this to make us see our limitations and that we had no other aid, in order that we should run to His mercy with all humility."[346]

It is certain that God is less generous with those estranged from Him than with those in His love. But even the worst sinners are not cut off from His saving mercy. They also receive the inspiration to pray and ask for the grace that would put them back into divine friendship. Some rigorists have held that eventually God withdraws this indirect help altogether from people who are obdurate in their vice. The accepted teaching is more lenient. No matter how sunk in bad habits or far from the practice of virtue, everyone receives—at least now and then— enough grace to be converted. It may be on the occasion of some personal tragedy, like the death of a loved one, or on being the object

---

[345] St. Alphonsus Liguori, *Exposition and Defence of the Faith* (Dublin: J. Duffy, 1846), 6:113.

[346] St. Bernard, *Lenten Sermons*, 5.

of an act of heroic generosity, that the urge to call upon God occurs. If the sinner responds, God will restore the soul to spiritual life.

The main purpose of the sacrament of Penance is to afford sinners the opportunity to be reinstated in grace. Christ said that He came to call sinners to repentance, and He instituted a sacrament to continue His work of mercy. When the Albigenses claimed the contrary, the Lateran Council decreed that "if after receiving Baptism, anyone shall fall into sin, he can always be restored by true contrition."[347] The Council of Trent compared the divine stimulus to a sharp excitation. "Those who have received the grace of justification but have lost it through sin can be justified again when, awakened by God, they make the effort to regain through the sacrament of Penance and by the merit of Christ the grace they have lost."[348]

Yet not only members of the household of the faith but all men, whether in the Christian tradition or not, are given sufficient light and inspiration to find their way to God after they had strayed from His law. As everyone is obligated to trust in God's mercy and hope in His forgiveness, so no one is denied the promise of divine grace to return "to His Father's house."

Unbelievers

The historical origins of Catholic teaching on God's providence regarding unbelievers stem from the Reformation. Luther and especially Calvin were adamant towards the unregenerate, which followed logically from their concept of selective predestination of some for heaven and of others for hell.

> We call predestination God's eternal decree, by which He determined with Himself what He willed to become of each

---

[347] *DS* 682; *CCC* 1428; cf. *Lumen Gentium* 8§3.
[348] *DS* 1542; *CCC* 1468.

man. For all are not created in equal condition; rather eternal life is foreordained for some, eternal damnation for others. Therefore as any man has been created to one or the other of these ends, we speak of him as predestined to life or to death.

As Scripture clearly shows, we say that God once established by His eternal and unchangeable plan those whom He long before determined once and for all to receive into salvation, and those who, on the other hand, He would devote to destruction. We assert that, with respect to the elect, this plan was founded upon His freely given mercy, without regard to human worth; but by His just and irreprehensible but incomprehensible judgment He has barred the door of life to those whom He has given over to damnation.

Now among the elect we regard the call as a testimony of election. Then we hold justification another sign of its manifestation, until they come into the glory in which the fulfillment of the election lies. But as the Lord seals His elect by call and justification, so, by shutting off the reprobate from knowledge of His name and from the sanctification of His Spirit, He, as it were, reveals by these marks what sort of judgment awaits them.[349]

According to Reformed theology, therefore, those whom God foreordained for damnation never came to the faith because He never gave them the first grace of invitation to believe in His name. He "shuts them off" from revelation and thus marks them already in this life as predestined to be lost.

The Jansenists accepted this version of God's salvific will and, without changing any of the essentials, pushed its implications to their limit. "It is Semi-Pelagian," Jansenius professed, "to say that Christ

---

[349] Calvin, *Institutes,* III, 21, 5–7.

died or shed His blood for all men without exception."[350] His followers were later censured for saying the same thing in different words.

> Christ gave Himself for us as an oblation to God, not for the elect alone, but for all and only the faithful.
>
> Pagans, Jews, heretics and others of the same kind receive no influence whatsoever from Jesus Christ. You may therefore rightly conclude that they have nothing but a bare and helpless will without any sufficient grace.[351]

Pasquier Quesnel refined the doctrine to its climax. "Faith," he claimed, is the first grace and the fountain head of all graces. There are no graces given except through faith."[352] So absolute is God's antecedent will against those to be damned that they receive no grace whatever, whereas men predestined to glory are first led to faith and through faith to all the riches of divine love.

Besides the Church's censure of Jansenism, the Catholic mind on God's providence towards unbelievers was expressed at length in two documents of Pius IX, both directed to meet the crisis of indifferentism which claimed that one religion is as good as another, and that a man can be saved if he just follows the dictates of reason with no concern for faith in a supernatural revelation.

The day after his solemn definition of the Immaculate Conception, Pius IX gave an allocution to the several hundred bishops who had assembled in Rome for the occasion. After exhorting them to oppose the teaching of those who claim that human reason can penetrate the mysteries of God, he admitted that another error was threatening the welfare of Christians. Its thesis was that no connection with revealed

---

[350] *DS* 2005; *CCC* 74; cf. *Dei Verbum* 7.
[351] *DS* 2304–5.
[352] *DS* 2426–27.

truth is necessary for salvation, but only a purely natural form of religion. After refuting this naturalism, he went on to explain that we may not establish limits to the divine mercy but "hold it as certain that those who labor in ignorance of the true religion, if that be invincible, will never be charged with any guilt on this account before the eyes of the Lord."[353]

Against the background of this possibility, that people who are invincibly ignorant of the true faith can be saved, the Pope published a second statement which explicitly declared the operation of grace among those who are unbelievers by the standards of Judaeo-Christianity.

> Those who labor in invincible ignorance of our most holy religion and who, carefully observing the natural law and its precepts, which God has inscribed in the hearts of all, and being ready to obey God, live an honest and upright life can, through the working of the divine light and grace, attain eternal life, since God, who clearly sees, inspects and knows the minds, intentions, thoughts and habits of all, will, by reason of His supreme goodness, never allow anyone who has not the guilt of wilful sin to be punished by eternal sufferings.[354]

The unbelievers of whom the Pontiff spoke and whom we are inquiring are negative infidels because their unbelief is not due to a culpable rejection of the true faith. A preferable term might be "a-fidelity," since infidelity implies a culpable refusal to believe. This corresponds to what patristic tradition called perfidy or positive, not merely negative, unbelief.

---

[353] *DS* 1646. See *Sources of Catholic Dogma* (Fitzwilliam, NH: Loreto Publications, 2002). Also cf. *Lumen Gentium* 16; cf. *DS* 3866–72 (for English translation of latter, see *Companion to the Catechism of the Catholic Church* (San Francisco: Ignatius Press, 1994), 360–62.

[354] *DS* 2866.

Since people in this condition represent the majority of mankind, it is more than academically important to examine how they can be saved. The fact is admitted in Catholic theology, but the full explanation is still in dispute. Ultimately the problem is how such persons acquire the supernatural faith without which no one can be justified. A broad range of theories has been stimulated by the legitimate concern for the destiny of millions of these nominal pagans.

One theory argues that only habitual but not actual faith is necessary for adults to be saved. If a man does what he can to follow his conscience, God will give him the infused virtue of faith and dispense with the need of also actually believing in supernaturally revealed truths. But this is pure speculation and quite contrary to Christian tradition, since to reach heaven "the act of faith as well as habitual faith is necessary for those who can exercise their free will."[355]

Cardinal Billot also evaded the problem by suggesting that infidels may be rational enough on the lower level of secular knowledge, but they are moral infants on the higher plane of religious culture. They are consequently not responsible for their actions and God will treat them as children, with the prospect of going to a species of limbo after death. Not many authors are sympathetic with this solution, mainly because it seems to contradict the known moral development of non-Christian peoples and raise a possible exception to the status of a normal occurrence.

A daring suggestion would have God accept the pseudorevelation of a false deity as the equivalent of the true faith, and infuse sanctifying grace as a result. But that idea is untenable because it allows God to confer justification on the strength of two objective errors: intellectual assent on the word of a legendary god, and belief in the attributes of a deity who does not exist.

---

[355] St. Thomas Aquinas, III *Sententiarum,* 25, 2, 1.

The most widely held solution of where the infidels get their faith begins with the established fact of a primitive revelation at the very dawn of history. Although heavily obscured in the centuries of transmission, this primordial speaking of God to the human family has been sufficiently diffused and substantially preserved throughout the world to become the basis of religious faith, distinct from the propagation of Judaism and Christianity.

We speculate as to when and how God gives the first actual grace to such an infidel, which, if he accepts, will lead him to the "great grace" of justification. Some say he receives the initial impulse shortly after reaching the age of reason; others delay the gift to later in life. Its form might be almost any inspiration to acknowledge God and one's dependence upon Him, with a corresponding desire to invoke His aid. If he cooperates with this "beginning of salvation," he will receive further related impulses until he receives the gift of salutary faith—believing at least the minimum truths necessary for salvation as revealed by the word of God. Acts of faith will lead to hope, and hope to charity, with the infusion of sanctifying grace if an act of perfect love is made.

PROCESS OF JUSTIFICATION

Catholics take for granted that for an adult to be justified he should personally contribute to the process. Basic to his contribution is the belief in certain truths of revelation on which he builds the structure of his faith and without which justification is impossible. Until the Reformation no one seriously questioned these principles. In the words of St. Augustine, "He who made you will not justify you without you. He therefore made you unknowing, but He justifies you willing."[356]

Augustine's faithful disciple St. Fulgentius was equally explicit. "Faith," he wrote, "is the foundation of all good. It is the beginning of

---

[356] St. Augustine, "Sermo 169," *MPL* 38:923; *CCC* 1847.

human salvation, and without it no one can obtain a place among the children of God, because without it no one can obtain the grace of justification in this world or possess eternal life in the next."[357] What Fulgentius meant by faith is clear from his commentary on the Creed, which follows this prologue.

With the advent of Protestantism, however, a new concept arose of how we become justified. Since human nature was said to be completely deprived of its spiritual powers for good, nothing a man could do prior to justification would affect his relationship with God. A composite statement of this doctrine was framed in the Formula of Concord, originally written in 1576 and published at Dresden in 1580. Its position is clear. Man is unable to contribute anything to his regeneration.

> The understanding and reason of man in spiritual things are wholly blind, and can understand nothing by their proper powers. We believe, teach, and confess that the yet unregenerate will of man is not only averse from God, but has become even hostile to God, so that it only wishes and desires those things, and is delighted with them, which are evil and opposite to the divine will.
>
> We repudiate, therefore, the teaching that, although unregenerate, man, in respect of free-will, is indeed, antecedently to his regeneration, too infirm to make a beginning of his own conversion, and by his own powers to convert himself to God, and obey the law of God with all his heart; yet if the Holy Spirit, by the preaching of the word, shall have made a beginning, and offered His grace in the word of man, that then man, by his own proper and natural powers, can, as it were, give some assistance and co-operation, though it be but slight,

---

[357] St. Fulgentius, "De Fide, ad Petrum," *MPL* 65:671.

infirm, and languid, towards his conversion, and can apply and prepare himself unto grace, apprehend it, embrace it, and believe the Gospel.[358]

Negatively, then, man cannot offer anything to the oncoming grace of God, to meet it with his untrammeled will and thus, together with grace, predispose himself for conversion. Positively, though, there is something whereby he apprehends his justification, in the sense of recognizing God's infinite mercy. This absolute trust in the merits of Christ and the confidence that they are applied to him is the fiducial faith which alone justifies. "It is a great thing," said Luther, "to hold and believe in sincere faith that my sins are forgiven and that through such faith I am righteous before God."[359]

Concretely fiducial faith is the answer to man's tortuous quest for peace of soul. The righteousness of Christ, which I lay hold of and trust has been imputed to me, with no works or deeds on my part, is "our whole being." The fundamental postulate of this theory is the familiar Reformation concept of conversion by grace alone (*sola gratia*). Modern confessional Lutherans use two terms to describe those who teach any kind of human cooperation in conversion; they call them Semi-Pelagian or synergistic (*syn,* together, and *ergon,* work) and spare no effort to expose what they consider hostile to the Scriptures. "Synergism of all shades turns the Biblical doctrine of justification by faith into the Roman, the pagan, doctrine of work-righteousness, even though the term *sole fide* be retained. Luther was right in declaring that Erasmus, the champion of the *liberum arbitrium* (or the *facultas applicandi se ad gratiam*), was defending the very foundation of the Papacy."[360]

---

[358] *Formula of Concord,* art. 2.
[359] Luther, *Werke,* Vol. XIII, 2495.
[360] Franz Pieper, *Christian Dogmatics* (St. Louis: Concordia Pub. House, 1950), 2:509.

If feeling on the subject can run so high in the twentieth century, it must have been higher in the sixteenth. It was. And that is why the Council of Trent devoted large sections of its decree on justification to this single topic, stressing three elements impugned by the Reformers: that adults must somehow vitally prepare themselves for the grace of conversion, that their preparation includes real dogmatic faith (assent of mind to revealed truths), along with other acts of the will under the impulse of grace, and that the fiducial faith on which Luther and his confreres placed so much emphasis was inadequate of itself to restore the soul to divine friendship.

Trent went to the heart of the issue by focusing attention on the will and insisting that the volitional faculty was not inert but quite capable of collaborating with grace. It censured those who said that "the free will of man, moved and awakened by God, in no way cooperates with the awakening call of God by an assent by which man disposes and prepares himself to get the grace of justification; and that man cannot dissent, if he wishes, but, like an object without life, he does nothing at all and is merely passive."[361]

The actual method by which a man turns from sin to God was outlined in a lucid paragraph that summarizes the whole justification process, with its inclusive accent on grace from the side of God and voluntary effort from the side of man.

> Adults are disposed for justification in this way. Awakened and assisted by divine grace, they conceive faith from hearing and they are freely led to God. They believe that the divine revelation and promises are true, especially that the unjustified man is justified by God's grace "through the redemption which is in Christ Jesus." Next, they know that they are sinners; and,

---

[361] *DS* 1554; *CCC* 1993.

by turning from a salutary fear of divine justice to a consideration of God's mercy, they are encouraged to hope, confident that God will be propitious to them for Christ's sake. They begin to love God as the source of all justice and are thereby moved by a sort of hatred and detestation for sin, that is, by the penance that must be done before Baptism. Finally, they determine to receive Baptism, begin a new life, and keep the divine commandments.[362]

It is immediately apparent that the start of justification is belief in God's revealed word or, as Trent has it, "faith is the beginning of man's salvation, the foundation and source of all justification, without which it is impossible to please God and to be counted as His sons."[363] For unless a man first believes with the mind, he cannot logically trust and still less love with the will. This antecedent acceptance of revelation is the *sine qua non* condition for that hope in the divine promises which the Reformers stressed to an extreme.

One remarkable feature of Trent's handling of fiducial faith is that it never questioned the need for confidence in the divine goodness. Undoubtedly a sinner must approach the throne of mercy with implicit hope that God will forgive his sins; but first comes faith, which, according to St. Paul, is "the substance of things to be hoped for." Yet even faith and hope alone are not enough; they must be supported by sorrow and animated by charity to fructify in justification. What may not be held is that "justifying faith is nothing else than confidence that divine Mercy remits sins for Christ's sake, or that it is confidence alone which justifies us."[364] This is tantamount to claiming that man has nothing of his own which can be offered to God to dispose himself for conversion.

---

[362] *DS* 1526.
[363] *DS* 1532.
[364] *DS* 1562.

It also denies what the Scriptures are eloquent in affirming. God wants the sinner to turn to Him in a voluntary acknowledgment of his guilt and a readiness to do penance for the sins of the past.

SUFFICIENT GRACE

Closely associated with the idea of fiducial faith as the unique source of justification was the Reformation theory on sufficient grace. In the system of Luther and Calvin all grace was intrinsically efficacious, that is, it never failed of its effect but always produced the results intended by God. This means that man, for his part, is too weak (in fact impotent) either to cooperate and merit or to resist the divine impulses received in the soul. And this leaves no alternative but that God on His part has foreordained some for heaven, to whom only efficacious grace would be given, and others for hell, on whom no real graces are conferred.

As with justification, the Council of Trent spelled out the existence of actual graces that are truly and yet purely sufficient to perform salutary acts. Their true sufficiency is evident from the fact that "no one should say it is impossible for the just man to keep the commandments of God," because "God does not command the impossible; but when He commands, He cautions you to do what you can, and also to pray for what you cannot do." His providence is unfailing, "for God does not abandon those who have been justified by His grace, unless they abandon Him first."[365] Conversely, however, people are liable to sin, and not only through infidelity. "The grace of justification, once received, is lost not only by unbelief, which causes the loss of faith, but also by any other mortal sin, even though faith is not lost."[366]

The same set of correlatives pertains to people who are not in the state of grace. It cannot be said that "the free will of man, moved and

---

[365] *DS* 1536.
[366] *DS* 1544.

awakened by God, in no way cooperates with the awakening call of God," as though "man cannot dissent if he wishes," and refuse to cooperate with the divine invitation.[367]

Accordingly help is certainly given by God, either to persevere in divine friendship or to obtain it. Therefore the grace received is truly sufficient. On the other hand, in both cases a man may turn his back on the help proffered and either lose justification or fail to reach it, in which case the grace was purely sufficient and not efficacious.

Jansenius followed in the wake of Reformation thought. The first of his five basic propositions stated that "there are some of God's commandments that just men cannot observe with the powers they have in their present state, even if they wish and strive to observe them; nor do men have the grace which would make their observance possible."[368] This is a diplomatic way of saying that when a man sins he did not have truly sufficient grace. Then the Bishop of Ypres went a step further. "In the state of fallen nature," which is our present lot, "internal grace is never resisted."[369] Again a euphemism for claiming that all grace is efficacious.

In condemning Jansenius, the Church revindicated the existence of divine aid which God seriously intends man to cooperate with and produce salutary acts while giving us free will to reject and consequently render sterile God's offer. Of course God foresees that the benefit offered will be spurned, but that is clearly not His purpose in conferring the gift. He really wants it to be received and fructify in use. We also admit that God might have given an efficacious grace with which the same man would have cooperated; but the fact that He did not grant the greater benefit does not prove that the grace offered was not a true gift and was so intended by God.

---

[367] *DS* 1554; *CCC* 1993, 2002.
[368] *DS* 2001.
[369] *DS* 2002.

Behind the existence of purely sufficient grace stands the reality of human freedom. Deny freedom while admitting some kind of special divine help and grace becomes invariably efficacious. Both the Reformers and Jansenius had only necessitating grace, although in somewhat different ways. With Luther and Calvin, grace was never resisted because man's freedom was extinguished in spiritual matters. He was physically incapacitated either to reject or (freely) to cooperate and thereby merit. With Jansenius, free will was so weakened that concupiscence invariably dominated, unless grace came along. When it did, there was no resistance because of moral impotence to do anything but follow the lead of the infused "conquering delight."

EFFICACIOUS GRACE

The subject of efficacious grace is so involved, that some preliminary clarification of terms seems necessary to avoid further complicating what historically is one of the most vexatious areas of theology. Efficacious grace may be understood in a popular or in a technical sense. Popularly conceived, all grace is efficacious because it has the power (*virtus*) to procure a given effect, which is to terminate in a freely placed, salutary action. In this way even purely sufficient graces are efficacious, since otherwise they would not deserve to be considered grace.

In a more restricted sense, however, grace is efficacious in what theologians call first act (*actu primo*) or in second act (*actu secundo*). There is nothing mysterious about the distinction. It is better to reverse the sequence and begin with graces that are efficacious in second act, which means insofar as they actually flow into salutary acts. In other words, when the grace de facto obtains salutary consent from a man's will, it is said to be consequent upon freedom and efficacious in second act.

But that is not the only kind of efficacy they enjoy. Graces may also be efficacious because they will infallibly produce salutary acts, so that their efficacy is prior to the consent of the will. This kind of grace is said to be efficacious in first act, and is the focus of our discussion.

If we scrutinize the efficacy we find it can be equated with a certain kind of infallibility. Before a man consents to a grace which God sends him, it had a threefold infallible connection with the salutary act that was produced. Objectively it is true that this grace would produce this salutary action; knowledgeably God infallibly foresaw that this grace would produce this given act; and affectively God freely willed to give this grace, which He also foreknew would have this salutary effect.

This triple infallibility is indispensable to understand God's salvific will. On the first level it means that efficacious grace is infallibly connected with a forthcoming consent of the human will; in terms of knowability it is the assured and unthwartable instrument in the hands of the Creator's goodness towards His creatures, on whom He confers these favors of benevolence. It should be noted that this is no mere possible contingency. It is a condition that results from an actual decree of God, by which He chooses out of a multitude of gifts that He might bestow an efficacious grace instead of one that would have been inefficacious.

Notwithstanding the infallibility prior to consent, an efficacious grace does not take away internal liberty. We are not compelled to accept it. And although a deep mystery shrouds the explanation of how this is possible, the fact is absolutely certain. Indeed it was exactly on the crucial problem of how to safeguard human freedom, while admitting antecedent certitude of consent in the knowledge of God, that conflicting theories of efficacious grace arose in Catholic theology.

As early as Pelagian times, the Church declared that while "God is the author of all good desires and deeds, of all efforts and virtues, with which from the beginning of faith man tends to God," nevertheless "free will is not destroyed by this help and strength from God, but is freed; so that from darkness it is brought to light, from evil to good, from sickness to health, from ignorance to wisdom."[370] Centuries later the same affirmation of man's liberty under the influence of grace was made to meet the challenge of the Reformers and Jansenists.

Yet, along with our liberty to consent is always the prior infallibility that such consent will be given. St. Augustine strenuously defended human liberty, observing that "the freedom of the will is not taken away, because it is helped; but it is helped because not taken away."[371] But against the Pelagians his accent was on the infallible certainty that comes from the eternal divine decrees. "If the sacred Scriptures are carefully examined," he said, "they show that the wills of men are to such an extent in the power of God that He makes them turn where He wants and when He wants."[372]

St. Augustine's teaching was the common possession of the Fathers, and found expression in all the major pronouncements of the Church. "God so acts in us that we both will and do what He wills," was directed at the Pelagians.[373] The same insistence was made when the ascetical Semi-Pelagians questioned man's complete dependence on God, antecedent to the first whisperings of grace.

> If anyone argues that God awaits our will before cleansing us from sin, but does not profess that even the desire to be cleansed is accomplished through the infusion and workings of the Holy Spirit, he opposes the Holy Spirit speaking through Solomon, "The will is prepared by the Lord" (Proverbs 8:35). He also opposes the apostle's salutary message, "It is God who

---

[370] *DS* 248.
[371] St. Augustine, "Epistola 157," *MPL* 33:677; *CCC* 1742.
[372] St. Augustine, *Treatise on Grace and Free Will*, 41; *CCC* 155, 1949, 2022.
[373] *DS* 248.

of His good pleasure works in you both the will and performance" (Philippians 2:13).[374]

Both elements are therefore kept intact in the Catholic system. For
it is inconceivable that grace, which is bestowed to perfect man's
nature, should destroy that nature by denying the freedom of will that
is connatural to an intellectual being. Whatever subtleties later entered
the controversy about efficacious grace, Catholics were at one in
believing that human liberty exists and is not, as Luther said, a mere
fiction, and that God is the ultimate master of man's destiny through
the efficacious graces He confers according to His eternal decrees. In
the relative stress on either truth arose different schools of thought
within the Church, yet never a doubt that "God certainly wishes all
men to be saved and to come to the knowledge of the truth, but not in
such a way that as to take away from them their free will."[375] Grace
without freedom would make us pawns of a blind Fate, and freedom
without grace would erase the supernatural order and remove God
from the providential care of His own creatures.

---

[374] *DS* 374; *CCC* 308.
[375] St. Augustine, *The Spirit and the Letter,* 58.

8

ANALYSIS OF EFFICACIOUS GRACE

In order to appreciate the meaning and importance of the celebrated controversy about efficacious grace, we must see its beginnings in their historical work. Apart from the circumstances to which it gave rise, the centuries-old discussion between two major religious orders in the Church might well seem to be "wrangling about a theological subtlety." If the subject under dispute was subtle, the issue at stake was far from useless. In fact on its clarification depended the substance of the Catholic faith.

Commentators on the disputation *De Auxiliis* sometimes underrate the significance of the problem by considering it only a domestic argument with no relevance to the Christian life. It is highly relevant, and the early disputants were not "wanting in a sense of humor" for taking too seriously what should have been an academic debate.

HISTORY OF THE QUESTION

The origins of the issue go back to early Reformation times, when the original Reformers revised the traditional concept of the supernatural to proclaim a new type of grace which supplied for the inherent freedom that man was said to have lost with the fall of Adam. The Council of Trent took cognizance of this theory and laid heavy stress on the fact that, in spite of his normal weakness, man's nature remains substantially sound; that grace neither substitutes anything for liberty nor does it negate autonomous human choice.

In the spirit of Trent, St. Ignatius Loyola (1491–1556) drafted his Rules for Thinking with the Church, which he incorporated into the Spiritual Exercises as a ready norm for giving retreats and directing the consciences of the faithful. Three of these eighteen norms of Catholic orthodoxy deal expressly with the relation of grace and free will, and became the *vademecum* for his followers in the Society of Jesus.

> We should not make it a habit to speak much of predestination. If somehow at times it comes to be spoken of, it must be done in such a way that the people are not led into error. They are sometimes misled, so they say, "Whether I shall be saved or lost, has already been determined, and this cannot be changed whether my actions are good or bad." So they become indolent and neglect works that are conducive to the salvation or spiritual progress of their souls.

> In the same way, caution is necessary lest by much talk about faith and much insistence on it without any distinctions or explanations, occasion be given to the people, whether before or after they have faith informed by charity, to become slothful and lazy in good works.

> Likewise we ought not to speak of grace at such length and with such emphasis that the poison of doing away with liberty is engendered.

> Hence, as far as possible with the help of God, one may speak of faith and grace that the Divine Majesty may be praised. But let it not be done in such a way, above all in times which are as dangerous as ours, that works and free will suffer harm, or that they are considered of no value.[376]

---

[376] St. Ignatius Loyola, "Rules for Thinking with the Church," *Spiritual Exercises of St. Ignatius,* (Chicago: Loyola Press, 1951), para. 367–69, 160–61.

The best tradition about the origin of these Rules is that they were written about 1537, or some fifteen years after Ignatius had his mystical experiences at Manresa and eight years before the convocation of the Council of Trent. As an integral part of the Exercises, which are permeated by the same spirit, the Ignatian emphasis on man's freedom in confrontation with God became part of the tradition in the Jesuit order and is still one of its typical orientations in spiritual theology.

St. Ignatius's concern was not an empty fear because the principles laid down by the Reformers were not sterile theories. In the lifetime of Luther, one of his disciples, John Agricola (1494–1566), developed a system of religious thought which has since become known as antinomianism, from the Greek *anti* (against) and *nomos* (law). Its basic tenet is that Christian people are freed from the obligations of the moral law, and it was derived by Agricola from Luther's idea of justification: If good works are not necessary for salvation, neither are evil works detrimental to achieving man's destiny.

Luther reacted against Agricola and forced the latter verbally to retract, but the theory was carried on by others. It became part of the religious structure of the Anabaptists in Germany and Holland, and through them of the English (and later American) Dissenters. If Protestant authorities officially repudiated antinomianism, it was only because they rightly saw the consequences of pushing the Reformed denial of human liberty to its logical conclusion.

Before Molinism came on the scene, the first shadows of the later conflict were already cast at the stronghold of Baianism in the University of Louvain. Leonhard Lessius (1554–1623), a native of Belgium, taught at Louvain from 1585 to 1600, where he soon found himself in opposition to the dominant followers of Baius on the efficacy of divine grace. He saw the dangerous consequences of the Louvain chancellor's ideas and, while opposing them, constructed a system of his own, which was closely akin to that of Molina, who had not yet published his classic treatise.

In 1587 Lessius's zeal cost him the humiliation of having the Louvain theological faculty spurred by Baius to censure thirty-four of his theses on grace and predestination, culled from his writings. Baius had not forgotten that twenty years before the Jesuits had secured his own condemnation under St. Pius V.

Similar tension had built at the University of Salamanca, where certain Jesuits were charged with heresy by the Dominican theologian Domenico Banez (1528–1604), spiritual director of St. Teresa of Avila. However both the Louvain and Salamanca situations might have cleared with minimum friction except for the appearance in 1588 of the *Concordia Liberi Arbitrii cum Gratiae Donis* by the Jesuit writer Luis de Molina (1535–1600). A native of Spain, Molina had entered the Society of Jesus at eighteen, and after ordination taught at the universities of Coimbra and Evora until 1583. He then spent several years in writing at Lisbon, where he published the *Concordia*. In 1590 he retired to Cuenca, where he remained until, in the year of his death, he was appointed professor of moral theology at Madrid.

There was something of a furor over Molina's book while it was still in manuscript. The Salamanca faculty wished to prevent its publication, but their protests did not move the censor of the Inquisition, Bartolomeo Ferreira, who gave the volume a glowing imprimatur. In this he stated that the work contained nothing that was not in accordance with the Catholic religion, and that many passages from the Councils and Holy Scriptures were explained in a most satisfactory manner.

Destined to become the focus of heated controversy, the *Concordia* was favorably received in wide circles and, even before Molina's death, new editions came out in Cuenca, Venice, Lyons, and Antwerp. A contemporary theologian at Valladolid admitted that the book contained nothing fundamentally new that could not be found in Augustine and Thomas Aquinas, yet Molina was the first to treat of the reconciliation of grace and freedom at such length and with so much detail, by solving the difficulties that theologians needed to meet the crises of Protestantism. Lessius pronounced enthusiastically in favor of Molina, observing that he defended the same opinion on efficacious grace. The judgment of Lessius is particularly valuable because St. Francis de Sales, who was later declared a doctor of the Church, declared that he shared Lessius's views on the doctrine of predestination, which completely excluded the physical predetermination of Banez.[377]

Yet Molina's *Concordia* was new in many ways, and excited criticism not only outside the Jesuit order but also within its ranks, notably from St. Robert Bellarmine. However Bellarmine was not against the main thesis of Molina, and later defended him stoutly against his critics in Rome.

The principle part of the struggle against Molina was undertaken in 1590 by Domenico Banez, whose name is as firmly attached to the Dominican theory on grace as that of Molina is to the corresponding Jesuit position. Banez was an ardent follower of St. Thomas, down to the smallest details. Among the Dominicans who founded the so-called Neo-Scholasticism, he ranks with Francisco de Vittoria as an outstanding theologian, a shrewd dialectician, and a profound student of metaphysics.

During the years 1590–1594, the Spanish Inquisition was preparing a supplement to its Index of prohibited books for Spain. Banez urged that Molina's treatise on grace should be included among the forbidden books. The attempt failed, and in the sequel Molina passed from a defense of his book to an attack on Banez, stating that the latter's

---

[377] St. Francis de Sales to Lessius, Aug. 26, 1618 in *Oeuvres de St. Francois de Sales* (Annecy: Nierat, 1912), 18:272–73.

teaching on grace and free will was not reconcilable with the Council of Trent. He charged that the Lutherans had started from the same principles as Banez and ended by denying human freedom. To bolster his indictment, Molina drew up a list of texts from Luther and Calvin, flanked them to those of Banez and one of his disciples, Zumel, and stated that Banez was the first to introduce these ideas into Spain. About this time, the Spanish Inquisition examined Molina's work and gave it formal approval.

During the seven years from the first publication of the *Concordia*, a veritable civil war of theology was waged throughout Spain, with the Dominicans writing and speaking against Molina, and the Jesuits defending his orthodoxy against what they said were distortions of his doctrine. The climax was reached when the Jesuits appealed to the Grand Inquisitor of Spain, who was told by Rome that since a question of faith was involved, and a matter of no small importance, the decision belonged to the Holy See and no one else must interfere. A papal letter of August 15, 1594, was received by the two religious orders, instructing them not to discuss efficacious grace in public or private under penalty of excommunication.

Unfortunately the tension had mounted to the breaking point, so that Philip II decided to intervene once again. Conferences were held between civil and ecclesiastical authorities and peace was temporarily achieved, only to be broken when Banez addressed a memorial to Clement VIII on October 28, 1597, in the name of the General of the Dominicans and the Dominican order. He asked that the papal prohibition be removed in favor of the Dominicans, since Banez took for granted that his doctrine was the ancient teaching of Augustine and Aquinas, whereas the teaching of the Jesuits was an innovation.

Clement VIII ordered Robert Bellarmine, who was then the Pope's adviser, to study Banez's memorial and report on it. Bellarmine's opinion was that the Dominican scholar assumed what still had to be proved, namely that his theory could be considered as the Church's tradition. He believed the cardinal issue was whether Banez's physical predetermination was compatible with the Scriptures, Councils, and ancient Fathers, which the Jesuits denied and especially argued for its contravention at Trent. St. Robert felt it would be rash to condemn the Society of Jesus outright: let there first be a hearing of both sides and allow the final decision to the Apostolic See. He further thought it would be better to lift the prohibition against speaking about efficacious grace, allowing discussions on an academic level, with substantial proof and without incriminating charges of heresy from either side.

Meanwhile a massive report was also sent to Rome from the Spanish Inquisition, transmitting the opinions of five bishops and four scholars (none Dominican or Jesuit) on the relative merits of Molina and Banez. The opinions were scattered: some were strongly for one, some for the other, and some blamed both for innovations. Thus the final stage was set for the great duel between the two. Writing years later, the Jesuit General Oliva observed that the issue had been very useful to the Church, but that while the controversy lasted the very existence of the Society of Jesus was in the greatest danger (*gravissimum discrimen*).

During the subsequent proceedings, two different attitudes were held on the precise question under scrutiny. From the first, the Jesuits held it was not important to defend all of Molina's theses. They considered the fate of a single book incidental to the dogmatic issue at stake, that is, whether physical predetermination was true or false. But the Dominicans wished to avoid this vital problem, on which not all members of their own order were in agreement. They wanted everything to center around Molina's *Concordia,* and not only the specific area of grace and free will, but everything Molina taught.

Representatives of the two orders met before the papal commission in the Congregation *De Auxiliis,* so-called because the auxiliary function of grace was under dispute. Three series of meetings were held between 1597 and 1607. In the first series, the decisions were highly critical of Molina and the Jesuits, urging the Pope to condemn their teaching. The final process was conducted under Paul V who dissolved the Congregation on September 5, 1607. His decision was to leave the final judgment to the Holy See while enjoining charity on the contending parties.

The *De Auxiliis* was unique in theological history. Each debate lasted several hours. At the first meeting, the Dominican Alvarez and the Jesuit Valencia disputed for a full four hours. The report for July 27, 1602, states that the disputation lasted uninterrupted for seven hours. Sixty-eight distinct meetings took place under Clement VIII; at thirty-seven the theologians disputed, while the cardinals and consultors deliberated at the others. All told eighty-five congregations were held under Clement VIII and Paul V. What raised these discussions to a historic level was the personal assistance of the Pope at the various meetings, and the sincere effort made by the Holy See to settle the issue in one direction or the other, while finally deciding, in the words of Paul V, that "in treating of this question, neither side may condemn the position opposite to his own or charge it with any censure. Even more he desires that they abstain from using harsh epithets that betray animus towards one another."[378]

Numerous efforts were subsequently made to evoke a papal decision beyond that of Paul V, but they did not succeed. Among the most dramatic was the appeal by the Jansenists against the Molinists, citing certain judgments of one or another consultor of the *De Auxiliis* as showing the true mind of Paul V although lacking his definitive approval. In 1654 Innocent X issued a solemn decree which con-

---

[378] *DS* 1997.

demned several Jansenist publications and passed judgment on the pretended declarations of his predecessor. Among the forgeries was a supposed Constitution of Paul V condemning Molina by formal definition. Innocent X decreed that "no trust at all is to be placed" in these documents, and that "nothing can or ought to be alleged on either side by anyone whatsoever"[379] in favor of their position.

A half century later the faculty at Louvain petitioned Innocent XIII to make a public declaration in favor of their traditional doctrine, including a doctrinal statement that grace is efficacious by itself, and that predestination before foreseen merits has not been weakened by the condemnations of Baius and Jansenius. Innocent replied that "We do not think it opportune at present to demand a more elaborate discussion of divine help than that which was instituted by our predecessors, Clement VIII and Paul V."[380]

When Benedict XIII in 1727 reconfirmed the privileges of the Order of Preachers, he forbade anyone to say that the doctrine of St. Thomas or his school was impugned by the condemnation of Jansenism. He then added that "having discovered the mind of our predecessors, We do not wish either by our own or their praises conferred on the Thomistic school, which we approve and confirm by our repeated judgment, that there be any disparagement of the other Catholic schools which think differently from the same in explaining the efficacy of divine grace, and whose merits are also clear to the Holy See."[381] He renewed the decrees of Paul V and forbade anyone "to brand with any mark of theological censure the schools that have different opinions" from the Thomistic position.

In 1748 his successor, Benedict XIV, came to the defense of the Molinists in a detailed statement to the Grand Inquisitor of Spain. It is

---

[379] *DS* 2008.
[380] Ibid.
[381] Ibid.

the latest authoritative declaration on the subject, which briefly summarizes the various schools of thought permissible in Catholic theology on the efficacy of grace.

> You know there are manifold opinions in the schools on the famous questions about predestination and grace, and on the manner of reconciling human liberty with the omnipotence of God. The Thomists are said to be destroyers of human liberty and followers not only of Jansenism but of Calvinism. However, since they meet the charges with eminent satisfaction, and since their opinion has never been condemned by the Holy See, the Thomists carry on without hindrance in this matter, and it is not right for any ecclesiastical superior in the present state of affairs to force them to change their opinion.
>
> The Augustinians are reported as the followers of du Bay and of Jansenism. They represent themselves as defenders of human liberty, and strenuously answer their critics. Since their opinion, too, has not been condemned by the Holy See, no effort should therefore be made to compel them to give up their theory.
>
> The followers of Molina and Suarez are condemned by their adversaries as Semi-Pelagians. But the Roman Pontiffs have not passed judgment on the Molinist system, which they presently defend and may continue to do so.[382]

Benedict XIV's reference to Suarez indicates the stage of development that Molinism had reached by the middle of the eighteenth century. By that time the accepted Jesuit theory on grace had become known as Congruism, a modification of Molina. It was elaborated by

---

[382] *DS* 2564.

Suarez, Vasquez, and Lessius, and became the quasiofficial teaching in the Society of Jesus under the Generals Vitelleschi and Piccolomini, in the mid-seventeenth century.

However, as early as 1613, the Jesuit General Claudius Aquaviva told the teachers of theology in the Society to lay greater stress on the Congruistic phase of efficacious grace. As will be seen in the theological analysis, Congruism steers a middle course between pure Molinism and Banezianism, without relinquishing the basic features of Molina's theory. Aquaviva was led to his decision by the representations of St. Robert Bellarmine, besides others, who felt that Molina's defense of free will might undervalue the primacy of grace, which is the decisive factor in the economy of salvation.

ANALYTIC COMPARISON

As indicated in Benedict XIV's letter to the Grand Inquisitor, there are three principal theories of efficacious grace permissible in Catholic thought: the Thomistic, more commonly known as Banezianism; the Augustinian, because its defenders said it was based directly on St. Augustine; and Molinism, whose historical development into Congruism was recognized in the Society of Jesus within a decade after Molina's death.

Banezianism

The true founder of the Thomistic theory of grace was Domenico Banez, whose name is commonly attached to the system, although he personally felt it was not an interpretation but a restatement of the doctrine of St. Thomas.

Banez started with the universal principle that God is the First Cause and Prime Mover of all things in creation. They depend upon God not only for their existence and faculties but for every one of their acts. "No second cause can operate," he declared, "unless it has been efficaciously determined by the First Cause."[383]

There are no exceptions to this divine causality. Whatever creatures do comes within the scope of God's primal operation. Whether the creaturely acts are good or bad, necessary or free, they depend upon the Prime Mover, without whom nothing can occur. God adapts Himself to the special nature of each creature, whom He moves accordingly. However this divine action is not simultaneous concursus, by which God together with the secondary cause influences an effect. It is a prevenient concurrence, which acts logically on the cause prior to acting on the effect. Like a workman using his tools, God moves and applies the secondary cause to produce the effect.

This application of the divine power to all secondary causes is called premotion or physical predetermination. It is a predetermination because it moves uniquely to that one determined act to which God has decreed to move a creature.

Transferring these norms to theology, Banezianism teaches that a twofold help of grace is needed for a salutary act. One help is less powerful and perfect; it predetermines the soul to certain indeliberate supernatural acts and functions by way of stimulus or excitation. The other help follows on the previous, and is more perfect and powerful, assisting the will to perform deliberate acts of free choice. The first kind of grace is called sufficient or stimulating (*excitans*), the second type efficacious, or assisting (*adjuvans*).

These two graces, sufficient and efficacious, are essentially different, since the former gives only ability (*posse*) whereas the latter produces activity (*agere*). "Sufficient grace in a Thomistic sense is one that gives a man the power of doing something good; in order to have

───────────

[383] Domingo Banez, *Scholastica Commentaria in Primam Partem Summae Theologicae S. Thomae Aquinatis* (Madrid: Editorial F.E.D.A., 1934), 1, 14, 13; *CCC* 308.

him actually do well or rightly use this ability, he needs another more powerful grace."[384] This "more powerful" grace is called efficacious grace. It confers not only the power to act but the act itself. By definition, it includes the free consent of the will, whereas merely sufficient grace lacks that consent.

More closely examined, efficacious grace is that additional divine aid which physically predetermines the human will, without taking away our free choice, both as to the exercise of our freedom and its specification or choice of a given object. "It never happens that the power which sufficient grace confers would either act or obtain its main effect, unless it were supplemented by an efficacious grace."[385] This efficacious grace is a determination because it is absolutely impossible for the will, under its influence, not to perform the act which God has determined; it is in every sense a *pre*determination since it comes before our consent, for the sake of that consent, and in order to effect a consent. It is physical because it produces its effect by virtue of its own reality, intrinsically woven into its nature, and independent of any circumstance or consent of the free agent.

If a man resists sufficient grace, he sins.[386] For a sin to take place, two decrees are required on the part of God: an eternal decree permitting the sin in this case and moreover the man to remain with sufficient grace only; another decree predetermining the sinner to the material element in the sin. Both factors are verified antecedent to God's foresight of what choice the created agent will make. The sequence is something like this. God confers a sufficient grace on some person; He predetermines the individual to the material part of this sin, by which he resists the grace offered; thereby the man sins formally, consequently

---

[384] Charles Rene Billuart, *De Gratia,* diss. V, a. 4.
[385] Ibid.; *CCC* 1742.
[386] *CCC* 679.

rendering the grace merely sufficient. In penalty for this sin he is deprived of the efficacious grace that would have predetermined him to place a salutary act.

The relation of efficacious grace to predestination in the Banezian system follows naturally on the foregoing. God wants all men to be saved, unless a universal salvation would impede the achievement of higher divine ends or purposes. Antecedent to His prevision of their good or bad use of freedom, by a free and absolute decree on God's part, He chooses certain persons for a definite measure of eternal glory. The rest of the human race He omits from this decree, which is technically called a negative antecedent reprobation. It is reprobation because it is not predestination to glory. It is negative and not positive because (other than Calvin) the object of the divine resolve is not eternal punishment but exclusion from the beatific vision. It is antecedent because God's will on their fate is determined (in human language) before He foresees their merits or demerits.

God absolutely predetermines to give the help of efficacious graces, by which the predefined meritorious acts of the elect will infallibly take place. This predetermination is called extrinsic. But when God puts it into effect in time by means of physical premotion, as explained above, it becomes intrinsic predetermination, i.e., built into the free human will. As regards the negative reprobates, God orders their lives in such a way so that they receive only such graces as are finally merely sufficient. They do not die in the state of grace.

While there are minor variations to the theory, substantially Banezianism postulates a threefold infallible connection between efficacious grace and salutary acts. The first nexus arises objectively from the internal force of premotion, as an instrument of divine omnipotence; given predetermination to a certain salutary act, it is inconceivable that a man would fail to consent. On the level of cognition, God foresees the future free actions of creatures in His eternal volitional decrees, in which He knows with infallible certainty the free actions of creatures predetermined by Him. In terms of His divine purpose, God absolutely and efficaciously wills that salutary good works be performed, and consequently ordains to confer intrinsically efficacious grace to make that effect come to pass.

Before going on to evaluate the Banezian theory, it may be useful to summarize. The Thomistic explanation of how grace and free will are reconciled begins with the premise that God has eternally predetermined that some people should be saved, and to realize this aim confers effective (efficacious) graces on these elect. He therefore physically affects their free wills, and thus secures that they decide freely to cooperate with His grace. There is an inner power in efficacious grace which infallibly insures that the predestined freely consent to perform such salutary actions as will merit heaven. Consequently efficacious grace is essentially different from merely sufficient grace, which confers the power or ability to place salutary acts, but no more. Before this bare potency can be reduced to action, another and different divine help must be received, namely efficacious grace. Since God has eternally willed the free consent of His chosen ones to the efficacious graces He confers, He thus ineluctably brings about the salvation of those who are included in His loving decree. All the rest who do not come within the ambit of this election are permitted, through the abuse of their freedom, not to attain heaven. The divine motive for this negative reprobation is that God willed to manifest His goodness not only by means of His mercy, but also by means of His justice.

On its credit side, Banezianism is in the Augustinian tradition of safeguarding the sovereignty of God and the gratuity of grace. It has the merit of constructing a system of grace that is perfectly consonant with the principle that God is the First Cause of all created activity, and that mankind, in its existence and operations, is utterly dependent upon God.

However, the problems to which it gives rise are neither few nor unimportant. At the head of these difficulties is how to reconcile physical predetermination with authentic human freedom. Howsoever defined, liberty must include the inner power of self-determination, of doing something or not doing it, of willing or not willing, or assenting or dissenting. It must be able to determine itself in such a way that, before decision, it is undetermined; otherwise it could not be the autonomous faculty that reason and revelation hold it to be. "Man has free choice," wrote St. Thomas, "otherwise counsels, exhortations, precepts, prohibitions, rewards, and punishments would all be pointless."[387]

In the Banezian system, before efficacious grace is received there is no real power to perform a salutary act. After its reception there is no corresponding ability to do anything but that act. Prior to its own determination, then, the will is already, by logical priority, determined to the one act for which it has been given an efficacious grace. When asked for his judgment by Clement VIII, Robert Bellarmine observed that "This opinion does not seem to save free will, nor can it be distinguished from the formulae used by the modern heretics." Yet he prudently added, "I do not, however, dare to condemn it absolutely, as I know it is defended by great men."[388]

At the time the controversy *De Auxiliis* was raging, contemporary writers spoke of the Protestant reaction to the prospects that Banezianism would be canonized and Molinism condemned. Followers of the Reformation eagerly gave ear to the rumors that Molina had already been censured. Scribani, the Jesuit rector at Antwerp, wrote that "I can

---

[387] St. Thomas, *Summa Theologica,* I, 83, 1; *CCC* 311.
[388] Xavier-Marie Le Bachelet, *Auctiarum Bellarminianum* (Paris: Gabriel Beauchesne, 1913), 143–47.

find no words to describe the expressions of joy with which this news has been received by the heretics of our city. Some of them have gone so far as to congratulate themselves that the view of Calvin as to free will has at last been recognized as true."[389] The fact is that an impassable difference separated the Banezian from the Calvinist theories on grace. Calvin denied freedom and built a whole theological structure on this premise; whereas Banez and his disciples resolutely defended human freedom under the impulse of grace. But better than speculative commentaries was the spontaneous reaction of the sectarians of the times, who thought (mistakenly) that the opponents of Molinism were proponents of determinism.

Equally grave is the practical impossibility of retaining truly and merely sufficient grace in the Banezian hypothesis. Truly sufficient grace would be a misnomer if it did not really suffice for the performance of a salutary act. The sources of Catholic tradition and the common belief of the faithful hold that sufficient grace gives more than a bare supernatural potency which cannot be reduced to act. On the contrary, God confers it so that we might have both the potency to perform and to accomplish salutary actions.

In the Banezian system, sufficient grace is insufficient of itself for a man to act supernaturally. He also needs a substantially new grace, called efficacious. But then how do we square two opposing concepts of sufficiency: one that is truly adequate for something, and another that is inadequate unless supplemented?

All defendants of physical predetermination sincerely maintain that truly and purely sufficient grace exists. The Jansenists were condemned for denying the fact, and no Catholic questions the Church's teaching. But how do we retain a sufficient grace that does not derogate from the primacy and necessity of the grace that is efficacious? If it is given too

---

[389] Ludwig von Pastor, *History of the Popes* (London: Kegan Paul, 1912), 24:355.

much potency, in the sense of enough power to perform a salutary act, then what is called merely sufficient would conceivably become efficacious grace and produce salvific actions-which contradicts a first principle of Banezianism, that strictly efficacious grace is necessary for every salutary act we place.

Molinism

There are really two forms of Molinism, one proposed by Molina himself, and the other developed under the stress of debate with his critics. The modified form is called Congruism and will be examined later.

The best presentation of classic Molinism is in the words of the author, whose *Concordia* deserves to be rated one of the great books of all time. Its most salient feature is the scrutiny given to it by the highest authority in the Church; and from which it emerged dogmatically unscathed. It has been said that no book since the invention of the printing press has been subjected to such minute and ruthless criticism in every line. Yet not a syllable of its more than 300,000 words was censured or condemned by the Holy See. Opposition from all sides over a period of twenty years only gained its author the privilege of being numbered among those who have reasoned most deeply on the relations of man with God. Modern scholars outside the Christian tradition rank Molina alongside Augustine, Aquinas, and Calvin as one of the most influential exponents of predestination in the history of Christianity.

Molina traced his doctrine first along historical lines. He showed that the beginnings of a theology of predestination were occasioned by the Pelagian heresy, which attributed all things to our free will and declared that nothing else is needed for salvation. To answer Pelagius, Augustine, and his contemporaries, he "demonstrated from Holy Scripture that the origin of our salvation comes from God through His foresight and action, and that the beginning and perfection of our salvation depend upon the grace of God which is given to us through Christ. In other words, the gifts and means of grace are conferred not according to the effort of our free will but according to the pleasure of God."[390]

As a result of Augustine's lucid writing, and the Church's authoritative teaching, certain truths became commonly accepted in Catholic tradition. Thus "the following matters have been above controversy; there is in us freedom of will; no one, whether adult or child can attain eternal life except through grace derived from the merits of Christ; and no adult, by reason of his own powers and without the aid of supernatural grace, can be justified and attain eternal life. In God there is a foreknowledge of all future events and a predestination of the good to eternal life through grace, gifts and supernatural helps. The freedom of the will is related to all of these and is not in the least diminished or impeded by them."[391]

But more than this was "above controversy" in Molina's opinion. The ancient writers also agreed "it was not because God foreknew what would happen that those things which depend on the created will would take place. On the contrary, it was because such things would happen through the freedom of the will that He foreknew it. He would also foreknow the opposite, if the opposite was to happen, as was possible by reason of the freedom of the will."[392]

However, if "there was always common opinion" concerning these elements, one thing Augustine admitted was still lacking: to find a

---

[390] Luis de Molina, *Concordia Liberi Arbitrii cum Gratiae Donis, Divina Praescientia, Providentia, Praedestinatione et Reprobatione* (Paris: P. Lethielleux, 1876), 545–46; *CCC* 1987, 1996, 2007.

[391] Luis de Molina, *Concordia Liberi Arbitrii cum Gratiae Donis, Divina Praescientia, Providentia, Praedestinatione et Reprobatione* (Paris: P. Lethielleux, 1876), 547.

[392] Ibid.

solution by which human liberty might be reconciled with divine grace, divine foreknowledge, and predestination. Molina was therefore looking for the clue to solve the problem, so that, as he hoped, "an adult could work out his salvation as he chose" without being worried about "these three obstacles."

There was a higher than academic motive that prompted Molina to spend years in reflective research on the issue. He was frankly interested in converting those who had left the Church, ostensibly because they could not accept the Catholic doctrine on grace and free will. "A way would be opened," he hoped, "whereby they might more easily return to the unity of the Church."

Certain principles should guide the theologian in explaining how grace and freedom are compatible. Molina ventured the guess that "if these principles had always been given and explained, perhaps the Pelagian heresy would never have arisen, nor would the Lutherans have dared so impudently to deny the freedom of our will, alleging that it could not be reconciled with divine grace, foreknowledge and predestination."[393]

He proceeds to enunciate these principles, which he reduces to four. They are the backbone of Molinism and state in clearer terms than any commentary what the author of the *Concordia* meant when he said he was sure that his theory would have been unanimously approved by St. Augustine and the Fathers "if it had been proposed to them."

> The first and basic principle is the nature of the divine influence, both through its concurrence in the natural acts of the will, as well as through particular aids to supernatural acts. (Thus) the prevenient and auxiliary graces which are conferred upon us in our pilgrim state (on earth), are efficacious or inef-

---

[393] Ibid., 548.

ficacious for conversion or justification. They depend upon free will and the cooperation of our will. In fact, these graces are in our free will, either to render them efficacious by consenting to or cooperating with them towards those acts by which we are disposed to sanctification; or to render them inefficacious by refusing our consent and cooperation, or even to raise a contrary disagreement.

The second principle is the legitimate, or better the orthodox, explanation concerning the measure of the gift of perseverance. Two things are necessary for the gift of perseverance. One on the part of God: that He will have decided to give those aids with which He foresaw that the adult would persevere by His own free will. Another (on the part of man): that the free will of the adult is a necessary condition; for without it the (divine) will to confer such aids could not imply the will to confer the gift of perseverance, namely, that the adult of his own free choice would so cooperate with such helps that he might persevere, which it is clearly within his ability to do. Therefore it should not be understood that the gift of perseverance from God is of such a nature that it takes away the power of not persevering.[394]

The foregoing principles are the foundation on which Molina rested his case. But they involve another postulate, relative to the way God foresees the future, which had first been defined and scientifically demonstrated by Fonseca, the teacher of Suarez. Molina distinguished three types of foreknowledge in God: mere possibles, actual future events, and an intermediate, *scientia media,* which covers the futuribles, i.e., of things which are not, but which would be if certain conditions were realized.

---

[394] Ibid., 231, 548–49.

According to Molina, "God knew before the free act of His will what the created will would do in all circumstances, if He, God, decided to place such created wills (men and angels) in a particular set of circumstances. And to the contrary, He also foreknew if the created will should decide on an opposite course of action. On the basis of this principle, the freedom of the will is compatible with divine fore-knowledge."[395] This means that through the *scientia media* God knows from eternity what reaction a created will would make to every conceivable grace He might confer. When, therefore, in the light of this knowledge, He actually bestows a grace, this grace will turn out to be efficacious or merely sufficient, according as God foresees whether a man will freely accept or resist the divine aid. He has absolute power to give or withhold His graces in each individual case, depending on His own free decision.

One last step needs to be made in order to reconcile freedom of the human will with divine predestination. "God chose to create this order of things rather than another, and to bestow these aids rather than others, and by means of which He foresaw that some persons and not others will attain to eternal life," Moreover, "predestination has no cause or reason on the part of the use of the free will of the predestined and the reprobate, but is to be attributed solely to the free will of God. This follows logically from the fact that the will to create a certain order of things and to confer upon individuals certain aids, provides the basis for the predestination of adults, which depends on the use that God had foreseen they would make of their free will."[396]

The essentials of Molinism, therefore, are three. The first is its denial of any kind of predetermination, whether physical (in the Banezian

---

[395] Ibid., 549.
[396] Ibid.

sense) or moral, as understood by the Augustinians. The other two are its hypothesis of a *scientia media,* by which God foreknows the free future acts of creatures not in predetermined decrees but through the *scientia media,* and its concept of grace, which is extrinsically efficacious.

Beyond these basic features, two principal schools of Molinism have since arisen. Most Molinists—following Molina, Vasquez, and Lessius—teach a conditioned predestination (to heavenly glory only), that is, after and because of foreseen merits. Others prefer the modified form which Suarez and Bellarmine devised to meet the critics who charged that "pure Molinism" has something strange about it because it implies that the efficacy or inefficacy of grace depends on the arbitrary choice of a created will. If sufficient grace becomes efficacious only by the consent of man, how can we still call the resulting salutary act an effect of grace? They consequently held that predestination is antecedent to foreseen merits. According to them, God freely resolved from eternity, without considering the merits of men, to confer grace for the performance of good works (*gratia de congruo*) in accordance with such circumstances as He foresees will be favorable to their use. This latter theory is also called Congruism, although it differs only accidentally from pure Molinism.

Congruism

The essence of strict Molinism is that efficacious grace is not given *as* efficacious, i.e., in order that a good act might be performed, but grace is conferred *which* God foresees to be efficacious. Congruism, on the other hand, declares that efficacious grace is given *qua* efficacious, that is, in order that a salutary act be placed.

The nature of efficacious grace was explained in a famous decree of Claudius Aquaviva (1545–1615), General of the Society of Jesus, published in 1613, by which he directed Jesuit theologians to teach

Congruism as being more in agreement with the doctrine of St. Augustine and St. Thomas.

> Henceforth let our Fathers always teach that efficacious and sufficient graces do not differ merely in completed act (*actu secundo*), because the one obtains its effect by the cooperation of the free will and not the other. But they differ also in their first movement (*actu primo*), in this sense that, presupposing *scientia media,* God Himself, with the fixed intention of producing good, designedly chooses those determinate means and employs them in the manner and at the moment which He knows infallibly will insure that the effect will be produced. Consequently, if He had foreseen the inefficacy of these means, God would have made use of other means.
>
> That is why, morally speaking and considering it as a favor, there is something more in efficacious grace than in sufficient grace even in its first movement (*actu primo*). In this way God brings it about that we actually do something, and not merely gives us the grace to be able to do it. The same may be said of perseverance, which is undoubtedly a gift of God.[397]

Soon after the decree was published, a variety of interpretations arose, which prompted the next general congregation of the order (1616) to further explain Aquaviva's ruling. "There was no intention to declare," it was stated, "that God by His will predetermines or predefines any good work of ours independently of the free cooperation of our will. Nor was it meant to say that in efficacious grace there is some sort of real entity or some kind of physical mode in its first movement (*actu primo*), which is absent from sufficient grace. The

---

[397] Claudius Aquaviva, quoted in *Controversiarum de Divinae Gratiae Liberique Arbitrii Concordia.* ed. G. Schneemann. (Friburgi Brisgoviae: Herder, 1881), 203.

decree only meant to say it was a special benefit of God to have given one man, e.g., to Peter, with the intention that he might do good thereby, a grace at such a time and place as God saw beforehand by His foreknowledge that the man would rightly use. This benefit He might not confer on another man, e.g., John, whom He gives a grace at such a time and place as He foresees the person will not put to use through his own fault."[398]

Commentators have pointed out that, according to this interpretation, all Molinists, including Molina and Lessius, have taught the same things. Nevertheless the decree of Aquaviva was not incorporated into the Jesuit Institute, nor is it now mandatory in the Society.

According to Congruism, sufficient grace is truly sufficient from the side of God because its inefficacy is attributable solely to the human will. No one questions that in this system the influx of efficacious, that is, congruous grace, fully safeguards the liberty of our wills, which the Congruists consider not as a mere abstraction but immersed in the complex circumstances of human life. God foresees what grace will prove efficacious in the context not only of chronological time or local place but of a man's temperament, native ability, weakness, education, past experience, association, and myriad factors that certainly influence the will without compelling it. He confers a supernatural grace that attracts the will and softens it, as it were, but—except for rare interventions like St. Paul's conversion—never compels us to do good.

Thus conceived, the difference between efficacious and sufficient grace depends not only on the will of man, but also on the will of God. He gives not only the grace which He knows to be efficacious, but *because* He foresees it will be efficacious. His selective choice of congruous graces, conferred under conditions so favorable to their efficacy that He knows we shall cooperate, vindicates the divine

---

[398] Ibid., 303–4.

sovereignty over His creatures and guarantees the absolute dependence on His will which is the hallmark of Christianity.

Syncretism

Other methods of reconciling grace and free will have been proposed and still enjoy some vogue in theological circles. Often they are joined in various combinations to produce a type of syncretism which draws either on Banezian or Molinist principles. Two especially are significant: the Augustinian theory of moral predetermination, and the Alphonsian hypothesis of a distinction between ordinary and onerous divine precepts.

The Augustinian system was first elaborated by certain members of the Order of St. Augustine in the eighteenth century to answer the Jansenist challenge without compromising the Catholic doctrine of free will. Actual grace, said the Augustinians, is the impulse of a holy love or heavenly delight, which may take on two different forms. When the grace is merely sufficient, the divine attraction is less than the pull of earthly self-love, and therefore no consent takes place. God gives the ability to perform a salutary act, if man desires to cooperate. However, to actually cooperate, he must receive a "conquering delight" in the form of efficacious grace. But all the while he remains perfectly free.

Efficacious grace morally predetermines the will to consent by attracting rather than physically impelling it to action. While the will responds infallibly to the inspiration of efficacious grace, it does not do so necessarily. In fact there would have been no need of such grace were it not for the fallen state of man and resulting concupiscence. Otherwise than in the Banezian system, the reason for efficacious grace is man's weakened condition, and not the hypothetical need of all secondary causes absolutely to depend on the First Cause for their action.

Augustinianism also differs from the Thomistic theory by admitting degrees in efficacy of the same grace, according to the circumstances in which a person finds himself, to the point where an identical help from God will be efficacious under one set of conditions and inefficacious if these conditions radically change. It therefore approximates Molinism, while transmitting the need of a *scientia media* and making grace intrinsically efficacious. Banezians favor the Augustinian explanation, but suggest that it does not go far enough; that the need for intrinsic efficacy in grace is not due simply to man's fallen state but to his created nature.

The name St. Alphonsus Liguori is commonly associated with a form of Congruism developed at the Sorbonne in the eighteenth century. This was later adopted by many Redemptorists, and is sometimes called mitigated Augustinianism. However, a careful distinction must be made between the theoreticians who first conceived the hypothesis or later explored it and the practical use to which St. Alphonsus put those elements in the Sorbonne system, which is the common possession of Catholic theology.

On its speculative side, the Sorbonne hypothesis is an attempted combination of Banezianism, Molinism, Congruism and Augustinianism. As summed up by a Redemptorist in the nineteenth century, "Grace is intrinsically efficacious, and in this we follow the Thomists and Augustinians as against the Molinists. Contrary to the Thomists we say this intrinsically efficacious grace is not physical but merely a moral motion. Intrinsically efficacious grace is required only for difficult salutary acts. For the easy acts, especially for prayer, sufficient grace, which is commonly granted to all, is the only grace required."[399]

Thus a middle ground is established in this eclectic system, whose critics are both Banezians and Molinists. They argue that the intrinsic

---

[399] Joannes Herrmann, *Tractatus de Divina Gratia Secundum S. Alphonsi M. de Ligorio Doctrinam et Mentem* (Rome: P. Cuggiani, 1904), 509.

and infallible efficacy of the divine decrees and of grace either is or is
not compatible with human freedom. If it is, why limit intrinsically
efficacious grace to difficult acts; if it is not, why admit it for them?
Salutary acts are supernatural and therefore require the advent of
grace. Their relative ease or difficulty does not change the function of
grace in its relation to the will.

However, it would be less than accurate to identify the speculative
side of Sorbonne Congruism with St. Alphonsus Liguori's ascetical
interest in the necessity of prayer. We must ask God, St. Alphonsus
would say, for efficacious graces when we are conscious of weakness
and find ourselves hard-pressed with severe temptation and trial. In his
treatment of the subject, he relies on the authority of Bellarmine and
Francis de Sales. He is not even remotely concerned about reconciling
grace and free will in the style of Banez or Molina. He wants to
explain in clear language the common teaching of the Church about
the need of prayer for salvation.

Liguori's trenchant insistence on everyone receiving sufficient
grace at least to pray, and thereby obtain further efficacious graces to
overcome grave obstacles, is borrowed from Bellarmine, whom he
quotes to the effect that all the Scripture exhortations to "be converted,
return, come, ask," would be "vain and mocking if God did not give
to all at least the grace to pray actually if they wish."[400] He concludes
with a graphic description of the just complaint that sinners might
make if this were not true.

> I am unable to understand how preachers can exhort the
> people to return to God, if even the grace of prayer is refused
> to some. For the people might answer, "Why do you exhort
> us to repentance? Ask God Himself to convert us, for we

---

[400] St. Robert Bellarmine, *De Gratia,* II, 4, Vol. 5 *Opera Omnia* (Paris: Ludovicum,
1874).

have neither the immediate efficacious grace to return actually to God, nor the mediate sufficient grace to obtain it by means of prayer."

I am likewise unable to conceive how the Sacred Scriptures can so strongly exhort men to listen to the divine inspirations if the grace of prayer be not granted to all. For they who are destitute even of the efficacious grace of prayer may say to God, "Lord, why do You tell us to do this? Make us do it Yourself, for You know we have not even the grace to ask You to make us correspond to Your invitation."

Finally I cannot comprehend how the reproof given to sinners in these words, "you always resist the Holy Spirit" (Acts 7:51), can be just, if they do not receive even the remote grace necessary for actual prayer.[401]

His conclusion is that since the grace of prayer is common to all, every excuse is removed from those who say they had no strength to resist the assaults of the flesh or the evil spirit, since they always had, as the Council of Trent declared, the grace of prayer by which "God does not command the impossible; but when He commands, He warns you to do what you can, and also to pray for what you cannot do."[402] To this principle, all theoretical systems of reconciling grace and free will would subscribe.

---

[401] St. Alphonsus Liguori, *Exposition and Defence,* 124; *CCC* 2744.
[402] *DS* 1536.

.

9

SUPERNATURAL MERIT

One of the best examples of how a basic concept in revelation has been clarified by Christian reflection is the idea of merit. The word itself occurs nowhere in Scripture, yet the inner meaning we commonly associate with the term reaches into the dawn of God's supernatural relations with man. In a true sense, the notion of merit is the watershed which divides Catholic Christianity from other forms of Christian belief. It distinguishes those elements of the faith that have remained constant over the centuries, even beyond Christ to the early patriarchs and prophets.

Woven into the texture of merit are such typically Catholic ideas as freedom of the will, good works, growth in sanctifying grace, the evangelical counsels, and intercessory prayer. They are neither conditions which make merit possible, or derive from meritorious actions nor assist the soul in meriting more effectively before God. A clear understanding of supernatural merit does more than educate the mind in the Christian religion; it offers motivation for fidelity in the spiritual life and, paradoxically, lie close to the center of the heroism of the saints.

RESOURCES IN FAITH

While the Old Testament is less "spiritual" about retribution for good and evil deeds than the Gospels or St. Paul, there is already some notion of reward for the virtues men practice in the first books of the Bible. A cryptic verse in Genesis tells how Henoch "walked with God and was seen no longer, for God had taken him away."[403] Since Henoch had lived in a manner particularly pleasing to God, he did not die as other people but was "taken away" as a reward for his virtue. Elias was also "taken away" riding upward in a fiery chariot. "He was taken into heaven because of his great zeal for the Law."[404]

Those who obey the commandments of Yahweh are frequently promised "life" as a recompense for their labors, while sinners are threatened with "death" as a punishment. When Ezechiel prophesied the destruction of Jerusalem, he was surely aware that both good and wicked men would be slain in battle, yet he promised life to those who fulfilled God's precepts faithfully and likewise to the sinners who return to the Lord.[405] The prophets also mention a "book of the living" in which the just are inscribed and from which the godless are stricken; and though earthly blessings are first concerned, future blessings after death are not totally absent.

By the time of the Wisdom literature, the doctrine of reward for the just had developed to a point that was only shades removed from its fulness in the teachings of Christ. The author of the Book of Wisdom was almost certainly stimulated by outside influences in the Hellenic world, as he built on the truths of the past. Yet his description of the lot of those who die in God's friendship is sharply different from Hellenism and the mystery religions of the East. Its purity is firmly rooted in the ancient prophets.

> The souls of the just are in the hand of God, and no torment shall touch them. They seemed, in the view of the foolish, to be

---

[403] Genesis 5:24; *CCC* 2569.
[404] 2 Kings 2:3–12; 2 Maccabees 2:58.
[405] Ezechiel 5–6.

dead; and their passing away was judged as affliction and their going forth from us, utter destruction. But they are in peace.

For if before men, indeed, they be punished, yet is their hope full of immortality; chastised a little, they shall be greatly blessed, because God tried them and found them worthy of Himself. As gold in the furnace, He proved them, and as sacrificial offerings He took them to Himself.

In the time of their visitation they shall shine, and shall dart about as sparks through stubble; they shall judge nations and shall rule over peoples, and the Lord shall be their King forever. Those who trust in Him shall understand truth, and the faithful shall abide with Him in love.[406]

The basic elements of merit before God are, therefore, apparent before the time of Christ. But the full flowering of its implications was not revealed until the Christian era. Eternal life, promised to those who serve God in this life, is variously called a reward, prize, crown, wages, retribution, and remuneration which the Lord will give to men according to their works. Every phase of man's service of the Lord has an ultimate reward. Those who fast and give thanks to God, those who believe and hope in God, those who love Him and through Him their neighbor, those who avoid sin and preserve themselves from the contagion of this world, those who are willing to give up all things to follow Christ will be rewarded.[407]

In the high point of Christ's teaching, recorded in the Gospels, a series of eight injunctions is set forth to His disciples, each of which is accompanied by a spiritual reward. After enumerating them, together with the promises attached to each, the Savior concluded: "Blessed are

---

[406] Wisdom 3:1–9.
[407] Merit as reward (Matthew 5:11), prize (Philippians 3:14), crown (James 1:12), remuneration (Hebrews 10:35), retribution (Colossians 3:23).

you when men reproach you, and persecute you, and speaking falsely, say all manner of evil against you, for my sake. Rejoice and exult, because your reward is great in heaven."[408]

If the reward promised to those who persevere is eternal, its measure is also conditioned on the good that a man has done before death, "when night comes and no man can work any longer." In the parable of the laborers in the vineyard, Christ explains both aspects of supernatural merit: the divine sovereignty in dispensing grace in this life and glory in the next, and man's collaboration with God's gifts for a longer or shorter time according to the dispensation of the Lord.

St. Paul is eloquent in extolling the absolute gratuity of Christian grace and man's complete inability to do any supernatural good without divine help. But he also recognizes the retribution which an equitable Providence has in store for those who struggle faithfully until called. "God will render to every man according to his works. Life eternal He will give to those who by patience in good works seek glory and honor and immortality."[409] Speaking of himself, he says, "I have fought the good fight, I have finished the course, I have kept the faith. For the rest, there is laid up for me a crown of justice, which the Lord, the just Judge, will give to me that day; not to me only, but also to those who love His coming."[410]

However the most incisive apostolic witness on the necessity of good works, and their correlative merit, is St. James, "Blessed is the man who endures temptation; for when he has been tried, he will receive the crown of life which God has promised to those who love Him."[411] Always in the New Testament, those who are faithful on earth are assured blessedness in heaven; they will become the

---

[408] Matthew 5:11–12; *CCC* 520.
[409] Romans 2:6–7.
[410] 2 Timothy 4:7.
[411] James 1:12.

makarioi, or happy ones, which the ancient Greeks primarily applied to the gods, whom they often simply called Makares, "those in perfect bliss." At the same time, the happiness promised was provisory and not inevitable. "Be faithful," Christ told John in vision, "and I will give you the crown of life."[412]

The Fathers of the Church expanded on the deposit of faith in the Scriptures, either to strengthen their own resolve to remain constant in God's service, or to console the faithful in their trials with the security of a heavenly reward. Ignatius of Antioch pleaded with the Roman Christians not to dissuade him from martyrdom, "Allow me to be eaten by the beasts," he wrote, "through whom I may attain to God."[413] Another martyr, the bishop Irenaeus, observed, "precious should be to us the crown which we gain in battle; and the more we obtain it by combat, the more precious it is."[414]

Tertullian (A.D. 160–220) appears to have been the first to use the term "merit" in describing the supernatural reward of virtue. "A good act," he declared, "has God as its debtor, even as an act which is evil, since the Judge is a vindicator of every cause."[415] Harnack made the incredible statement that Tertullian also first conceived the doctrine of merit.[416]

During the Pelagian conflict, Augustine wrote at length about the reward that awaits us if we rightly use the gifts of divine grace. God, he says, "gave us of His mercy, He will crown us in return. He is the donor of forgiveness, and the debtor of a crown. How can He be debtor? Did He receive something? The Lord made Himself debtor, not by receiving but by promising. We cannot say to Him, 'Return what You received,'

---

[412] Apocalypse 2:10.

[413] Romans 4:1; *CCC* 2473.

[414] St. Irenaeus, "Adversus omnes haereses," 4, 37, *MPL* 7:1104.

[415] Tertullian, "De Paenitentia," 2, *MPL* 1:1230.

[416] Adolph Harnack, *Lehrbuch der Dogmengeschichte* (Leipzig: Mohr, 1894), II, 179.

but, 'Grant us what You promised.' "[417] In the next century, the Council of Orange (A.D. 529) canonized a statement by St. Augustine, to the effect that "Reward is due to good works, if they are done; but grace, which is not due, must precede that good works might be done."[418] Thus even in the heat of Pelagianism, which insisted uniquely on merit without grace, the Church never lost sight of the law of divine remuneration by which God committed Himself to repay our efforts in corresponding with His will.

In the Middle Ages, the Schoolmen built on the patristic tradition a system of merit that has remained substantially the same to the present day. Two underlying principles supported the structure: that God rewards our good deeds supernaturally provided they are done from the infused virtue of charity, and that the faculty by which we merit is the free will. In a crisp sentence, St. Thomas summarized the doctrine. "Merit is attributed to charity, because the will, which charity perfects, is the first mover in the performance of meritorious works."[419] Consequently, "any deliberate action without exception done in the state of grace is meritorious."[420]

With the advent of the Reformation, with its theory of man's loss of spiritual freedom, the traditional doctrine of merit was charged with being against the Scriptures, and men like Peter Lombard and Aquinas were said to have corrupted the plain teaching of the word of God. In a lengthy treatise of his Institutes, under title of "Boasting about the merits of works destroys our praise of God," Calvin laid the foundations for the classic Protestant position on meritorious actions. He regretted that the term "merit" had ever entered the Christian vocabulary. "How much

[417] St. Augustine, "Commentary on Psalms," 83:16, *The Faith of the Early Fathers,* ed. and trans. William A. Jurgens (Collegeville, MN: Liturgical Press, 1970), 3:19; *CCC* 2007–8.
[418] *DS* 388; *CCC* 1996, 2008.
[419] St. Thomas, *De Veritate,* XIV, 5, 5; *CCC* 2011.
[420] St. Thomas, *II Sententiarum,* 40, 1, 5.

offense this term contains is clear from the great damage it has done to the world. Surely, as it is a most prideful term, it can do nothing but obscure God's favor and imbue men with perverse arrogance."[421]

He admitted that the ancient writers of the Church "commonly used it, and would that they had not given posterity occasion for error by their misuse of one little word." Then he proceeds to expound what he thinks the Fathers should have said if they had been more cautious.

Scripture shows what all our works deserve when it states that they cannot bear God's gaze because they are full of uncleanness. What, then, will the perfect observance of the law deserve, if any such can be found, when Scripture enjoins us to consider ourselves unprofitable servants even when we do everything required of us? For to the Lord we have given nothing unrequired, but have only carried out services owed, for which no thanks are due.

There is no doubt that whatever is praiseworthy in works is God's grace; there is not a drop that we ought by rights to ascribe to ourselves. If we truly and earnestly recognize this, not only will all confidence in merit vanish, but the very notion. We are not dividing the credit for good works between God and man, as the Sophists do, but we are preserving it whole, complete, and unimpaired for the Lord. To man we assign only this: that he pollutes and contaminates by his impurity those very things which were good. For nothing proceeds from a man, however perfect he be, that is not defiled.

Let the Lord, then, call to judgment the best in human works; He will indeed recognize in them His own righteousness but man's dishonor and shame.[422]

---

[421] John Calvin, *Institutes,* III, 15, 2.
[422] Ibid.

All the major confessions of the Reformation said the same thing, that any tinge of merit for our good works is derogation from the goodness of God. "To Him alone the glory," was not only a passing slogan; it was the avowed conviction that man contributes nothing of his own on the road to salvation, but is literally carried on the wings of the Most High.

It is small wonder, then, that the Council of Trent should have decreed so much on the question of merit from every angle that was challenged by the Reformers. Yet before delineating on what we deserve after being justified, it was important to clarify our naked condition before the infusion of divine love. We are justified freely, the Council declared, "in the sense that nothing that precedes justification, neither faith nor good works, merits the grace of justification for 'if out of grace,' then not in virtue of works; otherwise grace is no longer grace."[423]

That being granted, however, "when faith cooperates along with their works, the justified increase in the very justice which they have received through the grace of Christ and are justified the more, as it is written, 'He that is just, let him be just still.' "[424] For this reason, the Church begs the Lord in her prayers and liturgy, to "give us an increase of faith, hope, and charity." These virtues are not static possessions, but dynamic powers that grow in vitality with supernatural exercise.

With this in mind, those who are in the state of grace, whether they never lost it, or, having fallen, returned to God's friendship, should be confident that their labor has not been in vain.

> Eternal life should therefore be set before those who perse-
> vere in good works to the end and who hope in God. It should
> be set before them as being the grace that God, through Jesus
> Christ, has mercifully promised His sons, and as the reward

---

[423] *DS* 1532; Romans 11:6; *CCC* 2010.
[424] *DS* 1535; Apocalypse 22:11; *CCC* 1266.

which, according to the promise of God Himself, must assuredly be given them for their good works and merits.

They may be regarded as having truly merited the eternal life they will certainly attain in due time (if they but die in the state of grace), because Christ our Savior says, "He who drinks of the water that I will give him shall never thirst, but it will become in him a fountain of water, springing up into life everlasting."[425]

Christ has promised that a person who gives a drink of water to one of His least children will not be without a reward; and St. Paul taught that our present light affliction, which is for the moment, prepares for us an eternal weight of glory that is beyond measure. Nevertheless, although Scripture sets such a high value on good works, "a Christian should have no inclination either to rely on himself or to glory in himself instead of in the Lord, whose goodness toward all men is such that He wants His gifts to be their merits."[426] Moreover, since in many things we all offend, we should keep in mind as well the justice and severity of God as His goodness and mercy for whatever good we may have done.

Consistent with their principles, Baius and the Jansenists would not admit the existence of merit which derives from the autonomous will cooperating with divine grace. For Baius, "good works, performed by the sons of adoption are meritorious, not because they are performed by the spirit of adoption dwelling in the hearts of the sons of God, but only because they conform to the law, and manifest obedience to the law."[427] Since he denied true elevation of man's nature to the supernatural level, he also said it was Pelagian to claim that our good works do not merit heaven unless we are in the state of grace.[428]

---

[425] *DS* 1545, 1546; John 4:13.
[426] *DS* 1548; 1 Cor. 1:31, James 3:2; *CCC* 2008.
[427] *DS* 1913; *CCC* 2010.
[428] *DS* 1912.

His disciple Jansenius stressed the other side of the same theory, that whatever merit means it does not require true internal liberty to gain, on the prior assumption that we have lost the spiritual freedom that man enjoyed before the fall. "To merit or demerit," for Jansenius, "in the state of fallen nature, it is not necessary for man to have freedom from necessity, but only freedom from constraint."[429] This was an oblique way of stating that we have no genuine freedom of indifference, but only absence of external coercion, which, under the circumstances, is enough to "merit" or "demerit" before God.

Since the Council of Trent and the transit of continental Jansenism, the Catholic doctrine on merit has seen its largest development in the theology of the Church and the Communion of Saints. As the social character of Christianity became more prominent, the corresponding function of merit beyond oneself and for the benefit of others grew in importance until now it may be called a dominant feature of the Church's teaching. The encyclicals of Benedict XV on the missions, of Pius XI on the Sacred Heart, of Pius XII on the Mystical Body, John XXIII on Christian Unity, and several encyclicals of John Paul II, have one theme in common: that the faithful are called upon to labor, pray, and suffer by communicating their merits in union with those of Christ their Head for the upbuilding of the Kingdom of God on earth.

CONCEPT AND VARIETY

Medieval theologians under St. Thomas took the biblical notion of merit as a reward and analyzed its meaning in terms of justice and free will. "A man merits in as much as he does what he ought, by his free will; otherwise the act of justice whereby anyone discharges a debt would not be meritorious."[430]

---

[429] *DS* 2003.
[430] St. Thomas Aquinas, *Summa Theologica,* I–II, 114, 2, 1; *CCC* 2006.

The immediate problem that demanded solution was how we can be said to merit before God when all that we have and possess, and all our hope for the future, come to us from Him. In ordinary human relations, there is some equality between the man who does a good work and the one who repays him for his efforts. But between God and man there is the greatest inequality, since they are infinitely distant and all that man has is from God. Yet there is a solid basis for merit with God because, where other creatures attain their destiny necessarily, we do freely by choosing to use the means assigned us by the Creator as a condition for reaching the goal He set before us. "A rational creature moves itself to act by its own free will, hence its action has the character of merit, which is not so in other creatures."[431] They cannot be praised for acting nor blamed for refusing to act the way they do, whereas we deserve praise or censure—along with reward or punishment—according to our response to the will of God. We certainly owe the Creator our most dedicated service and perfect compliance with His commands, and in doing all this we are fulfilling a debt. At the same time, our service is not coercive and we are physically free to render it or not; if we do so, God has freely bound Himself to reward our generosity.

Taken existentially, merit is any morally good work deserving of reward. It implies that the action is somehow beneficial or honorable to another, and therefore calls for retribution from him either in justice or out of propriety. In theory, merit is the right or title to a reward, or that quality of a human act which makes it worthy of compensation. However that is not enough, because in addition to its worthiness the action must be recognized and accepted as meritorious by the person in whose favor I performed it. This has special relevance to our dealings with God, who rewards our deeds according to His judgment of

---

[431] St. Thomas Aquinas, *Summa Theologica,* I–II, corpus.

what we do conducive to His glory; His recognition and acceptation are paramount, and ultimately determine the quality of merit in our practice of virtue.

In every good work performed by a person in the state of grace we may distinguish three moral effects that differ considerably, although in certain respects they overlap. It will first of all be meritorious, namely graced with that quality which gives it a claim to reward. It will also be satisfactory, to the extent to which it repairs the offenses committed against God or removes some of the temporal punishment still due for past sins. It will finally be impetratory, in so far as the divine liberality is moved by the action to confer the benefits for which God is asked.

Consequently although the same act of virtue may be simultaneously meritorious, satisfactory and impetratory, each aspect has its own relationship to God. Merit looks to Him as rewarder and the action is deserving of recompense. Satisfaction placates His justice and presupposes an offense has been committed. Impetration successfully entreats the divine goodness and love.

These aspects are too closely related to be adequately distinguished without applying the familiar distinction between two kinds of merit, the condign (*de condigno*) and the congruous (*de congruo*). Synonymous with condign is deserved, adequate, justly due; and with congruous that which is fitting or becoming. On the difference between the two rests the whole theology of supernatural reward.

Merit is condign when there is a certain equality between the work done and its compensation, which may be reduced to a kind of demand in justice. In human affairs such merit establishes a clear and undisputed claim to a just return for service rendered. The recompense must be given because of a previous contract or promise, and to withhold it would be injustice. In our relations with God we cannot assert such absolute claim on His equity, because whatever we do is itself a gift from Him. Nevertheless, God has obligated Himself by a solemn covenant, in view of the merits of Christ, to bestow rewards in heaven and on earth in proportion to our fidelity to His will. As adopted sons of God and joint heirs with the Savior, we are able to merit heaven condignly with a positive title to the "wages" we earn in keeping the commandments.[432]

Congruous merit implies no previous contract or agreement, but only the kindness and generosity of the donor. Thus an employer may give his workmen a liberal bonus over and above their regular salary, not because they have a right to it but because he wants to show his appreciation of their services. Their salary would be merited condignly, whereas anything beyond would be gained congruously. Propriety suggests that employers occasionally favor their workmen with some evidence of good will; but if they fail to do so, they have not violated justice or done wrong to their employees.

In a comparable way God acts towards us in the supernatural order. Certain actions we perform He regards as worthy of merit in justice, which He has bound Himself to honor and on which we can depend with the surety of God's word. Others He prefers to consider dependent on His promise, perhaps, but not in justice. Thus a sinner making an act of perfect love congruously merits the state of grace, with something more than divine propriety but something less than strict equity. God does not owe him the grace of justification, but in His mercy has promised to infuse it under specified conditions and will be infallibly true to His promise.

Under less specified conditions, even though no formal promise has been made, we may still speak of congruous merit where the hope of receiving a benefit from God is not fidelity to His plighted word but

---

[432] *CCC* 2009.

the bonds of friendship with a soul in sanctifying grace. Such would be the guarantee of final perseverance in answer to humble prayer. The least favorable situation obtains in the case of a sinner estranged from God but still with some title to receiving aid when he prays or otherwise disposes himself to call upon the divine mercy. Theologians have coined the term fallible congruous merit to cover all such cases where the motive attributed to God is not faithfulness to His eternal pledge but liberality to all, even sinners, who invoke His name.

REQUISITE CONDITIONS

Keeping in mind the distinction between condign and congruous merit, the conditions required for each are correspondingly different. We may easily dispose of the latter because they are so minimal and obvious. In order to merit congruously, all that is necessary is that the act performed should be freely placed and not, for example, a pure reflex or thoughtless gesture; that it be morally good, since sinful conduct "merits," indeed, but in reverse; that the one meriting be still a wayfarer in this life, because no one can merit in any sense after death; and, most important, that supernatural grace be the driving power behind the action, for without true internal grace (whether actual or habitual) it is impossible to speak of merit of any kind.

Condign merit has requisite conditions attached on all sides: on the part of God that He has made a promise to that effect; on our part that we are still mortal, in the state of grace, and acting with complete human liberty. Further the action we perform must be morally good, and indifferent acts, if such exist, cannot be meritorious.

In the practical order, the conditions that affect us personally are the most pertinent. First of all, to be able to merit we must be still on probation in this life, since there can be no reward for good works after death. "It is appointed unto man once to die," wrote St. Paul, "and after this the judgment."[433] And the Council of Trent defined that the souls in purgatory are "outside the state of meriting or increasing in charity."[434] Christ Himself spoke of working while it is still day, before the night comes, when no man works.

We must also be in the state of grace. In the words of Trent, "nothing that precedes justification, neither faith nor works, merits the grace of justification"; and conversely, once a man enters into God's friendship he has the basis on which to claim heaven as his right if he perseveres. "As the branch cannot bear fruit of itself, unless it remains on the vine, so neither can you abide in me."[435] Unless we are united by theological charity with God and have Him dwelling in our souls, we lack the principle of supernatural merit in much the same way that a dead man cannot earn a wage. In order to deserve a heavenly reward we must be adopted sons of God, living with His life and operating on the same level by grace where He lives by nature. "If we are sons, we are heirs also," and the relation between the two, sonship and inheritance, is strictly causal; without the one there can be no promise of the other.

The inherent freedom needed to merit strictly before God follows on the divine option given us to serve Him with perfect liberty. When the rich young man asked Christ, "Good Master, what good work shall I do to have eternal life," the Lord answered him simply, "if you will enter into life, keep the commandments."[436] The force of this injunction is lost in English. The Greek original has *ei de theleis* "if you want to," which expresses a voluntary choice between two opposites, either to keep the divine precepts and reach heaven, or refuse to do so and fail to enter eternal life. Spiritual psychology confirms this condition, since

---

[433] Hebrews 9:27; *CCC* 1013, 1021.
[434] *DS* 1488.
[435] John 15:4.
[436] Matthew 19:16–17.

no one deserves to be rewarded (or punished) except for something that he himself did. If we examine our possessions, nothing is so uniquely our own as our free will, so that only what we offer God freely deserves to be praised (and rewarded) by Him as meritorious.

It would belabor the obvious to stress that only good actions receive merit, since the whole construct of man's salvation is based on the assumption that we are free agents capable of choosing between good and evil according to the will of God. Less clear is the position of some theologians who say that no action is condignly meritorious unless performed under the influence of supernatural charity. The trouble with the theory is that it can lead to some embarrassing practical consequences.

Such is the primacy of charity, it is said, that the *raison d'être* of merit consists in this virtue as its absolute and ultimate ground.[437] St. Thomas is quoted that "the precept of charity contains the injunction that God should be loved from our whole heart, which means that all things should be referred to God. Consequently man cannot fulfill the precept of charity unless he refers all things to God."[438] From this and like statements in the Fathers it is argued that the infused virtue of charity must have a positive influx in our good actions at the risk of losing their promised reward.

The most extreme demands require what is called a virtual flow of charity in our good works. This means that a previous act of charity continues *effectively* in what we are doing, although we are not necessarily conscious of this motivation when performing the good work. At the other end of the spectrum the majority of theologians believe it is enough to be in the state of grace and appeal to such authorities as Francis de Sales and Robert Bellarmine.

---

[437] *CCC* 2011, 2026.
[438] St. Thomas Aquinas, *Summa Theologica,* I-II, 100, 10, 2.

In practice, however, it makes no difference—or should not—unless the issue is misunderstood. Even the extremists who want a virtual intention flowing from charity into our good works allow that any previous act of charity will suffice, unless impeded by some disorder in the act, i.e., by a sinful element that implicitly erases the pure intention previously made.

SCOPE OF MERITORIOUS ACTIONS

On its negative side, a person in the state of grace cannot strictly merit the gift of final perseverance, which is a special gift that God reserves to Himself and yet promises to grant those who pray for it.[439] With this exception, however, we are able condignly to merit for ourselves the reward of eternal life, an increase in the beatitude which this heavenly reward implies, and, on earth, a growth in sanctifying grace with its concomitant virtues and gifts of the Holy Spirit.

Condign Merit

Nothing is clearer in the Scripture and the Church's tradition than the certainty of meriting heaven if we die in the love of God. But we not only gain heaven by our good works; we also determine the degree of happiness we will experience in the beatific vision—according to our greater or lesser correspondence with grace on earth. "The Son of Man is to come with His angels in the glory of His Father, and then He will render to everyone according to his conduct."[440] Or, as St. Paul told the Corinthians, "each will receive his own reward according to his labor."[441] Augustine explains the "many mansions" in heaven and the "full day's wage" paid to the laborers in the vineyard as descriptive of

---

[439] *CCC* 2016.
[440] Matthew 16:27.
[441] 1 Corinthians 3:8.

the two levels of celestial beatitude: the one absolute, which is common to all the blessed in their possession of God, symbolized by the *denarius* that all the workmen of the parable received, even those at the eleventh hour, and the other relative, which differs for each man depending on his works.

> Although one person may be stronger than another, or wiser, or more righteous, or more holy, "in the Father's house are many mansions." No one will be estranged from that place, where a home awaits every one according to what he deserves. True, they all equally receive the wage which the Householder commands to be given all who have worked in the vineyard. He makes no distinction between those who labored less and others who labored more. Their wages signify eternal life, where none lives more than another, because life has no degrees of measure in eternity.
>
> But the mansions signify the various dignities of merit in the one eternal life. "For there is one glory of the sun, another of the moon, another of the stars; for one star differs from another in glory. So also is the resurrection of the dead."[442]

St. Augustine illustrates the Church's tradition on still another point. By our good works on earth we merit varying degrees of the essential joy of heaven, which is the intuitive vision of the Trinity. At the same time, we also determine the measure of what are called the accidental joys, that are neither few nor insignificant.

Accidental happiness is enjoyed by the blessed through their company with Christ in His human nature, with the Mother of God, the angels and saints; through their reunion with families and former friends from their earthly life; through their knowledge of the

---

[442] St. Augustine, *Joannis Evangelium Tractatus* 67, 2.

created works of God. Moreover the union of the soul with the trans-figured body at the resurrection means an accidental increase of heavenly glory.

After the general judgment, therefore, "there will remain two cities, each with its own boundaries—the one Christ's, the other the devil's; the one embracing the good, the other the bad, with both consisting of angels and men. Among the former some will outrank others in bliss, and among the latter some will have a more bearable portion of misery than others."[443] Thus the divine equity follows mankind into heaven as well as hell, with happiness or suffering meted out with justice to the saved as well as damned.

In anticipation of heavenly glory, we also merit condignly an increase in sanctifying grace by our virtuous conduct.[444] "Set free from sin and become slaves of God, you have your fruit unto sanctification," the Romans were told by St. Paul.[445] And once justified, we are no longer children, tossed to and fro by every wind of doctrine, but should "practice the truth in love, and so grow up in all things in Him who is the head, Christ. For from Him the whole body derives its increase to the building up of itself in love."[446]

Good works promote every phase of habitual grace in the soul. The supernatural life of God is deepened in all its manifestations; faith becomes more clear and secure, hope more trustful and firm, and charity more fervent; the moral virtues of prudence, justice, temperance, and fortitude are made stronger; the gifts of the Holy Spirit intensify, and the indwelling is more profound; friendship with God grows in intimacy and the sense of divine sonship takes on a familiarity that only experience can prove. "Let us understand that he who loves has

---

[443] St. Augustine, *Enchiridion* 111.
[444] *DS* 1574, 1582.
[445] Romans 6:22; *CCC* 1995.
[446] Ephesians 4:15.

the Holy Spirit, and by having merits to have Him more, and by having Him more to love Him more."[447]

Congruous Merit

The scope of congruous merit extends to the farthest reaches of a man's life, and affects all persons who have attained the use of reason since it does not require the state of grace to be gained.

As might be expected, there is quite a difference between the generosity with which God responds to the good works of those in His friendship and those estranged from Him by grave sin. Only people in the state of grace can merit for others. One possible exception is gaining indulgences for the souls in purgatory. A few writers maintain that indulgences can be earned for the deceased even by persons in mortal sin, but their opinion is hardly probable and clearly opposed to the teaching of St. Thomas. However it would be enough that the state of grace be present before the end of the prescribed indulgenced work or prayer.

Sinners in mortal sin can merit congruously the graces they need to dispose themselves for returning to the divine friendship. The further question as to whether, being contrite, they also merit the actual justification is disputed among theologians, with the majority holding it to be possible under certain conditions, notably the outstanding merits before a man sinned gravely. Out of regard for these previous good deeds, according to Suarez, "God arouses the sinner to bring him out of his sin."[448]

The gift of final perseverance is in a class by itself. While a man is not in the state of grace we can hardly speak of him meriting to die in a condition he does not possess; at most he can dispose himself to receive efficacious graces to rise from the status in which he lives. But

---

[447] St. Augustine, "In Joannis Evangelium Tractatus," *MPL* 35:1838.
[448] Francisco Suárez, *De Divina Gratia* (Mogvntiae: Sumptibus H.M. Birckmanni, 1652), XII, 38, 6–7.

even the righteous merit the grace of dying a happy death only in the qualified sense of impetrating (by effective petition) what they have no right to, and what has not even been formally promised (to this individual) but rests ultimately on divine liberality in favor of those who love God.

Sanctifying grace enables a man to merit for himself and others the manifold graces that he and they need on the road to heaven. If it is surprising that our good works should obtain supernatural light and inspiration for other people as well as ourselves, we remember that "a man in grace fulfills the will of God, so it is congruous and in harmony with friendship that God should fulfill man's desire for the salvation of another. Of course there may sometimes be an impediment on the part of the one whose salvation the just man desires."[449] The one limitation is that we cannot merit the first actual grace in the process of justification for ourselves or anyone else, because without such grace no kind of merit is conceivable.

In the economy of God's mercy, the just man can earn temporal benefits for himself and others, in so far as the Lord foresees they are conducive to the spiritual welfare of those who receive them. The Psalmist makes no exception. "Revere the Lord, you His saints. They lack nothing, those who revere Him. Strong men suffer want and go hungry, but those who seek the Lord lack no blessing."[450] In the same strain, Christ enjoined that we should first seek the Kingdom of God and His justice, and "all these things will be added unto you."

PRAYER, SATISFACTION, AND MERIT

Theologians sometimes speak of merit in a way that seems to melt the distinction between meritorious actions and those which are reparative

---

[449] St. Thomas Aquinas, *Summa Theologica,* I–II, 114, 6; *CCC* 270.
[450] Psalm 33:10–11.

or impetratory. They describe the fruits of merit in this life as augmentative (increasing sanctifying grace), auxiliary (obtaining actual graces), satisfactory (remitting guilt and punishment due to sin), and impetratory (effectively petitioning divine help). The value of clearing up the concepts should be to better appreciate the dignity of merit and its universal application to every supernatural contingency. Otherwise there is risk of supposing that certain actions are somehow not meritorious, or at least the connection with merit may be hazy.

There is no problem regarding the augmentative and auxiliary fruits of merit, as explained above. The question is this. How are satisfaction and impetration related to merit? To what extent do their elements interweave, and how are they different?

Impetration and Merit

This is less complicated because the relationship between merit and impetration has been more fully developed. St. Thomas, in writing on the subject, says that "we impetrate in prayer things that we do not merit, since God hears sinners who beseech the pardon of their sins, which they do not merit."[451] In context he is talking about a person meriting the grace of final perseverance, which he declares is impossible, even for a just man, let alone a sinner. Evidently he refers to condign merit, and therefore holds that impetration and condign merit are not the same thing.

We further know that "impetration pertains to that which is requested and rests on favor (mercy and liberality) alone, whereas merit pertains to the end that a person earns and derives from justice."[452] Thus impetration looks to the person of whom a favor is asked, while merit looks to the intrinsic value of the work done. In one case what a man receives

---

[451] St. Thomas Aquinas, *Summa Theologica*, I–II, 114, 9, 1.
[452] St. Thomas Aquinas, *De Potentia*, 6, 9, 5.

is the result of divine bounty, in the other of God's equity. He owes us what we merit, He donates what we impetrate.

But if impetration is radically different from condign merit, is it also different from congruous? Yes, and no, according to the viewpoint.

The principal difference between merit and impetration is that the former applies only to persons on earth (in via) whereas impetration is possible also after death. Christ our Lord in His humanity, the Blessed Virgin, the angels and blessed in heaven, and the souls of the faithful departed pray and intercede before God and thus impetrate, i.e., obtain favors in answer to their petition. "Jesus has become surety of a superior covenant," we read. "He has an everlasting priesthood because He continues forever. Therefore He is able at all times to save those who come to God through Him, since He lives always to make intercession for us."[453] The same, in due measure, applies to all the saints, whose time of merit ceased at their entrance into eternity but whose power of petition is continually active.

Shifting the focus to ourselves, we can unite ourselves with the impetratory actions of the angels and saints, but especially with those of Christ in the Sacrifice of the Mass. We can merit graces for ourselves and others as a consequence. From the perspective of Christ the value of the Mass is infinite and has infinite capacity of impetration, but its effect in us is not only finite but also depends on our dispositions. We gain more or less of the graces obtainable according to the general norms which determine supernatural merit.

Moreover we combine impetration and merit in a single function every time we obtain a heavenly favor in answer to formal prayer. From the aspect of our petition to which God gave a favorable reply, it was impetration; from the standpoint of God's rewarding our supernatural act of praying, it was congruous merit. Indeed all our prayers in the

---

[453] Hebrews 7:22, 25; *CCC* 1364.

state of grace are meritorious and, when heard, may be equated with merit which looks to the divine liberality for its motive and power.

Finally the concept of impetration (and corresponding merit) should not be limited to formal prayers of petition. For it is quite possible to make all the actions of the day implicit requests of God, provided we have somehow directed our intentions to that purpose. The most familiar practice of this kind is the Morning Offering of the Apostleship of Prayer, approved and encouraged by the Church. In this prayer we offer "all my prayers, works, joys and sufferings of this day," for a host of petitions that we unite with the Sacrifice of the Mass. Thus all the requests of the members of the Apostleship, the numerous intentions for each day and month, and the specified intentions of the Holy Father are being petitioned throughout the day. The prayer encompasses every detailed action we perform, even though constant and conscious advertence to this intercession is impossible, and therefore theologically unnecessary.

Satisfaction

While prayer, merit, and satisfaction comprehend the whole of our good works, prayer is distinct from the other two because its effective value depends on the divine liberality, whereas merit and satisfaction mainly refer to God's justice and therefore have much in common, although they also differ widely.

In general, satisfaction means the voluntary undergoing of pain in order to compensate for the injury done to God by sin, and to remit the temporal punishment ordinarily due after sins have been forgiven.

Satisfactory works are necessarily penal, which follows on the nature of sin. After a man sins he remains guilty of the wrong committed. Consequently "the act of sin makes man deserving of punishment, in so far as he transgresses the order of divine justice, to which he cannot return except he pays some sort of penal compensation which restores him to the equality of justice. In accordance with divine equity, a person who has been too indulgent to his will, by transgressing God's commandments, suffers, either willingly or unwillingly, something contrary to what he would wish."[454]

St. Thomas requires three qualities for satisfaction, namely that the act performed be morally good, done for the honor of God "and penal, so that by it the sinner be deprived of something."[455] However it does not mean that whatever lessens the penalty or painful part of a satisfactory deed necessarily lowers the worth of his reparation. On the contrary, a person who more readily performs penance because of his readiness under the impulse of love for God increases the value of his satisfaction rather than lessens it.

Another difference, therefore, between merit and satisfaction is that the latter implies some element of pain or retrenchment, which merit, as such, does not require. Of course the same action may be simultaneously meritorious and satisfactory. Insofar as it satisfies the conditions of merit, it earns an increase of heavenly glory and sanctifying grace; and to the extent to which it meets the requirements of satisfaction it remits guilt and temporal punishment due for the sins committed.

This retrenchment, which must be at least objective, has to be voluntarily undergone, since satisfaction is a kind of active redemption, i.e., actively cooperating with the divine Redemption of which all men are the passive recipients. Thus we may patiently accept the trials and difficulties that God sends or assume certain works or practices that call for self-sacrifice.

It would be wrong, however, to suppose that some kind of infliction must be added to make an act satisfactory. The intrinsic effort expended in performing acts of virtue is enough; and then circumstances of time,

---

[454] St. Thomas Aquinas, *Summa Theologica,* I–II, 87, 6; *CCC* 1459.
[455] St. Thomas Aquinas, *Summa Theologica,* I–II, *Supplement,* 15, 1; *CCC* 1460.

place, personality, and duration will make further demands of sacrifice. Thus we have an immolation of intellect in acts of faith, of the will in obedience, of self-love when we love God and our neighbor, of the flesh in temperance and chastity, of the whole man in the observance of the precepts and evangelical counsels. Such immolation covers the complex of our lives, from the acceptance of a passing difficulty to the generous undertaking of great works for the glory of God.

Moreover, satisfaction differs from ordinary merit by reason of its purpose or function. It is directed to make good the offenses committed against the Creator. In place of turning away from God which characterizes sin, the sinner (or someone else for him) turns to God with sorrow for having offended the divine majesty, seeks to make up with love for ingratitude, and so obtains mercy from the Lord who invites sinners to repentance. The effects of this internal reparation may be the grace of conversion for oneself or another, or if the sins have already been forgiven, a deepening of divine friendship between the soul and God.

Closely connected with the preceding is the role of satisfaction to remit the punishment that sin brings in its wake. By placating the divine justice, we can be spared the sanctions that God inevitably visits on sinners in this life and in the next. Temporal punishments due to sin normally remain after forgiveness and, unless we expiate them, they will come to us unbidden as a purification or purgation in this life or after death.

The tie-in between sin and penalty is divinely ordained. "All punishment is just and inflicted for sin."[456] We suffer either for our own sins or for the sins of others. Vicarious suffering is familiar from human affairs, where we see one man undertake repayment of another's debt; and so in the spiritual order. We can volunteer to make expiation for other people's sins. In this way, altruistic satisfaction is

---

[456] St. Augustine, "Retractiones," *MPL* 32:583 sqq; *CCC* 271.

not unlike altruistic merit; we obtain for another a remission or amelioration of the sufferings he deserved for offending God. The whole idea of reparation to the Sacred Heart and suffrages for the souls in purgatory are built on this theological premise.

As might be expected, the Reformers had no sympathy with the idea that guilt can be removed without all the punishment being erased at the same time. Since they made fiducial faith the only remissive element in justification, they consistently held that all penalty, eternal and temporal, is remitted whenever a person is justified. Satisfaction in their vocabulary was useless, if not positively insulting to God's mercy—as though He would forgive a man's guilt without also removing all debt of punishment. The Reformation prejudice against indulgences and the Mass as a propitiatory sacrifice arose from these principles.

Taking issue with the Reformers, Trent examined and defined at length the subject of satisfactory merits. We may not say that "after receiving the grace of justification, the guilt of any repentant sinner is remitted and the debt of eternal punishment is blotted out in such a way that no debt of temporal punishment remains to be paid, either in this life or in purgatory, before the gate to the kingdom of heaven can be opened."[457]

In describing the varieties of satisfaction we can offer for past sins, the Council distinguished three levels: the penances sent from God and patiently endured; the penance imposed by the priest in sacramental confession; and "the penances voluntarily undertaken, such as fasts, prayers, almsgiving, or other works of piety."[458] Each is effective in its own way, and has its own relationship to merit.

The penitential providence of trials which God sends has been the theme of ascetical writers since before the time of Christ. "A great anxiety has God allotted, and a heavy yoke, to the sons of men. From the day

---

[457] *DS* 1580; *CCC* 1472–73.
[458] *DS* 1713.

one leaves his mother's womb to the day he returns to the mother of all
living, his thoughts, the fear in his heart, and his troubled forebodings
till the day he dies."[459] In the divine plan, these sufferings are meant to
be expiatory, provided we accept them patiently from the hands of God
as instruments of purification, to appease His offended justice and spare
ourselves and others more grievous pains in the future.

Sacramental satisfaction is imposed by the priest in the confessional and, according to common practice, fulfilled after absolution.
When the Jansenists held otherwise, that a person may not be
absolved until he had satisfied a long and rigorous penance, they were
condemned by the Church.[460] Unique among the works of satisfaction, the penance performed in connection with the sacrament has *ex
opere operato* efficacy. Its fruitfulness, in other words, depends
directly on the "power of the keys" and not on the dispositions of the
priest or penitent. Provided there is no obstacle, as when a person
commits a mortal sin subsequent to absolution and before he
performs his penance, the satisfactory power of the satisfaction takes
effect—though naturally more or less remissive according to the
penitent's dispositions.[461]

Most writers, including St. Thomas, hold that all our good works
take on *ex opere operato* satisfactory value from the sacrament of
confession. Among the reasons adduced is the Church's ritual practice,
after absolution, to have the priest pronounce a penitential formula.
"May the Passion of our Lord Jesus Christ, the merits of the Blessed
Virgin Mary and of all the saints, *whatever* good you do or evil
sustain, be to you unto the remission of sins, an increase of grace, and
the reward of eternal life. Amen."[462]

---

[459] Wisdom 40:1–2.
[460] *DS* 2306, 2635.
[461] *CCC* 1128.
[462] *Rituale Romanum.*

The most familiar kind of satisfaction is the one we freely undertake over and above the perennial trials, and distinct from the short penance said after confession. Trent singled out for special mention fasting, prayers, and almsgiving—which Christian tradition has favored since apostolic times. Bellarmine explains why this triad summarizes the penitential spirit. "One reason is that we should satisfy, as far as possible, through such things as are most completely our own." By sinning we claimed what was really not ours; so by satisfaction we deprive self in order to honor God. "We have three kinds of possessions: of soul, which we give by our prayers; of body, that we give Him through fasting; and of external good that we offer by giving alms. Another reason is that all vices can be reduced to the three mentioned by the apostle John: concupiscence of the flesh, concupiscence of the eyes and the pride of life. Fasting restrains concupiscence, almsgiving the concupiscence of the eyes, which is avarice, and prayer controls the pride of life."[463]

Viewed from the aspect of merit, the penance we offer by voluntary deprivation has the power of increasing sanctifying grace in the soul and thereby restoring (or even going beyond) the degree of supernatural friendship enjoyed by a soul before it offended God. It also has the efficacy of lessening or entirely cancelling the debt of punishment owed for past sins, not the least of which is the loss of those actual graces which God would have given to the sinner had he not committed sin. God would not have restored these graces except that the sinner satisfied the liability he incurred by his disobedience.

Everything dispossessive in our lives can assume satisfactory value. Prayer is generic for that radical self-immolation in which we acknowledge our basic contingency and utter dependence upon God, the only source of happiness and the fulfillment of all our desires. Fasting is

---

[463] St. Robert Bellarmine, *De Paenitentia,* IV, 6; *CCC* 1434.

generic for all bodily mortification and self-control, to be exercised in the very act of standing or walking and, under the influence of the will, affecting every motion and voluntary gesture of the body. Almsgiving is generic for every practice of charity, from sharing material things like money to giving another of the spiritual gifts we possess.

Perhaps more should be made of outgoing charity as a most salutary form of satisfaction. "Above all things," wrote St. Peter, "have a constant mutual charity among yourselves; for charity covers a multitude of sins."[464] It repairs, through the love of God which animates it, for the lack of love that lies at the root of sin. It calls upon humility to compensate for pride; generosity to make up for self-indulgence, patience to atone for anger, effort to redress for indolence, and possibly pain to amend for sinful pleasure. "Your own profit," wrote Chrysostom, "lies in the profit of your neighbor, and his in yours."[465] The mutual charity that men show one another is not only constructive of a healthy society, it is supernaturally expiatory.

The duty of making reparation for sin allows of no exception. "All men are obliged to make reparation," declared Pius XI, because all have sinned.

> It is true that the proud philosophers of this world deny this truth, resurrecting in its stead the ancient heresy of Pelagius, which conceded to human nature a certain inborn goodness that, by our own powers, lifts us up to ever higher levels of perfection. Born of human pride, these false theories were condemned by the Apostle who warns us that, "we were by nature children of wrath."
>
> As a matter of history since the beginning of the world men have recognized, in one way or another, the duty of making

---

[464] 1 Peter 4:8.
[465] St. John Chrysostom, *Homilies on First Corinthians* 33, 24.

reparation. Impelled by a kind of natural instinct, they have tried to placate the Deity by offering Him public sacrifices.[466]

What reason itself suggests, revelation confirms, that our sinful nature calls for atonement, to repay the honor due to God and repair the injury done to mankind, individually and collectively, by the accumulation of constant sin.

As with merit, so in satisfaction, we offer the expiatory value of our good works for ourselves as well as for others. In much the same way, the satisfaction we offer for ourselves, in the state of grace, is condign and due to us with that justice by which God has freely bound Himself. "Be converted to me with all your heart," He said through the prophet, "and turn to the Lord your God. For He is gracious and merciful, patient and rich in mercy, and ready to repent of the evil."[467] Vicarious satisfaction, however, is congruous, and depends on the divine mercy exclusively, along with the dispositions it meets in the person for whom reparation is offered.

Indulgences are distinctively important. "An indulgence is a remission before God of the temporal punishment due to sins whose guilt has already been forgiven, which the faithful Christian who is duly disposed gains under certain prescribed conditions through the action of the Church which, as the minister of redemption, dispenses and applies with authority the treasury of the satisfactions of Christ and the saints."[468]

Historically indulgences were already being granted in apostolic times. From the first to about the seventh century, they appeared under

---

[466] Pius XI, *On Reparation to the Sacred Heart* [*Miserentissimus Redemptor*] (1928), 8.

[467] Joel 2:12–13.

[468] Paul VI, *On Indulgences* [*Indulgentiarum Doctrina*] (1967), Norm 1; also *Code of Canon Law* (*Codex Iuris Canonici*), trans. Canon Law Society of America (Washington, D.C.: Canon Law Society of America, 1983), Canon 992; *CCC* 1471.

the guise of a mitigation of public penance or a partial remission of the canonical penance imposed by the Church according to the gravity of the crime. Mitigation was necessary in view of the severities prescribed. A penitential of the seventh century ordered that "a man whose child dies on account of neglect without Baptism shall do penance for three years; in the first with bread and water, in the other two without delicacies and without marital relations." And "he who gives a blow to his neighbor without doing him any harm, shall do penance on bread and water one or two or three forty-day periods."[469] Other sins and faults were to be expiated accordingly, but the practice became unmanageable, not only because the penances were extreme but their number and variety (several thousand) made application often impossible.

A significant feature of their mitigation was the reason for granting such "indulgences." They were offered to the faithful "in view of the merits of the martyrs," whose intercession with God even before death, was to supply for the external penances of their fellow members in the Church. The principle involved has more than historical interest, since it forms the basis for the idea that a short prayer or visit to the Blessed Sacrament is equivalent to one hundred days, or several years of expiatory value of the ancient canonical penance.

Hence comes the respect that indulgences have always enjoyed among Christians. Private works of satisfaction, especially for the Poor Souls, depend mainly on the dispositions of the one who does them; but joined to an indulgence they draw on the treasury of the Mystical Body, where the whole Church, Head and members, contribute in a special way to the efficacy of the good work performed.

---

[469] *Medieval Handbooks of Penance,* trans. John Thomas McNeill and Helena Margaret Gamer (New York: Columbia University Press, 1938), 105, 108.

DIFFERENCE AND INCREASE

Christ Himself indicated the difference in merit between the actions of two persons when he commented on the rich who were putting their gifts into the treasury of the temple, in contrast with the poor widow who contributed only two mites. "Truly I say to you," He remarked, "this poor widow has put in more than all. For all these out of their abundance have put in as gifts to God; but she out of her want has put in all that she had to live on."[470]

The norms which determine how much merit accrues from a given action apply equally to prayers and works of satisfaction, since the same principle obtains in all of man's relations with God. St. Thomas analyzed the norms on the basis of the nature of merit, which derives from the elements that constitute it. He is speaking of condign merit and, by analogy, of condign satisfaction.

> Since merit does not consist in a habit but in act, and not in any kind of act but in one animated by the state of grace; since moreover every meritorious act proceeds from the will—merit therefore must receive something from grace, something from the will, and something from the object of the action, whence the type of act is determined. Consequently we can measure the efficacy of merit from these three factors: from grace, the will and object.
>
> For as an act is informed by greater charity and grace, it is to that extent more meritorious; also the more voluntary is an act, the more it has of the essence of merit and is more praise-worthy; and finally, the more arduous is an object, the higher is the merit of the act—though the comparison is always understood about one of these factors, with the others being

---

[470] Luke 21:3–4.

taken as equal. However the fact that something arduous increases the degree of merit does not arise from the difficulty but from the dignity of the labor; for the more sublime a thing, the more it is beyond the reach of a man's efforts.[471]

Theologians and spiritual writers have used these principles to develop a system of values that are the common possession of Christian asceticism. They usually combine the first two norms of St. Thomas into one, as "conditions on the part of the one who merits," and take the third alone, as "conditions on the part of the act itself." Minor differences of theological opinion will be transmitted, most of which can be resolved by keeping in mind the proviso laid down by Aquinas, that no single factor *ipso facto* increases that total merit of any given action we perform. But taken singly each element contributes to the whole meritorious value. A man may have more grace at the time he places a salutary act, but may perform it more sluggishly than someone else who has less of the divine life. Again, an act of temperance, which is lower in the scale of virtues than theological charity, may be more meritorious in a given instance than an act of love, because the will behind the exercise was greater. In other words, the norms of increase in supernatural merit are to be understood objectively, so that, *other things being equal.* The factor in question intensifies our merit before God.

Determining Factors in the Person

The most influential element which determines the degree of merit (and satisfaction) is the possession of sanctifying grace. Hence, *ceteris paribus,* the more habitual grace we possess, the greater is our power of meriting. Underlying this norm is the idea of "personal dignity," that

---

[471] St. Thomas, II *Sententiarum,* 29, 1, 4.

explains many otherwise mysterious things in the spiritual life. As we know from human experience, the value of an action depends in great measure on the dignity of the one who performs it, and on the esteem that we and others have of the person in question. In the supernatural order, nothing excels the dignity of a soul in the state of grace, and, from all we know of the Church's teaching, God looks with favor on a person according to the amount of His own life which the soul possesses.

Accordingly if we possess a higher degree of divine indwelling, we are worth more in the eyes of God. Our actions are more agreeable to Him and to that extent more meritorious. One feature of this principle is that it increases merit by geometric proportion. As our good works multiply, sanctifying grace grows apace; and as grace intensifies, the same good works become productive of greater merit.

Besides, this intensity of divine life will normally exert a corresponding influence on our actions. Apart from the idea of "personal dignity" before God, the whole complexus of possessing a deeper faith, stronger hope, and more ardent charity conspires to improve the quality of what we do. All these factors tend to increase merit.

Purity of intention is closely related to the possession of grace. Christ set down the standard when He said, "Take heed not to practice your good before men, in order to be seen by them; otherwise you shall have no reward with your Father in heaven."[472] Merit can be lost if no purity of intention is present, and its value grows with the singleness of purpose—to please God—that motivates our actions.

A pure intention involves two aspects that need to be kept distinct: the purity of the motive with which we perform a salutary action and its nobility. The first refers to the absence of self-interest or lesser motives than seeking to please God, the second has to do with how much supernatural charity influences what we are doing.

---

[472] Matthew 6:1; *CCC* 1752–53.

Generous motivation is paramount in the gaining of merit, and understandably determines the supernatural reward that comes to us from God. Nevertheless it does not follow that if any other motive intrudes than the single one of seeking the divine glory, the action is without merit, or worse, even sinful. If a lower motive like vainglory should enter, it is highly questionable whether such an imperfection is always connected with venial sin. In practice it is recommended to bolster one's motivation from several sides, and increase merit in the process while protecting it. Thus an act of patience prompted by respect for the person concerned and by the desire to atone for one's sins has the combined value of the two virtues converging on a single object, and safeguards the will from becoming soiled through selfishness.

Since charity is the wellspring of spiritual conduct, every act we place under its inspiration will have meritorious value in the measure of divine love that moves us. Theoretically, then, since an act of theological charity is the most noble act of the virtues and highest in merit, acts of the other virtues will become more meritorious as more charity is put into them. However a caution must be made. At least two propositions of Fenelon have been censured, to forestall the suspicion that there is something wrong if charity is combined with some other less altruistic virtue. "There is a habitual state of the love of God," said Fenelon, "which is pure charity and without any admixture of self-interest. Neither the fear of punishment nor the desire of reward has any longer a place in it." And from another angle, "in the state of a contemplative or unitive life, we lose every self-interested motive of fear and hope."[473]

Accordingly merit is not increased if, eliciting an act of virtue motivated by the love of God, I *exclude* the motive of other virtues or abstract from them. The increase derives rather from subordinating such motives as hope and fear of God to the dominant one of love. In fact,

---

[473] *DS* 2351, 2352.

"charity cannot exist alone without the exercise of the other virtues, just as the other virtues are not perfect without charity because they do not perfectly unite one with God."[474] A common practice is to renew the pure intention occasionally by making aspirations of the love of God.

Fervor or voluntary intensity also raises the meritoriousness of our acts. Another way to express the same idea is that the greater wilfulness we expend in performing a good action, the greater liberty it indicates and the higher merit it deserves, just as in bad actions increased advertence and freedom mean greater culpability. Half-hearted effort merits in proportion to its lack of volitional energy, just as whole-hearted generosity gains proportionally. "For the love of God," St. Ignatius urged his sons, "be not careless or tepid. Try to maintain a holy, discreet ardor in work and in the pursuit of learning as well as of virtue. With one as with the other, one energetic act is worth a thousand that are listless, and what a lazy man cannot accomplish in many years an energetic man usually achieves in a short time."[475]

A person's state in life may also affect the worth of his actions. Persons living under vow, whether in the religious life or the priesthood or by a private commitment to God, are directly concerned.

When a person takes a vow he makes an act of religion, which is the chief of the moral virtues, whose object is to worship God as the ultimate source of creation. "Hence the works of the other virtues, like fasting, which is an act of abstinence, or continence, which is an act of chastity, are better and more meritorious if they are done in fulfillment of vow, since they thus belong to the divine worship, being like sacrifices to God. Wherefore St. Augustine says that not even virginity is honorable in itself, but only when consecrated to God and cherished by godly continence."[476]

---

[474] St. Thomas Aquinas, *Summa Theologica*, II–II, 184, 1, 2; *CCC* 2102–3.
[475] St. Ignatius, *Letters*, 123.
[476] St. Thomas, *Summa Theologica*, II–II, 88, 6.

Furthermore, a vow implies offering God not only one or more actions but giving Him the very power behind the activity, since a person binds himself so that in the future he cannot do something else, just as "he gives more who gives the tree with its fruit, than he that gives the fruit only."[477] His will is thereby fixed on the service of God, since the essence of a perpetual vow is to consecrate oneself irrevocably to the divine will. As in things evil, a man is more wicked if he is obstinate in committing sin, so is he better and his actions are meritorious if he is dedicated in doing good.

Determining Factors in the Action

Along with the subjective aspects of virtue that contribute to greater merit are the objective elements of the actions themselves. This stands to reason because what counts with God is not only our intentions but also our deeds; they have their share in the reward that is due to us.

The intrinsic excellence of an act of virtue is one determining factor since we know that the virtues have a hierarchy of values which is independent of the circumstances under which they are practiced. Between the theological and moral virtues, the former are superior, and within them theological charity is the highest.[478] Consequently other things remaining equal, there is more credit with God in performing an act of faith than one of temperance, and of charity than of faith. We have to practice all the virtues, of course; but on the bare level of their relative worth, some are higher than others and correspondingly more meritorious.

Two practical items may be pointed out. Given this hierarchy of objective value, it follows that a man should take every reasonable opportunity to practice the higher virtues and not allow himself,

---

[477] Ibid.
[478] *CCC* 1826.

unnecessarily, to devote all his time and energy to a lesser when he could also be practicing the higher.[479] On the other hand, the complexities of daily life are such that most people have little choice on the kind of virtues they practice, say prudence for a teacher or justice in an administrator. Yet they can profit from the higher virtues of faith and charity by animating their practice of prudence and justice with motives that draw upon faith and the love of God. In fact, this is the main reason why a life under vow is *per se* more pleasing to the Lord than the same life without such consecration. The difference is that by his vows a man's whole life is dominated by the virtue of religion, which looks exclusively to the honor and glory of God.

Quantity or frequency of an act, and its duration, are also meritorious elements. Certainly we would call a man more generous if he gave a thousand dollars to some worthy cause than if he gave only ten; or if he helped a poor family for a year instead of only for a day; or if he never failed in kindness to anyone, than if he were kind only to one or two.

However, as we know from Christ's comment about the widow's two mites, the quantitative aspect of our good actions is relative; it depends on numerous other factors that may completely reverse the picture, where a dollar's gift to charity may be more worthy supernaturally than many times that sum. Perhaps the best explanation is to say that the quantity of a good act—its amount, frequency, or duration—is a factor less in determining than in manifesting merit. It shows greater virtue and will deserve better of God, not necessarily in contrast with other people's actions, but by comparing a man with his own ideals and capacity for action. My half dollar in the Sunday collection may be more meritorious than someone else's ten dollars; however it would also be less meritorious if, through selfishness I gave only a fraction of what I could afford.

---

[479] *CCC* 1827.

More critical than the foregoing is the function of difficulty of hardship in the performance of virtue. Do they also increase merit and why?

At the outset it must be said that difficulties are not of themselves meritorious. The contrary opinion of the Jansenists was born of the strange theory that a man's nature is so fallen it can only follow its own concupiscence and clash with every moral good, unless divine grace comes along and efficaciously supplies for human depravity. Condemned by the Church for postulating this unnatural tension, they took refuge in believing that the opposition they experienced was just another facet of the same principle. "The suffering of persecution and punishments that a person endures as though he were a heretic, sinner and criminal is normally his final probation and most meritorious, because it makes him more conformed to Jesus Christ."[480] Indeed, for Quesnel it too often happens that the holiest men in the Church are treated as the least worthy, in accordance with the universal law of conflict.

The Catholic interpretation is quite different. Difficulties inherent in the practice of virtue tend to increase merit, not because they are obstacles to be overcome but because they invoke greater love of God, more generosity, and more strenuous effort. St. Thomas compares the lot of man before and after the fall to point up the issue involved.

> In his pristine condition, man commonly would have had greater grace than after he had sinned. His will therefore would have been more ready to act, since there was no resistance. Consequently the actions of a man in his primitive state were more efficacious for merit than afterwards, if we consider his conduct regarding the same object in both cases. This would be

---
[480] *DS* 2498.

true although a man has more trouble performing a given act since the fall than before.

The reason is that an arduous task increases the degree of merit not by reason of the difficulty but of the nobility of the act, except obliquely, to the extent that what is difficult calls for greater attention and requires greater effort of the will.[481]

Unlike charity and voluntariness, then, difficulty is not the essence of merit. Yet there is a close relation. It either implies an exalted object which is difficult to reach because it is high, or at least evokes greater will power and generosity because it is difficult to do.

Keeping these distinctions in mind, it remains true that difficulties in the spiritual life have much to do with raising the merit of our conduct. It is assumed that the hardship is not culpable, otherwise the bad habits induced by years of sin would make the simplest act of virtue heroic in a dissipated will. Stated more broadly, the source of hardship can be extrinsic to the action, arising from culpable personal defects. Sinful habits, uncontrolled passions, evil inclinations, or lack of prudent vigilance, then, clearly, are difficulties which lower merit instead of increasing it.

But if the difficulties are intrinsic to the action, i.e. part of its very nature, or at least not culpable in the person here and now; they add to the meritorious value of good actions done under such trying circumstances. Thus if the work to be done is arduous or sublime in itself, if doing it means overcoming severe temptations and external or even internal trials arising from temperament or physical conditions, the merit in performing what God wants will gain a greater reward.

The statements of the saints in their hunger for suffering must be interpreted in the light of these principles, at the risk of misunderstanding what William James crudely dismissed as "pathological

---

[481] St. Thomas Aquinas, II *Sententiarum*, 29, 1, 4.

self-immolation." Among the mystics especially, we find an incredible desire to endure trials that seem to the natural man inhumanly extreme. St. Margaret Mary is a classic example, as revealed in her letters.

> I consider the hours I have spent without suffering as lost. Indeed, I assure you that I do not wish to live long unless I have the happiness to suffer.
>
> It pleases the Lord to keep me in a state of continual suffering, my strength so exhausted that it is with extreme difficulty I carry my miserable body of sin. When I behold my suffering, it seems to me that I feel the same joy the most avaricious and ambitious do in seeing their treasures multiply.
>
> I know of nothing that so sweetens the prolongation of life as constant suffering in loving. Let us then suffer lovingly and uncomplainingly, esteeming as lost the moments passed without suffering. Who can hinder us from becoming saints, when we have a heart to love and a body to suffer?[482]

The clue to this attitude toward suffering is the word "love" that constantly recurs in the writings of the saints. In the history of God's dealing with men, those whom He chooses for closest intimacy He visits with the greatest trials to purify them from inordinate taste for creatures and dispose them for graces of a high order. They, in turn, responded to this economy by using the difficulties that other people avoid, to deepen their volitional effort in serving God under His visitations.

In the Spiritual Exercises we have the philosophy of hardship in the supernatural life reduced to a definite plan. Ignatius built on the premise that a soul in love with God will seek to be like Him as far as it can.

---

[482] François Léon Gauthey, *Vie et Oeuvres de Sainte Marguerite-Marie Alacoque* (Paris: Ancienne Librairie Poussielgue, 1920), Vol. II, Letters 11, 39, 86, 92; *CCC* 2031.

It is a matter of faith that God became man, and in His human nature underwent the most trying experiences of poverty, humiliation, the Passion, and finally death on the Cross. If I love Christ, I want to follow in His paths, which means to have a habitual disposition of preferring poverty to wealth, contempt to honor, and labor to a life of ease.

Yet, even in the sublime heights of the Third Mode of Humility, Ignatius does not forget the meritorious value of this following of the Master. The reward he envisions is an increase of the divine life in the soul, making it more pleasing to God, as well as more graces for others, merited congruously in favor of people whose salvation may depend on the sacrifices of those who are God's chosen ones.

10

INFUSED VIRTUES AND GIFTS

In *The Clerk's Tale* by Chaucer, we are told that "natural goodness comes of God, no strain of blood can give it, no, nor ancestor."[483] This was a poetic way of saying that so-called virtue is not born of nature but comes as a gift of God, who endows some people with qualities of mind and heart that others, after a lifetime of effort, never acquire.

But there is no poetry in the Catholic belief that part of the divine life we obtain in sanctifying grace is the possession of certain enduring powers—infused virtues and gifts—that raise man to a supernatural orbit of existence which is as far above nature as heaven is above earth. Grace gives us abilities of thought and operation that are literally born, not of the will of flesh nor of the will of man, but of God. Nowhere else does the true character of the supernatural appear more evident than in the endowments of infused virtue which some people possess and others do not, making some capable of spiritual actions which others cannot perform.

The soul is the substantial form of the body, which gives man all that is properly human and places him essentially into the natural order.[484] Sanctifying grace, by analogy, is the accidental form of the soul, which gives the same man all that is properly divine and puts him habitually into the family of God. Comparing the two, the soul is the

---

483 Geoffrey Chaucer, *The Clerk's Prologue and Tale.* (New York: Cambridge University Press, 1966).
484 *CCC* 365.

foundation of natural existence, and sanctifying grace is the principle of supernatural life.

Yet we know that the soul is not all we have in the body. The soul itself has various powers through which it operates and by which it gives expression to its rational nature. Even so, by a divine consistency, the "soul of the soul," as sanctifying grace has been called, must have channels for the deiform life that God pours into the just. These are the virtues, theological and moral, according to their respective purposes: like the native abilities through which mind and will come into contact with the visible world around us, and the world, in turn, with us; so grace brings us into contact with the supernatural and with God.

Moreover the powers of nature are possessed of certain instincts or impulses, which are natural propensities that incite animals (including man) to the actions essential to their existence, preservation, and development. In like manner the powers of supernature are endowed with spiritual instincts or gifts by which the Holy Spirit directs souls to follow His inspirations easily and more securely towards the attainment of their heavenly goal.

THEOLOGICAL VIRTUES

Etymologically "virtue" seems to be derived from the same root as the Latin *vir* (man) and *vis* (power), suggesting that in its primitive sense virtue implied the possession of such masculine qualities as strength and courage and, in the moral order, of goodness and human perfection.

The Scriptures have several equivalents for the Vulgate *virtus,* notably *ischus* (strength or power), *dunamis* (might), and *arethê* (moral excellence or perfection). In the Hebrew Old Testament there is no specific word for virtue, but in the Old Testament books written originally in Greek the word *arethê* is used to mean moral goodness or a particular moral quality.[485] In the New Testament the Greek word for virtue is used only five times; twice to describe the powers of God, twice meaning moral vigor, and only once of moral virtue in particular.[486]

But if the specific term was used only seldom in the New Testament, the concept of a divinely infused power which God confers on the elect appears throughout the letters of St. Paul and in the two epistles of St. Peter.

The theological virtues are identified as unique possessions conferred specially on the soul by God. "There abide faith, hope and charity," St. Paul wrote to the Corinthians, "these three; but the greatest of these is charity."[487] In the introduction to his first letter to the Thessalonians, he told them he was "mindful before God our Father of your work of faith, and labor, and charity, and your enduring hope in our Lord Jesus Christ."[488]

These are not passing favors but permanent endowments, since those who possess them are urged to "put on the breastplate of faith and charity, and for a helmet the hope of salvation."[489] The faithful are to use them as their constant weapons in the battle against evil, and their protection against the wiles of Satan. They are said to "abide," in the manner of enduring principles of action; and among them, charity "never fails," because it continues into eternity.

Not everyone receives these gifts, but only those who are the friends of God. "Having been justified by faith, let us have peace with God through our Lord Jesus Christ, through whom we also have access by faith unto that grace in which we stand, and exult in the hope of the

---

[485] Virtue as moral goodness (Wisdom 4:1; 5:13; 2 Macc. 6:13), and as particular moral quality (Wisdom 8:7).

[486] Divine powers (1 Peter 2:9; 2 Peter 1:3), moral vigor (2 Peter 1:5), and moral virtue (Philippians 4:8); *CCC* 1803.

[487] 1 Corinthians 13:13.

[488] 1 Thessalonians 1:3.

[489] 1 Thessalonians 5:8.

glory of the sons of God." In spite of tribulations, "hope does not disappoint, because the charity of God is poured forth in our hearts by the Holy Spirit."[490] Faith, hope, and charity, therefore, proceed from the state of grace, which they manifest and through which the divine life is made to grow.

In the patristic period, the theological virtues were the subject of frequent writing and, in Pelagian times, of controversy. The commentaries of the Fathers on St. Paul offer a complete treatise on every phase of faith, hope, and charity; and St. Augustine's *Enchiridion* or *Manual of the Christian Religion* was always referred to by him as "a book on Faith, Hope, and Charity." For Augustine, therefore, a summary of these virtues was an epitome of the essentials of Christianity.

However a scientific study was not made until the Middle Ages, in the great *Summae* of Peter Lombard, Peter of Poitiers, William of Auxerre, and Alexander of Hales, terminating in the definitive work of St. Thomas. The latter's treatment of the theological virtues remains the standard and figures extensively in all his major writings, especially the *Summa Theologica*.

Meaning and Comparison

St. Thomas defines virtue as "a good habit bearing on activity," or a good faculty-habit (*habitus operativus bonus*).[491] Generic to the concept of virtue, then, is the element of habit, which stands in a special relation to the soul, whether in the natural order or elevated to the divine life by grace.[492]

The soul is the remote principle or source of all activities. Faculties are the proximate sources built into the soul by nature. Habits are still more immediate principles superadded to the faculties either by

---

[490] Romans 5:1–6.
[491] St. Thomas Aquinas, *Summa* I–II, 55, 4; *CCC* 1806.
[492] *CCC* 1804, 1810.

personal endeavor or by a supernatural infusion from God. Consequently the soul helps the man, faculties help the soul, and habits help the faculties.

Habits reside in the faculties as stable dispositions or "hard to eradicate" qualities that dispose the faculties to act in a certain way, depending on the type of habit. If the habit is acquired it gives the faculty power to act with ease and facility. If it is infused, it procures not readiness in supernatural activity, but the very activity itself. Natural or acquired habits result from repeated acts. They do not give the power to act, but the power to act readily and with dexterity. Thus in the natural order, the faculty without the habit is simply power to act. The faculty with the habit is power to act with perfection. Since custom is parent to habit, it is called second nature. Faculty is like first nature, and habit the second.

Not every habit is a virtue. It is if the habit improves and perfects a rational faculty as to incline it towards good—good for the faculty, for the will, and for the whole man in terms of his ultimate destiny.

There is a broad sense in which we can speak of the natural dispositions of any of our powers as innate virtues, but this is a loose rendering and leads to confusion. More properly the infused virtues should be contrasted with the acquired, in which the autonomous will of the individual plays the dominant role. My consistent effort to concentrate on a given course of action, repeating the process over a long period of time and in spite of obstacles, gradually develops a tendency to perform the action spontaneously and almost without reflection, yet with a degree of perfection that someone else without the virtue cannot duplicate.

The infused virtues are independent of this process. They are directly produced by God in the operative faculties of a man, and differ mainly from the acquired because they do not imply the human effort that determines the faculty to a particular kind of activity, namely, facility induced by repetition. God Himself pours in (*infundere*) the infused virtues, not by compulsion or overriding the free will and without dependence on us. Augustine says that virtues "are produced in us by God without our assistance." They are supernatural gifts, freely conferred through the merits of Christ, and raise the activity of those who possess them to the divine level in the same way that sanctifying grace elevates their nature to a share in the life of God.

Among the infused virtues, however, some are concerned directly with God and operate in a field where unaided reason cannot work. They are called theological. Others have as their object not God Himself, the final end of all things, but human activities that are penultimate and subordinate to the final end. They are called moral. Four of them, prudence, fortitude, temperance, and justice—are primary and are called cardinal (*cardo,* hinge) in human conduct.

The necessity for theological virtues appears from a simple analysis of man's elevation to the supernatural order. Our final happiness may be considered in two ways. One, obtainable by the use of our native powers of mind and will, is commensurate with our human nature. The other is immeasurably higher, surpassing nature, and is secured only from God by the merciful communication of His own divinity. To make it possible for us to attain this higher destiny in the beatific vision, we must have new principles of activity, which are called theological virtues. These virtues are called theological because their object is God and not, as in moral virtues, merely things that lead to God. Because they are infused in the mind and will by God alone, unlike the habits acquired by personal exercise, they would never be known to us except through divine revelation.

Reflecting on the data of Scripture and tradition, we find a striking reasonableness in the kind of virtues that God infuses in the soul. They direct us to supernatural happiness in the same way that our natural inclinations lead to our connatural end, i.e., in two ways. First we must have a light for the mind, both of principles and practical knowledge. Second we must have rectitude for the will so that it can tend naturally toward the good as defined for us by reason.

> Both of these, however, fall short of the order of supernatural happiness, where "the eye has not seen, nor ear heard, neither has it entered into the heart of man, what things God has prepared for those who love Him." Consequently in both cases man had to receive in addition something supernatural to lead him to a supernatural end.
>
> For his intellect man receives supernatural principles, held by means of a divine light, which are the articles of belief accepted on faith. His will is directed to the same end in two ways, as an intentional drive moving towards that destiny to attain it (which is hope), and as a kind of spiritual union that somehow transforms the will into the goal it is seeking (which is charity).[493]

Accordingly, the theological virtues supply for the mind and will what neither faculty has of itself, the salutary knowledge, desire, and love of God and His will, without which there could be no supernatural *order,* which means the voluntary choice of suitable means to reach the heavenly goal to which we were elevated. These virtues make us well adjusted to our last end, which is God Himself; hence they are called theological. They not only go out to God—as all virtue worthy of the name must do—but they also reach Him. To be well adjusted to our destiny we must know and desire it. The desire demands that we are in love with the object to which we are tending and are confident of obtaining it. Faith makes us know the God to whom we are going, hope makes us look forward to joining Him, and charity makes us love Him.

---

[493] St. Thomas Aquinas, *Summa Theologica,* I–II, 62, 3.

Unlike the virtues known to philosophy, faith, hope, and charity are not applications of the golden mean between extremes. In Aristotle's language, a moral virtue is a certain habit of the faculty of choice, consisting of a mean (*mesotês*) suitable to our nature and fixed by reason in the manner in which a prudent man would fix it. It is a habit which consists in a mean between excess and defect. Courage, for example, keeps the mean between cowardice and reckless daring; sincerity between ironical depreciation and boastfulness, modesty between shamelessness and bashfulness, and just resentment between callousness and spitefulness.

But a theological virtue can be measured either by what the virtue demands or by what our capacity allows. Concerning the first, "God Himself is the rule and mode of virtue. Our faith is measured by divine truth, our hope by the greatness of His power and faithful affection, our charity by His goodness. His truth, power and goodness outreach any measure of reason. We can certainly never believe, trust or love God more than, or even as much as, we should. Extravagance is impossible. Here is no virtuous moderation, no reasonable mean; the more extreme our activity, the better we are."[494]

Nevertheless there is a valid sense in which even the theological virtues observe a kind of mean, or better a center of gravity to which they tend. As far as God is concerned, it is simply not possible to believe in Him, trust Him, or love Him too much. From our viewpoint, we should exercise these virtues according to the measure of our condition. For instance, Christian faith goes midway between heretical extremes. Pelagianism, on one hand, dispenses with divine grace while Jansenism, the opposite extreme denies free will: Christian hope must choose a path among the numerous prospective means of salvation; and Christian charity must find a balance in the myriad opportunities for loving God.

---

[494] Ibid., 64, 4.

FAITH

In the words of St. Paul, "faith is the substance of things to be hoped for, the evidence of things unseen."[495] Thus faith is basically a virtue of the mind, which becomes enabled to assent, on the word of God, to whatever truths He has revealed. The intellectual character of faith becomes clear from a cursory analysis of the Pauline definition.

The apostle calls faith the substance (*hupostasis*) of things to be hoped for, or as the New English Bible has it, "faith gives substance to our hopes." Taken objectively, faith is the substance of our hopes because it is the basis of all merit, and consequently the ground of our hope to obtain the heavenly promises in which we believe. It also gives substance to our hope by defining the nature of the blessings we desire and gives us a foretaste of what they will be. Faith gives a firm conviction in the objective truths communicated by God. Because we know that we know what He has revealed, we have absolute assurance that our will is not hoping in fabulous myths or aspiring to airy dreams.

But faith is also the evidence (*elegchos*) of things unseen, i.e., it "makes us certain of realities we do not see." The first meaning of *elegchos* in ancient Greek literature was "proof," and "argument to convince." Consequently the things which are not seen are more than invisible to human eyes. They are beyond the capacity of the mind to comprehend. Yet by faith we know they are true because the word of God supplies for comprehension. He sees and understands and tells us what He knows. For "if we receive the testimony of men, the testimony of God is greater."[496] If we believe fallible men and guide so much of our lives by their equally fallible claims, why not the word of God, which is not fallible?

---

[495] Hebrews 11:1.
[496] 1 John 5:9; *CCC* 1814.

The roots of anti-intellectualism in Christianity may be found in the Gnostic theories of the first and second centuries, and in the classic Reformers who depreciated the mental element of faith. But the gravest challenge arose more recently under the form of Modernism. According to the Modernists, faith is not an operation of the mind but a function of the emotions and will. Its object is not the truth of revelation but a "feeling of dependence," which Schleiermacher (1768–1834) defined as the essence of all religion.

In a series of documents that have made theological history, St. Pius X condemned the Modernist version of faith, and then prescribed what has since become known as the Oath against Modernism. Published on September 1, 1910, the oath was to be taken by all clergy advancing to major orders, pastors, confessors, preachers, religious superiors, and professors of philosophy and theology in Catholic seminaries. The person declares, among other affirmations, "I hold with certainty and sincerely confess that faith is not a blind sentiment of religion welling up from the depths of the subconscious, under the impulse of the heart and the motion of a will trained to morality. Faith is a genuine assent of the intellect to truth received by hearing from an external source. By this assent, because of the authority of the supremely truthful God, we believe to be true that which has been revealed and attested to by a personal God, our Creator and Lord."[497]

There are two kinds of intellectuality to divine faith, which is the human response to God's revelation. Its very essence is intellectual, since we are assenting on faith with our minds to the objective truths communicated by the Lord. But at least logically prior to actual belief, we also use intellect to arrive at a reasonable conviction that God has really spoken some revealed truth.

---

[497] *DS* 3542; *CCC* 155–56.

Traditionalists like Bautain and de Lammenais would not credit the mind with this capacity to recognize revelation, and postulated instead a blind acceptance of what purportedly was revealed. They were censured by the Church, especially Pius IX, who stressed the indispensable need to know (however dimly) the preambles of the Christian faith.

> Lest human reason be deceived or err in a matter of such vital importance, it must diligently inquire into the fact of revelation, in order to become certain that God has spoken, and in order to offer Him "a reasonable service," as the Apostle so wisely teaches (Romans 12:1). For who does not or cannot know that complete faith should be reposed in God when He speaks, and that nothing is more consonant with reason itself, than to acquire and firmly adhere to whatever is known to have been revealed by God, who can neither deceive nor be deceived.[498]

Echoes of the same tendency to lower the role of reason antecedent to faith are still being heard among the Demythologists, who show a positive hostility to historical data as the legitimate foundation for Christian belief. Where St. Paul appealed to the resurrection of Christ as the crowning proof of His mission, Demythologists say "it would be wrong to raise the problem of how this preaching arose historically. That would be to tie our faith to the results of historical research. The word of preaching confronts us as the Word of God. It is not for us to question its credentials. It is we who are questioned, we who are asked whether we will believe the word or reject it."[499] Nothing, it is held, must weaken the "unprovability" of the Christian proclamation. If it could be proved, faith would be deprived of its essential *skandalon* and robbed of its character of decision. Demythologists also say that

---

[498] *DS* 2778.
[499] Rudolf Karl Bultmann, *Kerygma and Myth* (London: S.P.C.K., 1953), 41.

faith must not be delivered over to the vagaries of historical criticism, in the fashion of David Strauss and his kind.

As regards the second concern, Catholics agree that the iconoclasm of Strauss and the nineteenth-century Rationalists left nothing of the Gospels but a handful of disconnected phrases. Emphatically the faith should not depend on the gentle mercies of Hegelian dialecticians who conceive God Himself as only a progressive evolution of the Idea.

The first concern is an inversion of all that we know of God's dealings with man, and of what we should expect when He makes a revelation. The divinity of Christ and His consubstantiality with the Father, the Redemption, and Real Presence, the life of grace in our souls, and the beatific vision to which we aspire, are all mysteries and as such not penetrable to their essence by the light of human reason. Yet must our faith in these mysteries be reduced to a blind impulse and sheer instinct? Should it not be what the wisdom of God, not to mention His justice, requires of intelligent beings? Faith, on the testimony of Christ, is meritorious precisely because it can be freely given or withheld as an option. In opting for faith, the mind presents to the will the option of bidding our intellects to submit to the wisdom of God.

Paradoxes of Belief

From whatever angle we view it, faith is a bundle of paradoxes, each an apparent contradiction that on closer analysis reveals a profound religious truth. We believe with the mind, yet the will is essential to profess anything in Christianity. The principal objects of belief are complete mysteries hidden in the mind of God and faith is by definition assent to things that are not seen. No light is so penetrating as the *lumen fidei* in which those walk who sincerely believe. The preambles of faith which lead the mind to accept the word of God revealed are assurances, indeed, that God has spoken and that we can reasonably believe. But they are faint whisperings compared to the absolute certainty of faith itself. It was exactly that firmness of faith that Christ said could move mountains and that history shows to have been the stay of martyrs and other millions of the faithful under the most pressing trials.

The relation of mind and will in the act of faith derives from the various states of mind we can have, according to the amount of evidence present and the cooperation of the commanding will.

Faced by a proposition to which it is asked to give assent, the receptive mind can be affected in several ways. It may be swayed either to one side or the other. Either sufficient evidence is lacking for both, as in problems about which we have no clue, or the conflicting evidence appears to balance perfectly, leaving us in a state of *doubt*. Sometimes the mind tends more to one side of the proposition than to the other, yet without being entirely convinced. Although partially resolved in favor of one, it is not finally decided. This is *opinion,* i.e. accepting one side of a question while fearing the opposite may be true.

At other times we make up our minds in favor of one side, and reach a decision either from evidence of the subject under inquiry or from the influence of the will. Objective evidence may be immediate, when the truth of something appears infallibly certain without discursive analysis, as with the basic principle of contradiction and the fact of our own existence. More often it is only mediate, when we have to reason by deduction from general principles or by induction from individual cases. Scientific knowledge is always mediate; we do not immediately perceive the Pythagorean theorem or the ethical norm of the double effect.

However, it may happen that the mind cannot take a stand on the internal evidence, either immediately seen, as with principles, or mediately demonstrated, as with conclusions, but comes to a decision under the influence of the will, which resolutely and firmly chooses to adopt one side, because this is the right and advantageous course to take. The motive is enough to sway the will, though not the mind. Such is *faith*.

One person takes the word of another for the sake of prudence, or common sense, because the other person knows what he is saying and his judgment can be trusted. This is what happens with religious faith, where the mind is moved by revelation because of the divine promise of the reward of eternal life, though the mind remains blind to the inner evidence of what is proposed wherever the mysteries of Christianity are concerned. We can be unwilling about other acts, but we cannot believe unwillingly. St. Augustine explains that we may go into church, approach the altar, and take the sacrament without internal intention about what our body is doing, but we can make an act of faith only if we want to.[500]

Twice in the course of its history, the Church passed judgment on the liberty of divine faith when this was impugned or called into question. At the Council of Trent, freedom of belief was defined to answer the Reformation theory that man's free cooperation with God's grace was impossible before justification. Human nature in Protestant theology was so debilitated that man had lost the power of autonomous choice in matters of religion. As a result, faith was no longer the joint product of man's freedom and the help of God, but the sole effect of divine grace.[501]

At the First Vatican Council the liberty of faith was redefined, but now to answer the Rationalists who were so impressed by the inherent power of human reason that they denied the necessity of a volitional influx (under grace) to make an act of faith. The mind alone, they said, can assent to whatever is objectively true without the command of a free will. Certain German theologians were willing to admit the need

---

[500] St. Thomas, *De Veritate*, XIV, 1; St. Augustine, "In Joannis Evangelium", 26 MPL 35:1607.
[501] *DS* 1554; *CCC* 154.

of revelation to recognize the existence of the mysteries of faith, but, once revealed, the mind is quite able to understand their nature without further assistance.[502]

The paradox of mind and will correlating in belief is repeated in the combination of obscurity and clarity in the virtue of faith. Nothing seems more hidden that what we believe, and yet nothing gives more understanding to the human mind.

All sources of obscurity in faith are reducible to the absence of intrinsic evidence, but this may differ widely according to the different truths revealed. Every revealed truth, insofar as we believe it on God's authority and not because we see why it must be so, will lack the clarity of perception arising from intrinsic rational evidence. There will be quantitative defect in perceptible properties, because fewer elements are generally present in things believed than in things that are personally known. Thus an American knows quantitatively more about the United States than a European who depends for his knowledge of the United States on the testimony of others. There will also be a qualitative defect in the depth of perception. It is common knowledge that things believed do not naturally effect as deep a mental penetration as things personally experienced. A civilian, for example, cannot have the same realization of the horrors of war as the soldier who engaged in combat.

Strict mysteries, like the Trinity, Incarnation, and the life of grace, have an obscurity all their own. They have two transcendencies, i.e., ways in which they exceed the capacities of the rational mind, as part of their nature. Before revelation not even the existence of the mystery can be certainly known. After revelation, the existence is known only on the authority of God while the essence cannot be so understood that the intellect sees the inner nature of the thing revealed. This side of the beatific vision we cannot understand how there can be three persons

---

[502] *DS* 3035.

in one God, or the details of how the humanity of Christ can be simultaneously present in heaven and in all the Eucharistic species throughout the world. We accept the fact on the word of God. We do not see the ultimate reasons why.

In spite of this veil of mystery drawn across the dogmas of faith, there is also a perspicacity that no one but those who believe are allowed to possess. The insight they have is more than a cold mental perception: It is a vision that affects the whole of their lives and penetrates every corner of their being. Unless they are specially trained in the sacred sciences, they may not be able to give a full account of what this means, and still less defend their revealed philosophy against hostile criticism. Nevertheless their faith is the most real thing in their lives and they could no more act without it or ignore its illumination than a man could enjoy the colors of nature without opening his eyes.

Christians have an evidence of the truth of their religion for which nothing else can supply. They sense that the religion which has power to move them to action is true and to the extent it can renew the human heart it is divine. This is the secret reason why they believe, whether they are adequately conscious of it or not. Their lives are being changed daily in the direction of an unseen power, which only the infused light of God can explain.

They have the conviction that a Divine Presence is with them. This Presence comes stronger according to the length of time they have served God, and as they advance in holiness. They recollect that in the course of years they have become very different from what they once were. They are equally certain that much more than advancing age, outward circumstances, trials and experiences were responsible for the difference. "I think a religious man would feel it little less than sacrilege, and almost blasphemy, to impute the improvement in his heart and conduct, in his moral being, with which he has been favoured in a certain sufficient period, to outward and merely natural causes. He will be unable to force himself to do so: that is to say, he has a conviction, which it is a point of religion with him to doubt, which it is a sin to deny, that God has been with him." He is convinced that "God is present with him to an extent, with a fulness, in a depth, which he knows not."[503]

Above all, the virtue of faith produces a personal relationship with Christ that makes His character and conduct, His words, deeds and sufferings, the very food of our devotion and rule of life. What Paul said of himself, "I live now, not I, but Christ lives in me," is valid in its way for all followers of Christ. The *Imitation of Christ* by Thomas á Kempis is not just a manual of pious reflections that, after the Bible, has been more widely used than any other book in Christian literature: It symbolizes the light in which every believer walks in the company of the Savior, according to the measure of his faith, speaking with Him and contemplating His actions (historically in the Gospels and mystically in the Church) as a sure guide on the road to salvation. The whole gamut of Catholic worship and piety—assistance at Mass and reception of the sacraments, devotion to the Sacred Heart and the Spiritual Exercises, Friday abstinence and the Rosary, the liturgical life and evangelical counsels—are meaningful only on the premise of faith, a faith that sees behind the facade of external practices to the Person of Christ by whom the believer is motivated, who is within the believer, and to whom the believer spontaneously directs his thoughts and affections.

A final paradox is the disproportion between the moral assurance about the prelude to faith, that God has spoken, and the absolute

---

[503] John Henry Newman, *Sermons Bearing on Subjects of the Day* (London: Longmans, Green, 1902), 350.

certitude of the faith itself. Blaise Pascal, whose Jansenist leanings
made him exaggerate the weakness of man's intellect apart from
grace, asked "who will blame Christians for not being able to give a
reason for their belief, since they profess a religion for which they
cannot give a reason? They declare, in expounding it to the world,
that it is a foolishness, *stultitiam;* and then you complain that they do
not prove it! If they proved it, they would not keep their word; it is
in lacking proofs that they are not lacking in sense."[504] Pascal was
mistaken in depreciating the preambles of faith to the vanishing
point; but his mistake serves to emphasize the vast difference that
separates the bare reasonableness of believing and the unshakeable
conviction once the faith has been attained.

At the First Vatican Council, the question was raised how the less
educated among the faithful, who may not clearly understand the
motives of credibility and are unable to explain them, can be said to
make a rational act of faith in the Church's divine authority, and
through this in the whole *corpus* of Catholic doctrine. The answer was
given in the form of an analogy.

> The natural providence of God has disposed that the entire
> human race should have complete certitude about the basic
> rational truths, without necessarily being able to prove them
> scientifically. On philosophical analysis, of course, this certitude
> can be more fully explained and clearly reduced to first princi-
> ples, and correspondingly defended against opposing objections.
>
> In the same way, the wisdom and goodness of God in the
> order of supernatural providence has made the Catholic Church
> outstanding in certain characteristics, which do no require a
> scientific demonstration that is beyond the mental capacity of
> most people. Thus even uneducated persons (*rudes*) may have

---

[504] Blaise Pascal, *Pensees,* 194.

a kind of rational compendium of motives of credibility to arrive at full certitude. Once convinced in this way, they can clarify and amplify their conviction through scientific apologetics; but they can never be induced rationally to call this conviction into question by any arguments to the contrary.[505]

Theologians have been aware of the condition of such people, perhaps the majority of the faithful, and speculate not only how they get the faith but (for our purpose more important) how they rise so far above their native intelligence that "they can never be induced rationally" to question their certitude by any arguments to the contrary. The final explanation, as defined by the Church, is "the efficacious help of supernatural power," whereby the Lord "strengthens with His grace those whom He has brought out of darkness into His marvelous light, so that they may remain in this light."[506]

The virtue of faith, therefore, carries its own mysterious light which God supplies to sustain the faith of all believers, not only the more educated. But more than sustain, the Spirit so illumines those in whom He dwells that they become literally spiritual-minded. They are able to see those invisible beings who actually surround them, though without seeing them with bodily eyes. They see them by faith as vividly as others see the things of earth—the ground and vegetation, the sky and brilliant sun. They are also just as certain about this world of faith, as ever the natural man is about the world of sense. "Hence it is that, when saintly souls are favoured with heavenly visions, these visions are but the extraordinary continuations and the crown, by a divine intuition of objects which, by the ordinary operation of grace, are ever before their minds."[507]

---

[505] "Acta Concilii Vatican", *Collectio Lacensis,* Friburg: Herder, 1892, 7:533; *CCC* 812.

[506] *DS* 3014.

[507] John Henry Newman, *Meditations and Devotions,* 78.

HOPE

The virtue of hope is related to faith as desire is related to knowledge, or as the question was posed by St. Augustine, "what can be hoped for which is not believed?" If the object of faith is natural, the hope it inspires is the same; but when the truths believed are divinely revealed, the hope which aspires to possess them is supernaturally divine.

Hope implies seeking and pursuing, in other words, the appetite of desire and not of delight and enjoyment. Although hope and desire are often equated, they differ a great deal. Strictly speaking, when we desire something we look for any good that may be offered, and therefore respond to that instinctive urge which likes pleasure and shrinks from pain. But hope is for a difficult good, and responds to that higher part of our nature which is ready to tackle opposition. Moreover desires may be vague yearnings for an object without reckoning whether we can obtain it or not, whereas hope is always evoked by some good that can be secured and even inspires a sense of confidence of achievement.

Speculative theology distinguishes hope by the four qualities that characterize the things we hope for. Hopeful things are invariably *good;* we do not hope for what is evil. They are *future,* and in this hope differs from joy which implies satisfaction over something good already possessed. They are *difficult* of attainment, otherwise than mere desire which prescinds from the hardships involved. They are also *possible,* and therefore hope is the opposite of despair, which looks to a future prospective good that cannot be obtained.

Just as we speak of a human and divine faith, depending on the persons (man or God) on whose authority we believe, so we have two kinds of hope, natural and supernatural, according to the things desired and the persons from whom we expect to receive them. In the natural order, an object is possible either because we can secure it by our own efforts or because we rely on the help of friends, in which case two elements enter, the good hoped for, and the person who will support our desires. Supernaturally, however, no one is able of himself to grasp the supreme good of eternal life, whose very existence would be unknown except for a gracious revelation from God. To reach heaven we need divine help, so that hope as a theological virtue has a twofold object: the beatific vision we look forward to attaining, and the supernatural grace by which this heavenly goal is attained.

Essential Elements

The two basic elements of Christian hope are desire and confidence, so that hope itself may be defined as the confident desire of obtaining eternal beatitude. Already in the Old Testament, notably in the Psalms, we find this dualism expressed, where the just man looks forward to the consummation of happiness in the life to come. "I am sure," sings the Psalmist, "I shall see the Lord's goodness in the land of the living. Hope in Him, hold firm and take heart. Hope in the Lord."[508]

However, it was not until the fulness of revelation was made under Christ that the full meaning of hope became clear, since the clarity of what we desire determines the surety of what we hope for. Once the mystery of man's elevation to the divine life and the love of God in the person of His Son were made manifest, the wellsprings of desire to reach this high destiny were opened as never before. Compared with the glory that awaits us, the trials of our present existence are as paltry chaff, of which St. Paul wrote to encourage the Romans. "I reckon that the sufferings of the present time are not worthy to be compared with the glory to come that will be revealed in us." We who are the first fruits of the Spirit, "groan within ourselves, waiting for the (perfect) adoption as sons, the redemption of our body. For in hope were we saved. But hope that is seen is not hope. For how can a man hope for

---

[508] Psalm 26:11; *CCC* 1843.

what he sees? But if we hope for what we do not see, we wait for it with patience."[509]

Implicit in the notion of hope is that we do not see but accept on faith the glorification that awaits us. The will strives for what the mind, on the word of God, presents to us as desirable: In the same faith that we believe in heaven as the goal of our striving, we see the incapacity to reach that goal of ourselves. Trustful reliance on divine grace is more than a feature of supernatural hope; it is that quality without which hope would be a fabulous dream. The phrase "to hope in God" recurs in all the writings of Peter, Paul, and John, to impress the faithful that what makes them distinctive is not only the sublimity of their religion, or the certitude of their destiny, or even the purity of life to which God calls His chosen ones—but the confidence they should have of passing out of their "great tribulation" into the day of eternity. The effort they expend in serving God will be recompensed as only the Creator can reward those who are submissive to His name.

> The grace of God our Savior has appeared to all men, instructing us, in order that, rejecting ungodliness and worldly lusts, we may live temperately and justly and piously in this world; looking for the blessed hope and glorious coming of our great God and Savior, Jesus Christ, who gave Himself for us that He might redeem us from all iniquity and cleanse for Himself an acceptable people.
>
> According to His mercy He saved us through the laver of regeneration and renewal of the Holy Spirit; whom He has abundantly poured out upon us through Jesus Christ our Savior, in order that, justified by His grace, we may be heirs in the hope of life everlasting.[510]

---

[509] Romans 8:18–25.
[510] Titus 2:11–14, 3:5–7; *CCC* 1817.

Christians, therefore, are not as other men, who "have no hope," because the faith is lacking. They see through the eyes of God what the Lord has prepared for those who love Him, and this vision gives substance to the future which is closed, or at least uncertain, to all who do not believe.

In the centuries since the New Testament was written, the vagaries of philosophy apart from revelation have reached their zenith in the utter pessimism that characterizes a great deal of modern thought, sometimes in circles that are only nominally Christian but always among people who have lost their faith, and consequently hope, in the supernatural. "The universe is what it is," for Bertrand Russell, "not what I choose that it should be. If it is indifferent to human desires, as it seems to be; if human life is a passing episode, hardly noticeable in the vastness of cosmic processes; if there is no superhuman purpose, and no hope of ultimate salvation, it is better to know and acknowledge this truth than to endeavor, in futile self-assertion, to order the universe to be what we find comfortable."[511]

Cut off from the moorings of Christian hope, the alternative is stark pessimism which sees no finality in man's existence and no purpose beyond the grave. Among the ancient Romans, Seneca ventured the opinion that "death is the end of all sorrows," because once a man dies, "he no longer exists."[512] Modern naturalism offers nothing more hopeful.

Since the world is not ruled by a spiritual being, but rather by blind forces, there cannot be any ideals, moral or otherwise, in the universe outside us. Our ideals, therefore, must proceed from our own minds; they are our own inventions. Thus the

---

[511] Bertrand Russell, *Understanding History* (New York: Philosophical Library, 1957), 102.
[512] Seneca, *Ad Marciam de Consolatione*, 19.

world around us is nothing but an immense spiritual emptiness. It is a dead universe, purposeless, senseless, meaningless.

Nature is nothing but matter in motion. The motions of matter are governed, not by any purpose, but by blind forces and laws. If the scheme of things is purposeless and meaningless, then the life of man is purposeless and meaningless too. Everything is futile, all effort is in the end worthless. A man may, of course, still pursue disconnected ends, but his life is hollow at the center.[513]

If not all naturalists are equally frank (or clear), the reason is only because they have not followed their philosophy to its logical conclusion.

Object and Motive

The object of Christian hope is heavenly beatitude and the divine grace by which we aspire to the intuitive vision of God. Those who believe in Christ live "in the hope of life everlasting which God, who does not lie, promised before the ages began."[514] Faith and hope are theological virtues because both have God as their direct and immediate object; but where God is the object of faith as infallible truth, He is the object of hope because He is our highest good, towards whom the will of man constantly aspires and in whom alone it finds rest.[515]

Coessential with the tendency to reach God, hope relies on the divine goodness to furnish the instrumentalities of reaching Him. We desire to possess Him in eternity, and to receive the help He alone can give us in time. Both elements are a part of hope: the goal, which is

---

[513] Walter T. Stace, "Man Against Darkness," *Atlantic Monthly* 182 (September 1948): 153–58.
[514] Titus 1:2.
[515] *CCC* 215, 2052.

God, and the way, which is grace. Without the first, there would be no destiny. Without the second, there would be no means.[516]

Theologians differ in their ultimate analysis of the motive for hope. If we look upon hope mainly as the virtue of trust in God, and reliance on Him from whom we await the reward of eternal life, then the motive of hope becomes God as our Helper. For St. Thomas and the more common tradition since patristic times, hope is essentially a confident dependence on God's help. It does not include but presupposes the desire of union with God. It consists mainly in the expectation of a good which is difficult to obtain, namely the possession of God. The motive on our part is to receive the assisting divine Omnipotence which elevates our souls, weans them from seductive desires for earthly things, and bears them in the direction of heaven. God's promises, as revealed in the Scriptures, simply confirm the certainty of His aid.

If, on the other hand, hope is conceived primarily as an act of desire, then its dominant motive is that God is supremely able to enrich us. Scotus and the Franciscan school prefer to look upon hope in this light. The principal act of the virtue is the desire or love for God, not as He is in Himself but as our happiness and the terminus of all our wants. This emphasis is traceable to St. Francis himself, whose exhortations to the Friars were built on the same theme.

> Let us desire nothing, wish for nothing, take pleasure in nothing, and delight in nothing except our Creator, Redeemer, and Savior, the one true God, who is the plenitude of goodness, all good, complete good, the true and supreme good. For He alone is holy, just, true, and righteous; He alone is beneficent, innocent, pure, and from Him, through Him,

---

[516] *CCC* 1266, 1813.

and in Him is all pardon, all grace, all glory for the penitent and the righteous, as for all the blessed saints who rejoice together in Heaven.[517]

Objectively, of course, the virtue of hope comprehends two responses to God—trust *and* desire—and therefore includes both motivations—confidence in His help and yearning for Himself; nor is it possible in practice to separate the one from the other.

CHARITY

Christ our Lord told the disciples, and through them all His followers, "No longer do I call you servants, because the servant does not know what his master does. But I have called you friends."[518] In this statement of friendship, He was declaring the charity by which God loves those who are in His grace and the virtue by which they are enabled to love Him in return.

Sanctifying grace makes us friends of God, members of His Trinitarian family, and capable of knowing and loving Him in the beatific vision even as He knows and loves Himself. Friendship is bilateral. It implies a mutual loving between two persons, here between the soul and God. Theological charity is simply the virtue that gives this friendship expression, allowing us to reciprocate for the "loving kindness" that God is constantly showing to us.

Hope and charity both are directed to God, and both find their fulfillment ultimately in Him. But where hope is a form of self-interested love, whose motive is the desire to possess the *Summum Bonum* for oneself, charity is a disinterested love of benevolence for God

---

[517] St. Francis of Assisi, "The First Rule of the Friars Minor," 23 in *The Writings of St. Francis of Assisi,* trans. Ben Fahey, OFM (Chicago: Franciscan Herald Press, 1964), 52.
[518] John 15:15; *CCC* 1972.

Himself. The motive is not to have His goodness so we can enjoy it but His goodness as it, in itself, shines forth in Him.

The motive force of supernatural charity, then, is the absolute goodness of God, i.e., not relative to us but as it is in Itself. When we love God for His sake and not for ours, we seek no profit or utility from so loving Him as happens with the virtue of hope. Yet while excluding self-interest strictly so-called, we do not exclude from perfect charity a desire for union with the God whom we love, since this is necessarily part of every true love or friendship. In other words, the desire of possessing God is one thing (always present in hope), and the desire of union with God is another (always present in charity). When we love God perfectly, we want to love Him as He wishes to be loved, which cannot be otherwise than united with Him in the embrace of consummated charity.

The main element here is the motive that *psychologically* flows into the will to effect an act of perfect love of God. In this sense we eliminate all self-seeking motivation. However, it is quite another question whether objectively and *ontologically* it is possible to have any love among creatures, such as we are, where an object is loved only for itself and without benefit to the one loving. It is not possible, given our finite nature and the built-in perfectibility of every act of love we perform. Consequently our wills cannot love God, whether in hope or with theological charity, without ontological advantage and increased perfection to ourselves. Nevertheless the guiding and dominant motive in charity is not this benefit, which is never absent, but the sheer goodness of the Triune God.

It is the motive of charity, in the love of friendship, that most clearly distinguishes this virtue from all others and, in practice, even from those acts which may be acts of charity but which are not the perfect love of God. To clarify the obvious, the motive moves a faculty to action and determines its distinctive quality. Where the rational will is involved, the moving force must always be goodness, real or apparent, created or divine, otherwise the will remains unmoved.

What precisely is the divine goodness which Catholic theology says is the object that moves us to a perfect love of God? In general a good thing is suitable for the being in question, and among creatures always improves it. Thus food and drink are good for the body, and knowledge is good for the mind. The goodness of God is a composite of all His attributes: His wisdom and power, justice and mercy, beauty and liberality, in fact all the "qualities" that form His divine being and are therefore "good to Him" in constituting His infinite perfection. Most theologians teach that any divine attribute, even taken singly, when viewed under the aspect of its goodness to God, is an adequate motive for placing an act of perfect charity.

For practical purposes it is well to consider these perfections under two aspects, absolutely, as they are in God, and relatively, insofar as they produce some benefit in creatures. We do not mean that divine attributes like mercy and magnanimity cannot be the object of perfect love, although they bear a direct relation to the world outside of God. Everything depends on the aspect under which they are viewed. Seen as perfections proper to God, emanating from Him, deriving from the ocean of goodness which He contains, they are adequate motives for loving God with pure benevolence. But taken from our viewpoint as benefiting me, either personally or collectively as a member of society, the divine mercy and magnanimity are objects of hope or gratitude, but not strictly of theological charity. Of course charity may arise from hope and gratitude, and these will always be present along with charity, but the latter is itself caused by no personal benefit accrued or desired. Its guiding star is the divine perfections insofar as they are God's.

True love for God is spontaneously demonstrative, since genuine charity cannot remain sterile and our benevolence towards the Creator will not be unproductive. It shows itself internally by acts of affection and externally by effective deeds. The terms "internal" and "external" in this connection are misleading, but they have to be used, much as when we spoke of the difference between internal and external grace. Internal acts of affection are called such with reference to the will, and cover all the elicited (immanent) acts of volition, which begin and terminate in the will faculty.

In the hierarchy of acts of perfect charity, the highest are the joy and complacency we experience by reflecting on the perfections of God. Among those are His holiness and dazzling beauty, His wisdom and boundless power, His mercy and selfless liberality. When the mind attentively considers the infinite perfections of the divinity, it is impossible for the will not to be animated with the sense of complacency in this good. The first reaction of complacency, it may be said, arises unbidden at the very sight of an attractive object. But where God is concerned, "we promptly use the liberty we have to provoke our heart to redouble and strengthen its first complacency by acts of approbation and rejoicing. We enjoy the infinite perfections of God, deriving happiness and satisfaction from them as from an inheritance which belongs to us. By this means the divine perfections become in some manner our own property. We attract them to our heart, and they become a heavenly banquet that fortifies our souls."[519] In a word, we are pleased to see the greatness and beauty and goodness of God and, without envy, join with Him in rejoicing over His myriad possessions.

If this kind of complacency seems unreal or superfluous to the believing mind, it is only because the thought never occurs to Christians

---

[519] St. Francis de Sales, *Treatise on the Love of God* (Westminster, MD: The Newman Book Shop, 1942), 196.

to do anything but rejoice with God over His perfections. There is a complete "otherness" we naturally associate with loving God, and taking satisfaction in seeing Him as He truly is: We never dream of wanting to "deprive" Him of what He is or has, or claim for ourselves what belongs to Him.

But not every one reacts in this way, and one of the minor revelations that believers receive is the rude awakening about the way some people think and feel about God. We expect dialectical materialists to dismiss the Deity as an antiquated projection of suppressed desires, and teach that Communism has no place for religion. We may be surprised to learn that varying degrees of unsympathy with theism, which believes in and worships a personal God, is also found in Western thought. Men like Dewey and the Huxleys, Emerson, Royce and Einstein, Fichte, Freud, and Spengler have left a deep impress on the history of modern civilization, and that impress has not been theistic.

Sigmund Freud (1856–1939) represented religion as essentially wish-fulfilment. Religion, he claimed, originated in man's feeling of helplessness and need for protection, at a period in history when his intelligence was not yet fully developed. Man invented God by wishing Him into existence, in order to allay his anxieties in the face of life's dangers, including the crushing superiority of nature, which gave rise to the doctrine of Providence; and in order to insure at least a long-range justice, which produced the doctrine of immortality. Man invested God with the qualities of his human father toward whom he has a mixed attitude of love and fear. Like the father remembered from childhood, God makes everything turn out to man's advantage, consoling him in his tragic situation, and giving him answers to his curiosity. Religion, therefore, is an illusion, derived from our ignorant ancestors. "The comparative method of research," he wrote, "has revealed the fatal resemblance between religious ideas revered by us and the mental productions of primitive ages and peoples."[520] If American and English naturalists have been less crude, their impact on contemporary thinking has been equally influential if not more so. Like Freud, they leave no place for a Deity to whom our affections may turn with whole-souled dedication in acts of perfect love.

There is more than academic value in seeing how transcendent is the Christian religion, which enlightens the mind by faith to recognize with complete certitude the existence of a personal God; and inspires the will not only to trust God, but so generously to love Him that reflection on His goodness evokes sentiments of the purest and most selfless charity. A parallel reading of a work like Nietzsche's *Thus Spake Zarathustra* and Newman's *Apologia* would show the chasm that divides two contradictory philosophies of life or, in Augustine's phrase, the two loves that have created two cities: "self-love to the extent of despising God, the earthly; love of God to the extent of despising one's self, the heavenly city. The former glories in self, the latter in God."[521]

Parallel with complacency, love of benevolence urges a desire to increase the divine goodness as far as possible, since benevolence means just that—"to wish another well"—except that God is infinite and cannot be enriched by anything we do. If there is question of God's intrinsic perfections, His power, wisdom, and goodness, then, barring a fiction of the mind, we cannot desire to increase them because nothing can be added to infinity.

But there is no figment or hypothesis about desiring to increase God's external glory, which consists in the knowledge and love that rational creatures have for Him on earth, in purgatory, and in the beatific vision. The internal impulse to great sanctity and heroic work in the apostolate stems from this principle, that the glory of God

---

[520] Sigmund Freud, *The Future of An Illusion* (Garden City, N.Y.: Doubleday, 1957), 68–69.
[521] St. Augustine, *City of God* 14; *CCC* 1850.

admits of degrees and variations. In the measure of a man's love he will seek to increase the depth of his own and other people's knowledge of God, the intensity of his and their love, and the number of those who advance the ultimate purpose of rational creation—the loving acknowledgment of the Creator by His creatures.

Among the internal acts of supernatural charity, sorrow for sin follows consistently on the desire to see God honored and duly loved. When I think of my own sins and those of others, I am grieved at the injury done to the Divine Majesty and wish to make amends for the offenses committed against a loving God.

External acts of divine charity are the effective counterpart of internal affection. They are called external only in relation to the will, and include every form of activity (not excluding the most internal) that may be commanded or directed by the power of free will. In the history of Christian asceticism, they are an essential part of any true love of friendship, which consists not only in sentiments of affection but in the exchange of any goods that are separately possessed.

Basically these acts are of two kinds: those involving labor for the glory of God and those concerned with reparation for sin. On the first level, the desire to promote God's kingdom is manifested (beyond internal affection) by using every means at our disposal to advance in personal holiness, and doing everything in our power to increase the knowledge and love of God in the souls of others. In the same spirit, the sorrow we feel over sin moves us to the practice of penance and mortification, to expiate the injustice committed against the Divine Majesty and make satisfaction for man's ingratitude to God.

Love of Christ

Among the most satisfying truths of the Catholic faith is the fact that we can direct our affection for God to the Person of Jesus Christ and be certain that the love we express is not lessened but fortified by this method. Christ Himself told us that He is the Way, the Truth, and the Life. "In Christ," said Augustine, "you have all. Do you wish to love God? You have Him in Christ. 'In the beginning was the Word and the Word was with God, and the Word was God.' Do you wish to love your neighbor? You have him in Christ. 'The Word was made flesh.' "[522] The whole panoply of theological charity finds scope in the person of the Savior; in His divinity we have the primary object and the fulfilment of the first great commandment, "Thou shalt love the Lord thy God with thy whole heart"; in His humanity we have the secondary object, responding to the precept to love our neighbor as ourselves.

St. Teresa of Avila wrote at length on the importance of directing attention to the Savior and, indeed, to His humanity (united with the Godhead) as the way instituted by God for growing in His love. She warned from her own experience what a mistake it would be to think that as one grows in the spiritual life he should dispense more and more with the humanity of Christ, as though this were a hindrance to advancement in virtue. "Is it possible," she prayed, "that I could have had the thought, if only for an hour, that You, my Lord, could be a hindrance to my greatest good?" It is "a great matter," she added, "to have our Lord before us as Man while we are living and in the flesh." All the great saints acted in this way; they centered their love on the person of Christ and found in Him all that their souls desired.

> Seek no other way, even if you were arrived at the highest contemplation. This way is safe. Our Lord is He by whom all good things come to us; He will teach you. Consider His life; that is the best example. What more can we want than so good a Friend at our side, who will not forsake us when we are in

---

[522] St. Augustine, "Sermo 261," *MPL* 38.

trouble and distress, as they do who belong to the world. Blessed is he who truly loves Him, and who always has Him near him.

Let us consider the glorious St. Paul, who seems as if Jesus was never absent from his lips, as if he had Him down deep in his heart. After I had heard this of some great saints given to contemplation, I considered the matter carefully; and I see that they walked in no other way. St. Francis with the stigmata proves it, St. Anthony of Padua with the Infant Jesus, St. Bernard rejoiced in the Sacred Humanity, so did St. Catherine of Siena and many others.

What I would say is, that the most Sacred Humanity of Christ is not to be counted among the objects from which we should withdraw. Let this be clearly understood. I wish I knew how to explain it. We are not angels, for we have a body; to seek to make ourselves angels while we are on the earth is an act of folly. Our thoughts must have something to rest on, though the soul may go out of itself.[523]

There is profound wisdom in these injunctions. They accentuate a principle of spirituality that cannot be too strongly emphasized. Since Christ is true God, we not only may but should love Him with all the ardor reserved for the Creator, and be assured that His humanity is no obstacle but a help to supernatural charity.

It is a help because we have in the Person of the Savior the incarnation of the divine attributes, lived out for us in historical perspective, and manifested in flesh and blood. We know on faith that God is loving, merciful, forebearing, all wise, and infinitely powerful. But the man Jesus is God in human form. The love He showed by His death on the cross was no abstraction. His mercy in the parables of the Prodigal and the Good Shepherd and in the prayer for His enemies on

---

[523] St. Teresa of Avila, *Autobiography,* XXII, 5–14.

Calvary was no mere idealism. His patience with sinners and kindness towards those in distress and want were not speculation. His wisdom in the Sermon on the Mount and power in the miracles He worked were not idyllic representations but vivid realities, perceptible to the senses and palpable with all the materiality that only God-made-man could have devised. He wants us to profit from these evidences of the divine perfections in order to more easily love Him because we can witness Him in action so tangibly.

The Person of Christ as the object of divine love makes the practice of perfect charity and contrition simple for those who believe that Christ is God. This Person becomes the focus of affective volition every time we choose to do so. A single glance at the figure of Christ on the cross, or a passing thought in the direction of the Eucharist, are enough to evoke an act of benevolent love. He epitomizes in Himself all the goodness of the Divinity, manifested in every detail of His mortal and glorified life; and continues in the Mystical Body which He animates. All that is necessary on our part is the momentary recollection of this fact, even implicitly, and a responsive act of the will that reacts to the mental realization.

People sometimes wonder what sentiments are needed to express an act of the perfect love of God. The answer may be found in all the standard formularies approved by the Church, and summarized in the short sentence that was St. Francis of Assisi's most common exclamation, "My God and my all!"[524] At the same time, it is imperative to know that whatever formula is used, it can always be directed to Christ, the God-man, whether the name of the Savior is mentioned or not. The practice of the saints, however, was to explicate the Holy Name often when they addressed God in terms of affection.[525] St. Paul's desire "to

---

[524] *B.P. Francisci Assisiatis Opuscula,* ed. Luke Wadding (Antwerp: ex Officina Plantiniana apud Balthasarem Moretum, 1623), 119.

[525] *CCC* 2668.

be dissolved and be with Christ," and Ignatius of Antioch's "I am the grain of God, being ground by the teeth of beasts, that I may become the pure bread of Christ," are echoed in the history of Christian hagiography. The Christological concept of supernatural charity was explained in a prayerful reflection of St. Anselm. "My soul," he said, "attach yourself to God, obstinately attach yourself to Him. Good Lord Jesus, do not repulse my soul. It hungers for Your love, strengthen it. Grant that it may be sated with Your charity, enrich it with Your affection, filled by Your love. Grant that this love may wholly seize me and entirely possess me because You are, with the Father and the Holy Spirit, one only God, blessed for ever and ever."[526]

The devotion to the Sacred Heart, approved by the Holy See in solemn documents, is a practical implementation of this principle, that perfect love of God may find expression in the love of Jesus Christ. Conscious of the prejudice still lurking on this point, Pius XII declared "it is wrong to say that contemplation of the physical heart of Jesus is a hindrance to attaining intimate love of God, and that it impedes the soul in its progress to the highest virtue."[527]

This practice of associating acts of theological charity with the person of Christ has special relevance to perfect contrition, which for many people may be the only means of salvation, either because they are not Catholic or have not the opportunity of receiving sacramental absolution. As defined by Trent, "contrition is made perfect through charity and reconciles man to God."[528] The problem is how to insure that the sorrow is perfect. For those who believe in the divinity of Christ, reflection on His mercy and love, especially in His death on

---

[526] St. Anselm, *Meditationes,* XI, trans. W. J. Copeland, *Meditations and Prayers to the Holy Trinity and Our Lord Jesus Christ* (Oxford: J. H. Parker, 1856).

[527] Pius XII, *On Devotion to the Sacred Heart* [*Haurietis Aquas*] (1956), 102; *CCC* 2699.

[528] *DS* 1168; *CCC* 1492.

the cross, can be an effective, and relatively easy, way of inspiring the will to contrition based on disinterested love. Faced with the utter generosity of God who became man to redeem mankind by the shedding of His blood, a soul that believes what this means will be led to respond with like generosity and beg pardon for having offended such selfless Love.

Love of Neighbor

Although the primary object of supernatural charity is God Himself, it also includes the person loving as well as his neighbor.[529, 530] In fact, whatever increases the divine glory is indirectly related to the secondary scope of the highest theological virtue, and follows logically from the perfect love of God. If we love Him, we must love what He loves and for the same reason. Among the objects of His affection are ourselves and our neighbor. He loves us with complete selflessness and out of sheer liberality. Therefore within the ambit of true charity are included, besides God, all the persons touched by His beneficent will, notably myself and my fellowman. Yet even in loving ourselves the motive is not self-interest but to love God, here seen as the divine Rewarder in the exercise of His liberality towards me.

If legitimate self-love subordinated to perfect divine love offers no practical difficulties, love of neighbor as an instrument and index of the theological charity is a lifetime effort and its precept has been woven into the texture of the Christian religion. "This is my commandment," Christ told His disciples, "that you love one another as I have loved you."[531] On the last day the human race will be judged on the practice of fraternal charity, with the good entering heaven because they loved others, and the wicked condemned because they closed their hearts to

---

[529] *CCC* 1822.
[530] *CCC* 1022.
[531] John 15:12; *CCC* 1823–24.

the neighbor.[532] The first epistle of St. John is a treatise on the subject, rising to a climax that synthesizes the Christian faith.

> Let us therefore love, because God first loved us. If anyone says, "I love God," and hates his brother, he is a liar. For can anyone who does not love his brother, whom he sees, love God, whom he does not see? And this commandment we have from Him, that He who loves God should love his brother also.[533]

The correlation of these two loves, God and neighbor, is a matter of faith, already found in the Old Covenant. "Thou shalt love the Lord thy God with thy whole heart and with thy whole soul and with all thy strength and with all thy mind; and thy neighbor as thyself."[534] Christ repeated the injunction and confirmed it, "This do, and you shall live."[535] He further added that in this twofold precept are contained all the Law and the Prophets. St. Paul declared in a brisk sentence that "love is the fulfilling of the Law," and went on to explain in lyric language the excellence of divine love, whose manifestation in the love of neighbor comprehends all the virtues: patience, kindness, modesty, meekness, humility, selflessness, and generosity.[536]

Not only are these two loves always conjoined, but one is a proof of the presence of the other. "The surest sign that we are keeping these two commandments," according to Teresa of Avila, "is that we should be really loving our neighbor. For we cannot be sure if we are loving God, although, we may have good reasons for believing that

---

[532] *CCC* 1022.
[533] 1 John 4:19–21; *CCC* 1878.
[534] Deuteronomy 6:5–7.
[535] Luke 10:25–29; *CCC* 2055, 2196.
[536] 1 Cor. 13:1–13; *CCC* 1825–26.

we are. But we can know quite well if we are loving our neighbor. And be certain that, the farther advanced you find you are in this, the greater love you will have for God. For so dearly does His Majesty love us that He will reward our love for our neighbor by increasing the love that we bear to Himself, and that in a thousand ways. This I cannot doubt."[537]

The norm for loving our neighbour is deceptively simple: We are to love him as we do ourselves. "As yourself," therefore, is the divine mode of fraternal charity, which ascetical theology has invested with the qualities of truth, order, decisiveness, constancy, and generosity.

We should first of all love others truly, for their own sakes (out of love of God) and not for our own. Friendship may be spurious or genuine, depending on its character of selflessness. If we love a person out of utility, we give him up when no further advantage is to be gained. If we love him for pleasure, it is ourselves and not him we seek. Only if we love him for virtue's sake, i.e., to be of benefit to him, do we love truly.

We should love others ordinately, and not treat them as though they were the ultimates of our affection. Christ stressed this rule even where the closest bonds of human relationship are involved. "He that loves father and mother more than me, is not worthy of me; and he that loves son or daughter more than me is not worthy of me."[538] Love of neighbor must be subordinated to the love of God.

We should love others effectively, as do ourselves, doing them whatever good we can, and, where possible, protecting them from evil. "Let us not love in word, neither in tongue, but in deed and truth," and "without dissimulation."[539] The prototype of such affection is the divine love for us, which God effectuated in time, though He loved us from eternity,

---

[537] St. Teresa of Avila, *Interior Castle*, V, 3, trans. E. Allison Peers (NY: Image Books, 1961), 115.

[538] Matthew 10:37.

[539] 1 John 3:18; Romans 12:9.

bringing us out of nothing into existence, raising us to the supernatural order, and constantly serving our bodily and spiritual needs.

We ought to love patiently, calmly bear with people's defects, endure quietly whatever is disagreeable in them, and pardon readily the offenses they commit against us. This is the way we like to have others deal with us, or as we deal with ourselves. We prefer to have people overlook our faults, keep silent about them, ignore them and excuse them, and if possible, even keep them off their minds. The same standard is a divine mandate in our treatment of every person who enters our life. Patience joined to meekness are the keystone of enduring fraternal charity.

Finally we should love generously and without envy, rejoicing over the success of others as we do over our own. No aspect of charity is more difficult, as none is more pleasing to God. Envy has been described as a criminal sorrow over the good fortune of others. It is no coincidence that the earliest and longest extant document in Christian literature outside the Scriptures, the first-century letter of Pope Clement to the Corinthians, treats exclusively of this one vice, to which Christians as everyone else are readily prone. It was envy, Clement explained, that brought sin into the world when the devil tempted Eve; it was envy that moved Cain to slay his more successful brother, Abel; it was envy that brought death to the prophets of the Old Law, and finally death to Christ on Calvary. The lesson of history is the story of conflict, born in large measure on envy, where human pride is saddened at other people's happiness and seeks to destroy what it cannot share.

A brilliant insight into God's providence which invites us to communal charity is the bond of love by which He seeks perforce to unite the human race, through family ties and language, circumstances and every kind of need. Necessity is not only the mother of invention, it is the parent of selfless charity.

Effects of Sin

Theological charity is the mainstay of the supernatural life. When grave sin is committed, this virtue is lost, even though faith and hope may remain.[540] The reason is fairly clear. Every mortal sin means the deliberate choice of a creature in place of the Creator, a reversal of charity which by definition, adheres to God above all things.

Not only charity is lost by deliberate grave sin. Also lost are the gifts of the Holy Spirit and all the merits that a man may have gained during a lifetime of effort. The merits of a man in the state of enmity with God are technically called "mortified" (*mortificata*), which St. Thomas says have the same standing in the sight of God, even after sin, as they had when they were performed. But sin prevents the reception of the heavenly reward. Hence, as soon as the obstacle is removed, they can exercise once more the efficacy that belongs to them, leading to everlasting life.

Theologians agree on this revival of merits. The majority further say that everything is restored, just as it was before grave sin had been committed, along with the added merit of repentance. In a famous statement of Pius XI, those who return to God "repair and recover entirely the fulness (*copiam ex integro*) of merits and gifts which they had lost by their sins."[541]

Mortal sin does not, of itself, deprive a person of membership in the Mystical Body, unless the sin were against the faith. Consequently Catholics living in the state of sin but still believing and otherwise practicing their religion do not cease to belong to the Church: Although they are "dead members," they are members none the less. They still have a special bond of union with Christ and others in the Mystical Body not enjoyed by those who were unbaptized and do not profess the Catholic faith.

---

[540] *CCC* 1855.
[541] *DS* 3670.

The loss of supernatural charity, then, does not cut a person off from the Church. However, every sin weakens the hold on faith and a habit of sin tends to break down the faith altogether. Commenting on the situation in his own day, Bellarmine asked himself, "By what means is the faith preserved," and he answered, "through good works." And conversely, without subscribing to the Reformation theory that every sin is an act of unbelief, he added that faith is lost through evil works.

> A multitude of sins, a facility in sinning, and the practice of an evil life are the road and, as it were, the steps, towards infidelity. For men are so fashioned by nature that they easily and readily believe what they desire, what pleases and delights them. It is not hard to convince voluptuous and carnal-living people that priests should be married, that chastity is impossible, that fasting is superfluous, that selection in the matter of food is superfluous. It is not difficult to excuse usury before the avaricious, or simony among the ambitious, or fornication with the sensuous.[542]

This has been borne out by centuries of experience, and is proved in everyday life. In the degree to which a man strives to stay in the state of grace, he safeguards the power to believe; but self-indulgence through habitual sin blinds the intellect to Christian revelation, finally extinguishing the light of faith altogether.

INFUSED MORAL VIRTUES

Besides the theological virtues of faith, hope, and charity, a person in sanctifying grace receives an infusion of the moral virtues whose immediate object is not God Himself but the practice of human actions

---

[542] St. Robert Bellarmine, *De Lumine Fidei*, I; *CCC* 162.

conducive to man's final end. Most theologians, following St. Thomas, teach that just as faith, hope, and charity correspond in the supernatural order to natural knowledge, hope, and love, so there are other divinely infused habits to supplement and match these theological virtues. These habits are elevated counterparts of the acquired virtues of prudence, temperance, fortitude, and justice.[543]

In order to understand what the infused moral virtues are, it is useful to see what they mean naturally, since the infusion of these powers does not radically change their character but sublimates and raises their capacity to a higher than natural end.

The four cardinal virtues can be considered as either the main characteristics of every virtue or special types of virtue. In the patristic tradition, especially of St. Augustine, they are treated as elements of every true virtue. All directing knowledge is prudence, all balanced fairness is justice, all firmness of soul in misfortune is fortitude, and all moderation in the use of earthly values is temperance.[544] Accordingly no prudence is genuine unless just, courageous, and temperate; no temperance perfect unless strong, just, and prudent; no courage complete unless prudent, temperate, and just; and no justice true unless prudent, strong, and temperate.[545] That there should be four cardinal virtues is a matter of stress, and not, as medieval scholastics held, because they are specifically different habits dealing with diverse types of object.

More commonly, however, they are treated as special virtues, each occupied with its own proper type of situation, without denying that they overlap, or that one flows into the other. Thus fortitude is temperate and brave, for a man who can contain his lusts can well control himself in danger of death; and if he can face death unflinchingly, he can also withstand allurements.

---

[543] *CCC* 1804, 1810.
[544] St. Augustine, *Of the Morals of the Catholic Church*, 24.
[545] St. Gregory, "Moralum Liber," 22, *MPL* 76:22.

Aristotle was the basic source on which St. Thomas built the now familiar structure of the cardinal virtues, which are reduced to four because of the objective order of morality. The mind must first discover this order and propose its commands to the will. Prudence, or the habit of doing the right thing at the right time, is reason's helper. The will, in turn, must execute these commands in its own field. Justice, or the habit of giving everyone his due, is helper to the will in its own operations. Temperance assists the will in its management of the appetite's desire, and fortitude helps to manage the same appetite's aversions.[546]

Just as there are four faculties that contribute to our moral acts—intellect, will, appetite of desire, and appetite of aversion—so there must be four virtues to keep these faculties straight. Prudence is for the mind, justice for the will, temperance for the urge to what is pleasant, and fortitude for the instinct away from what is painful. The Latins summarized their function in the words, *circumspice* (look around), *age* (act), *abstine* (keep away from) and *sustine* (bear up with).

All other virtues in the moral order can be referred to this tetrad as their potential parts. In view of their practical value as possessions of nature (also infused by grace), it is worth examining the gamut in some detail.

The principle act of prudence is the practical executive command of right reason, and the following virtues come within its orbit: good counsel (*eubulia*), sound judgment (*synesis*) concerning the ordinary rules of conduct, and a flair for dealing with exceptional cases (*gnome*).

As regards justice, its classical type renders what is due between persons who may or may not be equal, but other virtues also come under the general heading of justice. Some render what is owing to another, but not as to an equal. Others deal with a situation where both

---

[546] *CCC* 1805–9.

parties are equal, yet the due or debt, though demanded by decency, cannot be enforced by law, and so is not an affair of strict justice. In the first category of these phases of justice comes *religion,* which offers our service and worship to God; then *piety* and *patriotism,* which renders our duty to parents and country; then *observance,* which shows reverence to superiors; and *obedience* to their commands. In the second category comes *gratitude* for past favors, and *vindication* when injury has been done; also *truthfulness,* without which social decency is impossible, *liberality* in spending money, and *friendliness* or social good manners.

The respective parts of fortitude, on the attacking side, are *confidence,* carried out with *magnificence,* which reckons not the cost, and *magnanimity,* which does not shrink from glory. On the defensive side is *patience,* which keeps an unconquered spirit, and can be protracted into *perseverance.*

Finally the subordinate kinds of temperance are *continence,* which resists lustfulness and evil desires concerned with touch; *clemency,* which tempers punishment; *meekness,* which tempers anger; *modesty* in our deportment, which includes disciplined study, reasonable recreation and good taste in clothes.[547]

Supernatural Infusion

The existence of supernatural equivalents for the natural moral virtues follows logically on all that the Scriptures say about man's condition in the state of sanctifying grace. The evangelist John and the apostle Paul emphasize the new life acquired by those who are justified. They are enabled to perform actions beyond the capacity of their native powers because of the new dispositions they received

---

[547] St. Thomas, *Summa Theologica,* II–II, 48, 1; 58, 5–6; 61, 1–2; 79, 1; 80, 1; 103, prologue; 128, 1; 143, 1; 144, 1; 145, 1; 147, 1; 161, prologue; 166, 2; 168, 2; 169, 1.

from the indwelling Spirit. These dispositions in the moral order are the infused virtues, directing the justified to a supernatural destiny in the beatific vision.

More than once St. Paul spoke of various types of these virtues as the special possession of those in the friendship of God. "I exhort you to walk," he told the Ephesians, "in a manner worthy of the calling with which you are called, with all humility and meekness, with patience," and "careful to preserve the unity of the Spirit in the bond of peace."[548] Timothy was reminded that "God has not given us the spirit of fear, but of power and of love and of prudence."[549] In a long exhortation to the Romans, the converts were urged to practice zeal and fervor, patience and perseverance, hospitality and condescension, peaceableness and justice.[550]

The Church's tradition reflects the same idea, that the souls of the just are graced with infused moral powers beyond the reach of acquired virtue. Early in the thirteenth century, Innocent III censured the Albigensian speculators for saying that "faith or charity or the other virtues are not infused in children since children do not give their consent."[551] At the Council of Trent, the justified were said to advance from virtue to virtue by mortifying the members of their flesh, showing them as weapons of justice unto sanctification by observing the precepts of God and the Church.[552]

In his letter on true and false Americanism addressed to the United States, Leo XIII singled out the infused moral virtues as especially potent in the spiritual life because they imply the operations of divine grace. He took issue with those who underrated these supernatural

---

[548] Ephesians 4:1–3.
[549] 2 Timothy 1:7.
[550] Romans 12:9–19.
[551] *DS* 780.
[552] *DS* 1535; *CCC* 2015.

powers. "It is hard to understand," he said, "how those who are imbued with Christian principles can place the natural ahead of the supernatural virtues, and attribute to them greater power and fecundity." At most the latter lead to human perfection, but only the former direct us to God. "For as the nature of man, because of our common misfortune, fell into vice and dishonor, yet by the assistance of grace is lifted up and borne onward with new honor and strength; so also the virtues which are exercised not by the unaided powers of nature, but by the help of the same grace, are made productive of a supernatural beatitude."[553]

Reflecting on the teaching of faith about the consistency of the supernatural order, Catholic theology has concluded to the necessity of infused moral virtues. It is obvious that a person in the state of grace performs actions of virtues other than just the theological, that is, justice, prudence, temperance, and fortitude. These actions are essentially supernatural; and therefore require, besides the state of grace, moral habits that are equally supernatural. Otherwise we should postulate an imbalance in the moral order, since God's ordinary providence uses secondary causes of the same kind as the effects produced. If we are to have truly supernatural acts of justice and chastity, for example, we should have infused supernatural virtues that proximately bring these actions about.[554]

In the last analysis, the main reason why there must be infused moral virtues, in addition to the theological, is the possession of faith in the person justified. A moral virtue, by definition, avoids extremes. It does not offend against right reason by excess or by defect. But once the faith is had, there is no question of limiting the practice of moral virtue by reason alone. Faith sublimates reason as the standard of moderation. Just as prior to faith there are acquired virtues commensurate with

[553] *DS* 3343.
[554] *CCC* 1810.

reason to assist the natural mind and will in the performance of morally good acts, so with the advent of faith there should be corresponding supernatural virtues commensurate with the light of faith to assist the elevated human faculties in the performance of supernaturally good actions in the moral order.

A slight problem arises from the fact that the infused virtues are necessarily spiritual. This would mean that the infusion must directly take place in the mind and will, in spite of the fact that two of the virtues, temperance and fortitude, involve the sense appetite. One explanation is to have the virtues immediately enter the spiritual faculties, in turn affecting the lesser powers as called upon for moral action.

Here, if anywhere, the familiar dictum that "grace does not destroy but builds upon nature" is eminently true. All that we say about these virtues as naturally acquired qualities holds good for the infused virtues, but much more. With the reason enlightened by faith, the scope of virtuous operation is extended to immeasurably wider horizons. By the same token, faith furnishes motives which reason itself would never dream of, and theological charity offers inspiration that surpasses anything found in nature.

GIFTS OF THE HOLY SPIRIT

Along with the infused theological and moral virtues, sanctifying grace also includes the gifts of the Holy Spirit, which were anticipated in the prophetic text of Isaias, when he spoke of the coming Messiah. "There shall come forth a rod out of Jesse, and a branch shall grow out of his roots. And the Spirit of the Lord shall rest upon him, the spirit of wisdom and understanding, the spirit of counsel and fortitude, the spirit of knowledge and piety, and he shall be filled with the spirit of the fear of the Lord."[555]

---

[555] Isaiah 11:1–3; *CCC* 712, 1830, 1831.

Although directly attributed to the Messias, the gifts are implicitly the common possession of all Christians, in God's friendship since Christ received them as the Second Adam to be dispensed to all who come under His influence and receive from the fulness of His grace.

In the Greek *Septuagint, Vulgate,* and other texts, seven gifts are named. But in the Massoretic text, produced by Jewish grammarians between the sixth and eighth centuries, the gift of piety is not mentioned. The last word *yirah* occurs twice, which the *Septuagint* and *Vulgate* render first as "piety" and then as "fear of the Lord." All evidence indicates that the Christian tradition of seven gifts, found in the ancient patristic writers was not derived from the *Septuagint* version of Isaias but attached to it. Thus the Syriac Church, which did not use the *Septuagint* or *Vulgate,* as early as the third century spoke of the "Spirit of the Lord which rested upon Christ with His seven activities, as related by the prophet Isaias."[556]

A parallel text familiar to the Fathers was the passage in Romans, that "whoever are led by the Spirit of God, they are the sons of God."[557] They argued that for the sons of God to act supernaturally, they must be directed by a higher than natural disposition that operates on a level commensurate with their divine dignity. This disposition is assured permanence by the infused gifts of the Holy Spirit, who disposes the souls of the just to be moved according to His will.

Until the Middle Ages, there were some who wondered if the gifts were really different from the virtues and not merely the virtues viewed from another aspect. St. Thomas found the clue in the scriptural term regularly used, namely "spirits," to describe the gifts as distinct from the virtues, which suggests that they come to us by divine inspiration, by way of motion from the outside. He further associated this with

---

[556] Aphrates, "Demonstratio: De Fide," 10, *Patrologia Syriaca* (Paris: Firmin-Didot et Socii, 1926), 1:22.

[557] Romans 8:14.

Aristotle's teaching about the two dynamic principles, one of which is within us, namely reason, and the other outside us, that is, God. Whatever is set in motion, Thomas reasoned, should be adapted to its mover. The higher and nobler the mover, the more necessary a better disposition: for instance, the higher a doctrine proposed, the more attentive and highly equipped should be the learners.

> The virtues perfect our inborn tendency to be set going by our reason in our inner and outward life. But we need higher dispositions in order to be stirred by the Divinity which transcends us. These dispositions are called Gifts, not only because they are infused by God, but also because by them we are prepared to be promptly responsive to divine inspiration: "the Lord God has opened my ear, and I was not rebellious, neither turned away back" (Isaias 1:5). Aristotle notices how persons touched by a divine instinct have no need to take counsel by human reasoning, for they are stimulated by a nobler principle. In this manner the Gifts arouse men to acts higher than the capabilities of virtue.[558]

If we would define the exact difference between the virtues and gifts, it lies in the need to have a supernatural counterpart for the natural instincts of mind and will. Even the infused virtues are not enough. They do not, by themselves, so perfect a man on the road to heaven that he has no further need of being moved by the yet higher promptings of the Holy Spirit. For whether we consider human reason and will in their natural powers alone, or as elevated by the theological virtues, they are still very fallible and require help. Wisdom is against folly, understanding against dullness, counsel against rashness, fortitude against fears, knowledge against igno-

---

[558] St. Thomas Aquinas, *Summa Theologica*, I–II, 68, 1.

rance, piety against hardness of heart, and fear of God against pride. The gifts of the Holy Spirit supply this help by giving us remedies against these defects and making us amenable to the promptings of His grace.

It follows, then, that the gifts, no less than the virtues, are necessary for salvation, at least to meet those critical situations when the mind and will, though elevated by ordinary grace, cannot cope with the problem or difficulty but require assistance that is ready at hand in the gifts. Moreover, according to the present economy of salvation, the special help we need to persevere in God's friendship includes immediate illuminations and impulses from the Holy Spirit. The infused gifts furnish us with the readiness to answer these divine invitations, and thereby save our souls.[559]

The function of the gifts cannot be understood without reflecting that God acts upon the soul in two different ways. In one case He accommodates Himself to the human mode of action. He gives light to see the best means suitable to perform a good work and strength of will to carry it out; yet we are left free to take the initiative on the basis of reason enlightened by faith. We are thus acting, through the virtues, under the impulse of grace.

At other times, however, God takes the initiative Himself, before we have a chance to reflect on a course of action, by sending illuminations and inspirations that call for immediate response. His movements affect us, as it were, from the outside, although deep in the soul and never without our consent. Hence the call for a supernatural responsiveness to these visitations, where the habitual disposition to react favorably and easily is one of the gifts of the Holy Spirit. They are in the nature of supernatural reflexes, or reactive instincts, spontaneously answering to the divine impulses almost without reflection but always with full consent.

---

[559] *CCC* 1303.

Christian theology has analyzed the gifts according to certain norms, clarified by St. Thomas and developed by later scholars. The analysis begins with the postulate that the gifts are infused habits which perfect a man by making him ready to follow the promptings of grace, just as the moral virtues perfect the appetitive powers so they conform to right reason. And just as it is natural for the appetites to be moved by the command of reason, so it is natural for all the forces in man to be moved by the impulse of God, as by a superior power. Consequently whatever human powers that can be the sources of human acts, can also be the subjects of infused gifts, even as they are of supernatural virtues. Such powers are the reason and appetite.

There are two kinds of reason, the speculative and practical, and in both we find the apprehension of truth (pertaining to its discovery) and the judgment concerning truth. In terms of the gifts, therefore, the speculative reason is perfected by *understanding;* the practical reason by *counsel.* For the speculative reason to judge correctly it receives perfection from *wisdom,* and for the practical reason *knowledge* is given.

As regards the volitional powers, whatever touches on our relations to other people is graced by *piety.* Whatever concerns ourselves is gifted with *fortitude* against the fear of dangers, and with *fear of the Lord* against inordinate lust for pleasures.

The first of the gifts is also the highest in dignity. It is wisdom that makes the soul responsive to the Holy Spirit in the contemplation of divine things and in the use, so to speak, of God's ideas for evaluating every contingency in the secular and spiritual order. Often the word "wisdom" is used to describe a fulness of knowledge possessed by a man through study and acuteness of mind. But this is far removed from the gift, which implies fulness of knowledge derived from an affinity to divine things, as when a person learns to know the Passion of Christ through suffering or the joys of virtue by personal experience.

Wisdom also differs from faith. Where faith is a simple knowledge of the articles of belief that Christianity proposes, wisdom goes on to a certain divine and explicit contemplation of the truths that the articles contain, which faith accepts without further development. Built into the concept of wisdom is the element of love that inspires contemplative reflection on the dogmas of belief, rejoices in dwelling upon them, and directs the mind to judge all things according to their principles.

The gift of understanding is a supernatural enlightenment given to the mind for grasping revealed truths easily and profoundly. It differs from faith because it gives insight into the meaning of what a person believes, whereas faith, as such, merely assents to what God has revealed.

Ascetical writers since Augustine have said that understanding characterizes the clean of heart, following the teaching of Christ, "Blessed are the pure of heart for they shall see God." This beatitude, they explain, contains two clauses: one refers to merit, namely cleanness of heart, the other to reward, namely seeing God. Both in a sense correspond to the gift of understanding.

> There are two stages of purity, one preparatory, the other final. Preliminary to the sight of God is a cleansing of the affections from inordinate desires, performed by the virtues and the gifts in the appetitive parts of man. Then there is a final development of purity, when the mind is purified from errors and phantasies, and receives divine truths without anthropomorphism or heretical distortion. This cleansing comes from the gift of understanding.
>
> Similarly, there are two stages in our seeing of God, one is imperfect, which though not gazing on God in Himself, well perceives what He is not. We know Him the better in this life the

more we appreciate how far He is beyond our comprehension. The other is perfect vision which sees His essence. Both visions correspond to the gift of understanding; the first to its beginning on earth, the second to its consummation in heaven.[560]

Sometimes called "the science of the saints," the gift of knowledge enables us, through some form of relish and warmth of charity, to judge everything from a supernatural viewpoint by means of lesser causes. Closely tied with this gift is the lesson of past experience, after a person has learned the emptiness of things created and the hollowness of sin.

Thus the function of knowledge is to help us pass judgment on creatures, which can be the occasion for our turning away from God. Sorrow for past mistakes answers to the gift of knowledge; then comes consolation when creatures are accepted as God would have us do. So that knowledge corresponds to the third beatitude, "Blessed are they that mourn, for they shall be comforted." Mourning is by way of merit, comfort by way of reward. In the measure that a person knows the vanity of this world, his comfort begins already now and is destined to reach fruition in heaven, when all things earthly will have passed away.

Counsel is a specialized gift which assists the mind and perfects the virtue of prudence by enlightening a man on how to decide and command individual supernatural acts. It refers primarily to prudent conduct in one's own case, and only secondarily in favor of others. Its proper object is the right ordering of particular actions, after the gifts of knowledge and understanding furnish the general principles. Enlightened by the Spirit, a person learns what to do in a specific case, what advice to give when consulted, or command to make if he is in authority.

Implicit in the gift of counsel is the native inability of reason, left to itself, to grasp all the facets of a concrete situation and see at a glance all

---

[560] St. Thomas Aquinas, *Summa Theologica,* II–II, 8, 7.

the contingent circumstances. It needs the help of God who comprehends all things, and who acts in the capacity of counsellor to the humble soul, as in human affairs when we consult others who have more experience or knowledge than we do. Speaking of this interior Guide, St. Augustine says that in the last analysis it is not external teachers who instruct us, "but Truth that presides within, over the mind itself; though it may have been words that prompted us to make such consultation. The One consulted, who dwells in the inner man, He it is who teaches, Christ, the unchangeable Power of God and everlasting Wisdom. No doubt every rational soul consults this Wisdom, but to each one only so much is shown as he is able to receive because of his own good or bad will."[561]

Hence, the importance of nearness to God and personal holiness in those whose positions require them to direct other people. The interior Counselor will advise them on how to advise others in virtue of their office, and the greater their sanctity the more claim they have on this divine consultation. Patristic tradition further associates counsel with the beatitude, "Blessed are the merciful, for they shall obtain mercy," The reason is that among all the virtues that counselors need, none stands higher than mercy—which knows how to be compassionate and forbearing under provocation, and communicates this spirit to those who come for advice. "The only remedy for great evils, the only way of plucking them out is to forgive and to give."[562] When persons come for help, no matter what their problems may be, two things will always be needed and the counselor should offer them by word and example: forgiveness of injuries real or imagined, and great generosity; both are covered by the concept of mercy.

Piety as a gift of the Holy Spirit aids and supplements the virtue of justice by disposing us to show reverence for God as a most loving

---

[561] St. Augustine, "De Magistro," 38, *MPL* 32:1215–20.
[562] St. Augustine, *Sermon on the Mount*, 1.

Father as men who are the sons of God. We respect and serve our parents through the virtue of piety. It is, therefore, analogous to the gift that prompts us to offer worship and service to God. He is the divine Parent of our souls in the natural and supernatural order.

Consistent with the same analogy, as the virtue of piety urges us to serve everyone related to us by the bonds of blood, the gift makes us ready not only to worship God but also to honor His children. "The saints are honored, misery is relieved, the Holy Scriptures are not contradicted, whether they be understood or not."[563] In a word, whatever is connected with God as the Author of nature and of grace comes within the scope of piety.

The characteristic feature of this gift is filial attitude towards God and a fraternal attitude towards the neighbor which it engenders in the soul, with special reference to our spiritual regeneration and incorporation in the Mystical Body of Christ. It makes us look upon God not only as Lord and Master but as the Originator of our being, naturally by creation and supernaturally by grace, and upon our fellowmen not as competitors in the struggle of life but co-equals under God as our common Maker and brothers in Christ through the saving merits of His Passion.

Fortitude as a gift goes beyond fortitude as a virtue by carrying to a successful conclusion even the most difficult tasks in the service of God. "This is beyond human power, for sometimes we are not strong enough to win through and override all evils and perils, which press us down to death. The Holy Spirit leads us to eternal life, which is the final achievement of all we do, the escaping from all ills and dangers."[564]

Two forms of courage are implied in the gift of fortitude: to undertake arduous tasks and to endure long and trying difficulties for the

---

[563] St. Thomas Aquinas, *Summa Theologica,* II–II, 121, 1.
[564] St. Thomas Aquinas, *Summa Theologica,* II–II, 140, 1.

divine glory. The two are quite distinct. There is a type of courage which anticipates grave obstacles while entering on a course of action, a state of life, or a new venture in the spiritual life or the apostolate. The obstacles are faced with a quiet trust in Providence that inspires the willingness to suffer in the prosecution of the plan. Fortitude of this kind is characterized by a dauntless spirit of resolution, firmness of mind, and an indomitable will.

Another form of courage does not pioneer in God's service but finds itself tried by unexpected trials, sickness, persecution, and external failure. Nevertheless it perseveres in the practice of virtue and unflinchingly carries on in spite of oppressive odds.

Both types are necessary for salvation, at least to the extent that perseverance in grace over a long period of time will call upon the deepest resources of courage in resisting the allurements of flesh, the wiles of the devil, and the seductiveness of worldly ambition. Not the least strength a man needs is to live up to his ideals in spite of the criticism and, perhaps, opposition he meets from those who should encourage him in the struggle for perfection. "When any Christian has begun to live well, to be fervent in good works, and to despise the world; in this newness of his life he is exposed to the condemnations and contradictions of cold Christians. But if he persevere, and get the better of them by his endurance, and faint not in good works, those very same persons who before hindered will now respect him."[565] His strength of character, born of the Spirit will become a grace of attraction for others to follow his example.[566]

The seventh of the gifts, and yet first in the rising scale of value, is the fear of the Lord which confirms the virtue of hope and impels a man to a profound respect for the majesty of God. Its correlative

---

[565] St. Augustine, "Sermo 38," *MPL* 38:548.
[566] *CCC* 828, 2030; cf. *Lumen Gentium* 40; 48–51.

effects are protection from sin through dread of offending the Lord, and a strong confidence in the power of His help.

There are various kinds of fear, only one of which is a gift of the Holy Spirit. Worldly fear is a fear of creatures that may lead a person to offend God, as when Peter was led to deny Christ because he was afraid of the bystanders in the court of the high priest during the Savior's passion. Slavish fear also should not be numbered among the gifts because it cringes only at God's punishments without detaching the heart from sin. If a man remains attached to sinful intentions but, out of fear of being punished, fails to carry them out, there is no merit in his conduct and no profit, except the possible restraint which keeps him from giving scandal or causing injury to his neighbor.

Even servile fear is not yet the infused gift, although it is certainly noble and praiseworthy. It not only shrinks from the pain that follows sin, but has the positive effect of detaching the will from affection for sinful creatures and keeping it attached to God. However, the gift cannot be based on this type of fear because, while good, it can be found in persons not in the state of grace. The useful fear of punishment may concur in disposing a sinner to justification through attrition. According to the Council of Trent, treating of attrition born of the fear of hell or God's punishments, servile fear is a grace of God. It is an impulse of the good Spirit, not, indeed, as dwelling within the soul but merely as moving it. Consequently servile fear is excluded from the gifts which abide only in those who possess the Spirit of God in sanctifying grace.

Unlike the servile kind, the gift of fear is filial because it is based on the selfless love of God, whom it dreads to offend. In servile fear, the evil dreaded is punishment. In filial fear, the fear is offending God. Both kinds may proceed from the love of God, but filial fear is par excellence inspired by perfect charity. In that sense, it is inseparable from divine love. When I dread the loss of heaven and the pains of hell, my fear, though servile, is basically motivated by the love of God, whom I am afraid of losing by my sins, since heaven is the possession of God and hell the loss of Him for eternity. To that extent, even servile fear cannot be separated from supernatural charity. On a higher plane, however, when the object of my fear is not personal loss, though it be heaven, but injury to the Divine Majesty; then the motive is not only an implicit love of God but love to a sublime degree. And this is the scope of the infused gift of the fear of the Lord.

To further clarify the meaning of this gift, we may recall that the sources of divine charity from which servile and filial fear arise correspond to the familiar difference between perfect and imperfect love. One is benevolence and the other is self-interest. In the pure love of benevolence, I love God for Himself alone, not for any benefit He can bestow upon me. To this corresponds the filial fear wherein I am afraid to offend God, whom I love above all things, because I know that sin would "deprive" Him of the only good I can give, which is the gift of my voluntary love. In self-interested charity, my love is egotistic. I love God because of the blessings, including Himself, that attachment to His will can bring me. To this corresponds the servile fear that causes me to dread the loss of those very things to which self-interested love inclines me.

Persons in the state of grace are therefore disposed by the gift of fear instinctively to shrink from causing injury to One whom they love more than themselves, and in whom they recognize a Father deserving of their deepest affection.

Moreover, the gift of fear is not only filial but also chaste, and in its chastity lies hidden that perfection of divine love which raises a soul from earth to heaven already in this mortal life. St. Augustine uses a powerful similitude to explain what this means. Suppose some chaste woman, he says, fears her husband; suppose another, an adulterous woman, also fears her husband. The chaste woman fears lest her husband depart, the adulterous wife is afraid lest hers come. What if both husbands are absent? The one fears that he might come, the other lest he delay in coming.

> He to whom we have been betrothed is in a certain sense absent. He is absent, who gave us as a pledge the Holy Spirit. He is absent who redeemed us with His blood. He is that Bridegroom than whom nothing is more beautiful. He is beautiful, and is absent. Let the spouse ask herself if she is chaste. Our Bridegroom is absent. Ask your conscience: do you wish that He come, or do you prefer that He delay?
>
> A chaste fear, then, has this quality, that it comes from love. But that fear which is not yet chaste, fears His presence and punishment. From fear a man does whatever good he performs, not from fear of losing that good, but from fear of suffering the contrary evil. He does not fear the prospect of losing the most beautiful Spouse of his soul, but lest he be cast into hell. This fear is good and useful; but it will not last forever. It is not yet that chaste fear which endures into eternity.[567]

Consequently, the gift of fear gives us the power to sublimate all lesser fears, including the salutary and much-needed dread of God's justice. In the measure that this gift becomes active through generous cooperation, we come closer to realizing the ideal of the Christian life, namely that charity casts out fear. Our love of God becomes so intense that gradually the dominant disposition is to fear losing the

---

[567] St. Augustine, "Enarrationes in Psalmos," 127, 8, *MPL* 37:1681–82; *CCC* 1041.

least particle of God's friendship. As we grow in charity, the dread of God's punishment flows into a calm assurance of ultimate salvation, and even becomes a strong desire, like St. Paul's, to be dissolved into and to be with Christ.[568]

---

[568] *CCC* 1011, 2086.

Index*

---

* Saints are listed under their personal names.